Math Guide

(Third Edition)

ISBN: 9781495933189

"SAT," "SAT II," "SAT Reasoning Test," and "SAT Subject Tests" are registered trademarks of the College Board, which has had nothing to do with the production of, and does not endorse, this book. "PSAT/NMSQT" is a registered trademark of the College Board and the National Merit Scholarship Corporation, which also has no connection with this book whatsoever, and does not endorse it.

Volume discounts available for teachers and tutors. Contact mike@pwnthesat.com for details.

To Pythagoras: I wish we could have chilled, bro.

All joking aside, there are some people I need to thank. I am overwhelmingly grateful to all the students who've listened to me babble while I refined this advice into its current form, and to my Beta testers, who pored over early manuscript drafts of the first edition and spotted a staggering number of typographical and grammatical errors. Special bonus thanks go to Suzanne, who picked up where the Beta testers left off; to Frank, who taught and inspired me; to Debbie, who encouraged me; and to my girlfriend Amy, who patiently endured me even though I was completely insufferable while writing this book, and who continues to endure me even though I'm pretty insufferable even when I'm not writing a book.

Table of Contents

Introduction

Although I've scored 2400 and work with kids on all three SAT subjects, I spend most of my SAT-related energy thinking about the math section. It's the section about which I've had the most arguments with people in my line of work and far outside of it. Emotions tend to run high on both sides, which I understand completely because my own philosophy on the section has changed so much since I was in high school.

I was a math guy in high school. I looked forward to math class every day. I loved the satisfaction I got from constructing an elegant geometrical proof; I thrived on the sturdy reliability of algebra. I won awards for the best math GPA. I couldn't wait to get to college and take harder, more demanding courses in advanced mathematics.

But of course, like everyone, I still got questions wrong sometimes. I'd subtract incorrectly, or forget to distribute a negative sign, and feel my stomach sink when my teacher handed me back a 95% when I'd been sure a 100% was coming.

Despite mountains of evidence indicating that I was fallible and likely to make a few mistakes under pressure, I brute-forced the math section on the SAT because I knew no other way. It's been too long for me to remember any of the questions and I'm fairly sure I never knew which ones I got wrong, but I do remember that I was devastated when my scores came back that I had only scored a 730 in math. I had done better than that in reading! FFFFFFFUUUUUUUUUUU.

Here's what I wish someone had told me then, and one of the first things I tell all my students now: *the SAT is not a math test*—at least not the kind you're used to. The SAT math sections are mostly multiple choice, for one. When's the last time you took a multiple choice math test? And then there's the fact that there's nobody looking at your work and possibly giving you partial credit when you don't get a question all the way right. Not to mention that SAT math sections are full of booby-traps, misleading diagrams, and intentionally difficult phrasing. Even questions that look a lot like straightforward system-of-equations algebra questions are put there not to see if you can *do* the algebra, but to see if you can spot the shortcut that lets you *avoid* the algebra.

Taking the SAT like you'd take a regular math test is like bringing a knife to a gun fight. Sure, a knife is a deadly weapon and with it you might get lucky, but that doesn't change the fact that the guy with the gun is going to be happy to see you.

Perhaps a less macabre way to put it is this: taking the SAT using only brute force math is like a Little Leaguer insisting on using a wooden bat, because that's what the pros use, even though it puts him at a huge disadvantage since all the other kids use metal bats. If that kid then complains that the best kids in Little League are doing it wrong, then he's basically asking that the playing field adjust to him, because he refuses to adjust to the playing field.

If you want to drastically improve your score, you're going to have to drastically change the way you take the test. I'm here to help.

What's changed in the 3rd edition?

This new edition of the *Math Guide* contains a number of improvements from the 2nd edition. Some of them (chapter title font changes) are completely cosmetic, and some are so minor (a sentence added here, a word deleted there) as to not warrant specific mention. Still, there are a few changes that are worth pointing out, mostly for the benefit of teachers and tutors who have been teaching out of the 1st or 2nd editions for a while.

The biggest change in this new edition is the addition of two new chapters: **Prime factorization** (page 92) and **Corresponding coefficients of equivalent polynomials** (page 156). The skills taught in these chapters are tested on the SAT only rarely, but rarely is not the same as never, so students who want to be prepared for every eventuality should pay close attention.

I have also added a new example question at the beginning of the **Plug in** chapter (page 31) to introduce the technique a bit more gently and without having to also review the concept of remainders. The remainders question that used to be the first example in the chapter is still there; it's just the second question now instead of the first.

I've completely redone the section about graphs and function notation (page 117) in the **Functions** chapter. There's now a mini-drill that provides much more practice translating from graphs to function notation than existed in previous editions.

The **Parabolas** chapter (page 142) now contains mention of the vertex form of a parabola, which is really just an application of the graph translation rules that have always existed in the **Functions** chapter.

The **Angles and triangles** chapter now contains a brief section about similarity and congruence (page 167). Those rules were only mentioned in a footnote in the previous editions. Congruence rules are still footnoted, as congruence is just a special case of similarity and I'm not into overloading students with redundant rules.

I changed problem #20 in the drill (page 190) at the end of the **Circles** chapter. The new one still has a rolling wheel just like the old one did, but I think it's a better question.

The **Working in three dimensions** chapter now has one more example (page 205) which illustrates the shortcut that the long diagonal of a cube will always be $\sqrt{3}$ times the length of the edge of the cube.

Finally, I've added an alternative solution to Example 2 in the **Probability** chapter (page 227) to reinforce principles discussed in **Counting and listing**.

How to use this book

I'm willing to guess that, if you're reading these words right now, then you're pretty interested in score improvement. What a coincidence! Me too!

I spend a lot of time thinking about the best way to help my students improve, without wasting tons of time, and without frustrating them more than is necessary. I started PWNtheSAT.com with that in mind, and this book, as an extension of that site, is forged from the same goals. I've helped *lots* of kids improve, so I know the methods herein work, but I also know that a cursory glance at the practice questions in here—or in any book—will not be sufficient to raise your score. You're going to have to put in a fair amount of effort to see the results you desire. You're going to have to be thorough. (The fact that you're reading the introduction bodes well.) I wrote this book to be read cover-to-cover, and although I'll outline another way to approach things at the end of this chapter, I still think that reading every page and doing every drill is the surest way to improve your score.

Make sure you're always accompanied by the following when you sit down to work.

Pencils

You should try to solve every single problem in this book *before you read its explanation*. If you just read my explanations, you'll forget what you read as soon as you turn the page. I want this book to work for you, so I want you to write all over it. Practice as you'll play: with a yellow, wooden #2 pencil, that you can erase if you make mistakes.

Graphing calculator

I'm partial to the TI-84, but whatever you already own and are comfortable with should be fine. As long as it doesn't have a QWERTY keyboard or an internet connection and as long as it doesn't beep or print, it should be fine on test day. Your calculator can probably do like ten million things, but here's a short list of tasks you should know how to perform on your calculator for the SAT:

➔ **Graph functions.** It won't happen often, but occasionally you'll be able to solve an SAT problem simply by graphing. It's up to you to spot these opportunities, but just spotting them won't help if you don't know how to use your calculator. Once you've graphed, you should also know how to:

⇨ Find the x- and y-intercepts of a function.

⇨ Find the intersections of two functions.

⇨ View a table of values.

⇨ Adjust window dimensions and scale.

➔ **Convert a decimal to a fraction.** This is all kinds of useful.

➔ **Work with exponents and radicals.** You should not have to fiddle with your calculator to figure out how to take the fifth root of something on test day. Know how to do so in advance.

➔ **Use parentheses.** It's not your calculator's fault if you enter 8^{x+4} as "8^x+4" instead of "8^(x+4)." That kind of careless mistake can really spoil an otherwise solid outing on test day.

The Official SAT Study Guide (AKA the Blue Book)

You should have a copy of The Official SAT Study Guide, 2nd edition or The Official SAT Study Guide with DVD. The books themselves are exactly the same except the covers, so I'll just be referring to them collectively as the "Blue Book" from here on out. You probably won't end up spending much time with the first half of the Blue Book, although it does contain some useful information and a few good practice questions. You're really buying the Blue Book for its second half, which contains 10 full-length tests written by the actual test writers—the first three of which were actually deployed in October 2006, January 2007, and May 2007, respectively. If you get the DVD version of the Blue Book, you get one extra practice test—from January 2008—on the DVD. In this book, I'll refer to the DVD test as Test 11.

Note that, because the first three tests in the Blue Book (and the one on the DVD) were actually administered, there's a little more statistical precision to them. They have real scoring tables, not score ranges like the other seven, and their questions are rated on a more granular difficulty scale. That's why, in the guides referred to in the preceding paragraphs, the question difficulty ratings for Tests 1, 2, 3, and 11 are numbered 1–5, while questions in the other tests are simply rated E, M, or H.

At the end of each unit in this book, I provide a list of Blue Book questions that can be solved with the techniques I've just described. These lists are meant to give you a rough idea of how often you can expect to use the techniques you're learning, and I encourage you to use them to mine the Blue Book for practice, but I recommend leaving at least the first five Blue Book tests untouched on your first run through this guide. You'll want to use those to take as full-length tests in one sitting to assess yourself as test day approaches.

I also include a brief companion to the Blue Book in the back of this guide. I call it the **Blue Book Breakdown** (page 357). It contains a list of questions by test, section,* and page number, and the techniques that work on them. The Blue Book Breakdown is good for:

→ **Keeping a record of your mistakes.** Build a database that reveals your strengths and weaknesses over time.

→ **Referring to after you take practice exams.** Make sure you're recognizing all the opportunities to employ your new bag of tricks.

About the question numbers in this book

You'll notice that the questions in this book are numbered strangely. Why, in the middle of a chapter, is there a question #17, when there was no #16 before it? Why are the questions in the drill at the end of a chapter not numbered in order?

It's a little quirky, I know, but I like to use question numbers to signal to you roughly how hard I think the question is and to subtly remind you to always pay attention to where you are when you're taking the test. On the real SAT, questions in a section go from easy to hard—#1 is easy, and #20 is hard. On average, each question is slightly tougher than the one before it. So when I call a question #17, I'm trying to tell you that I think it's moderately, but not maximally, difficult.

---

* In my Blue Book tables, I use the § symbol to denote "section."

Math sections come in three flavors on the SAT: 20-question, 18-question (that's the one with grid-ins), and 16-question. All the multiple choice numbering in this book is out of 20; grid-ins are numbered out of 18.

Alternative study plan

I know not everybody buys this book with months to go before their SAT, and therefore not everybody has time to read it cover-to-cover. *I still really think you should try—I think everything in here is important.* However, here's another path you might choose to take if you're in a hurry—but not like, a crazy hurry. This plan will still take a while. It's *barely* a shortcut.

1. **Take Blue Book Practice Test #1.** Correct and score it. That score is your baseline.

    a) Highlight every question you got wrong in the Blue Book Breakdown of Test #1 (page 358), and write down the techniques and relevant page numbers.

    b) Work through every chapter that you've written down more than once.

    c) Do the short drills at the end of each chapter. Use the solutions section towards the end of the book to understand any mistakes you make.

    d) *This is important:* Go back to the Blue Book now, and redo every question in the test you got wrong, making efforts to apply the concepts you read about in this book. New techniques won't be easy or feel natural the first time, but if you want to change your scores, you're going to have to change your approach.

2. **Read the General test-taking strategies section in this book (page 17).** You need to know how the test is designed, and how to use that to your advantage, and how not to fall into some of the most common traps.

3. **Take Blue Book Practice Test #4.** Yes, I know this is out of order. Only tests #1–3 have fully accurate scoring tables, so save #2 and #3 for the end of your prep. For this test, record your score as the exact middle of the range of scores you get from the scoring table. Repeat steps a) through d) above for Test #4.

4. **Do Diagnostic Drill #1 (page 235) in this book.** Use the answer key and technique guide at the end of the drill. Make special note of problem types you've been missing over and over again. At this point, it's safe to call those weaknesses. Reread the chapters corresponding to your weaknesses again, and use the guides at the end of each chapter to do all the problems contained in Blue Book Tests #7–10 that jive with those techniques.

5. **Take Blue Book Test #5.** Again, record your score as the middle of the range. Repeat review steps a) through d).

6. **Do Diagnostic Drill #2 (page 245) in this book.** Review it, and the weaknesses it exposes, to death.

7. **Take Blue Book Test #6.** Record your score as the middle of the range and repeat steps a) through d). As usual, take note of any weaknesses that persist. Use the guides at the end of each chapter aimed at your weakness to revisit EVERY question from Test #1 and Tests #4–10.

8. **Take Blue Book Test #2.** You're back to real, previously administered tests now, with accurate scoring tables. Take note of your improvement from the first test you took, and highlight any areas that still require attention. Reread the chapters for any remaining weaknesses *again* (yes, I know you're rereading them over and over again—repetition is a stepping stone to mastery) and revisit the relevant questions in every test except Test #3.

9. **OPTIONAL: Take Diagnostic Drills #3 (page 258) and #4 (page 270) in this book.** These drills are hard, so if you're not shooting for super-high scores, you needn't drive yourself crazy here.

10. **Take Blue Book Test #3.** Time it so that you're doing this a few days before (*not* the day before) your SAT. You want this to be an accurate prediction of your score on test day. Think of it like your dress rehearsal.

11. **Get in there and PWN the SAT for real.** Do it.

A brief note on practice tests

Practice tests are a necessary element of any SAT prep plan. The test itself is a harrowing and protracted experience, and if you haven't put yourself through rigorous simulations a few times before you sit down for the real thing, you'll be at a real disadvantage. People prep at different speeds, but as a general rule I recommend taking at least three full-length, all-in-one-sitting practice tests, and at least three others done a section or two at a time, throughout your prep process.[*]

The best practice tests are written by the test-makers themselves. That's why I very strongly recommend you purchase the Blue Book (see page 6). The College Board also makes a few practice tests available for free online. For links to those, go to http://blog.pwnthesat.com/p/free-college-board-practice-tests.html.

Anyway, once you've got your hands on the practice tests you need, here's how you take one. First, drag your lazy bones out of bed early on a weekend morning. Set your alarm to go off early enough that you'll have time to eat breakfast, take a shower, and be fully alert by about 8:30, when you should start testing.

Your bedroom isn't the *worst* place to practice, but if possible, get yourself to a public place that you can expect to be fairly quiet, but that will have some ambient noise—a public library is perfect. Part of the SAT experience is the fact that someone next to you might have the sniffles, or the hiccups, or...worse. A few minor distractions during your practice tests will help you to be better prepared when something noisy or smelly happens on test day.

Take the whole test in one sitting.[**] Yes, even the essay. And for Pete's sake, actually bubble your answers on the bubble sheet, rather than just circling them in your book. Bubbling actually takes time, and if you're doing an accurate simulation, you should account for that time. As you work, make sure to circle

---

[*] It's important to note that although practice tests are an important part of the prep experience, if you only take practice tests and do little else, your scores aren't likely to improve much. As a student of philosophy might say, practice tests are necessary but not sufficient.

[**] If you really want to go H.A.M., find an extra 25-minute section from another test (maybe your old PSAT practice book or something) to use to simulate the experimental section that all Blue Book tests are missing. So if, like Blue Book Test 1, your test is missing Section 4, give yourself an extra section to do between the 3rd and 5th sections.

any question you're uncertain about on your answer sheet. That way, even if you get it right, you'll remember that it's something you should revisit.

No finishing early and moving on to the next section. If the section's supposed to take 25 minutes, you work on it for 25 minutes. Give yourself a 5-minute break after the 2nd section, the 4th section, and the 6th section.

Once you're done, score that bad boy up. Scoring the test might seem simple, but it's actually a pretty important part of prepping for the SAT—to do as well as possible you need intimate knowledge of how the scoring process works. Blue Book tests have a worksheet at the end to walk you through it.

For the math questions you missed, go to the Blue Book Breakdown at the back of this book, and mark all your mistakes. This way, each time you take a practice test you'll be building a database of your weak areas, which you can then use to focus your prep.

We're only talking about math in this book, but this last point goes for all sections: *do not simply grumble about your score and then take another test.* Taking the test helps you build stamina, but reviewing the test is how you actually learn. A good rule of thumb is that you should take at least as long to review the test as it took you to take it in the first place. Go back and look at all your mistakes, and think them through until you'd be able to explain them to a total SAT neophyte. If there are any questions that, despite your best efforts at review, you still don't understand, ask someone for help.

As you work through this book, consider taking a practice test after each major section: Numbers and Operations; Algebra and Functions; Geometry and Measurement; and Data Analysis, Statistics, and Probability. Don't forget to track your Blue Book practice test progress in the Blue Book Breakdown (page 357)!

Miscellaneous review

There are some miscellaneous concepts that are tested on the SAT but that you won't find chapters about in this book. A great example is the occasional spatial reasoning question. Surely you've seen these—they contain a strange shape and might ask you which choice looks like that shape rotated 90° clockwise. I don't have a chapter on them because all you need to do is *actually rotate* your test book 90° clockwise, remember what the shape looks like in that orientation, and then rotate your test book back, and pick the right answer.

Please review this chapter carefully—you're probably already familiar with these concepts, but they're worth perusing because if you're shaky on any of them the SAT will exploit that weakness. And we don't want that. No, we don't want that at all.

I assume you already understand

→ **Basic algebra.** I'm talking "solve for *x*" type stuff here. In this book, I'm going to show you a lot of shortcuts through the more complex algebraic operations, but I assume that you come to the table with the basic ability to manipulate equations to get variables alone on one side, etc.

→ **Non-Cartesian graphs.** It's amazing how many questions of the "easy" variety on the SAT are really just "read the graph" questions. I include the odd bar graph, pie chart, and pictograph (where ✈ might represent 10 flights in a flights per day graph) in the "read the graph" category. To keep this book a remotely manageable length, I assume you're already skilled at understanding facts and figures presented in graphical form.

Make sure you know what's going on with

→ **Integers.** An integer is a whole number, not a fraction. Integers can be positive, negative, or zero. The following are all integers: –5, 31, 100, 0. The following are *not* integers: 0.5, $-\dfrac{2}{3}$, π.

➔ **Even and odd.** You should be able to predict what will happen when you perform basic arithmetic operations on generic even or odd numbers.

⇨ Odd × Odd = Odd

⇨ Odd × Even = Even

⇨ Even × Even = Even

⇨ Even ± Odd = Odd

⇨ Odd ± Odd = Even

⇨ Even ± Even = Even

⇨ *Zero is even.*

➔ **Positive and negative.** Again, duh, right? But know these cold.

⇨ Negative × Negative = Positive

⇨ Negative × Positive = Negative

⇨ *Zero is neither positive nor negative.*

➔ **Multiples and factors of integers.** The positive *factors* of 8 are 1, 2, 4, and 8. Positive *multiples* of 8 are 8, 16, 24, 32, 40, etc.

➔ **Prime numbers.** A prime number is a positive integer greater than 1 that has no positive divisors other than itself and 1. You should have the first few memorized. Here are all the prime numbers less than 100 (I've put the ones I think you should memorize in bold type): **2, 3, 5, 7, 11, 13, 17, 19, 23, 29,** 31, 37, 41, 43, 47, 53, 59, 61, 67, 71, 73, 79, 83, 89, 97.

⇨ 1 is *not* a prime number.

⇨ The only even prime number is 2.

➔ **Fractions.** Personally, I convert them to decimals whenever possible, but sometimes you can't escape working with fractions on the SAT. The top number in a fraction is called the *numerator.* The bottom number is called the *denominator.* Given a positive numerator and denominator ($a > 0$ and $b > 0$), the following points are true.

⇨ The greater the numerator, the greater the fraction: $\dfrac{a+2}{b} > \dfrac{a}{b}$

⇨ The greater the denominator, the smaller the fraction: $\dfrac{a}{b+2} < \dfrac{a}{b}$

➜ **Remainders.** Occasionally, you'll be asked about remainders on the SAT. It's probably been a while since you dealt with remainders, so here are two shortcuts:

⇨ If asked for a remainder, remove the decimal from the result you get when you divide, and multiply it by your original divisor. That's your remainder. Example:

$$13 \div 5 = 2.6$$
$$0.6 \times 5 = 3$$
$$\text{Remainder} = 3$$

You could also, of course, just do long division.

⇨ If you're given a specific remainder and a specific divisor, and you need to find a number that, divided by the divisor, produces the remainder, simply add the remainder to the divisor (or a multiple of the divisor). Sorry, that was the most confusing sentence ever. Here's an example: if you need a number that gives you a remainder of 5 when divided by 8, 8 + 5 = 13 will work just fine: 13 ÷ 8 = 1 R 5. In fact, 5 greater than any multiple of 8 will work: $8k + 5$, where k is a positive integer and therefore $8k$ is a positive multiple of 8, will always have a remainder of 5 when divided by 8.

➜ **Digit places.** In the number 5,764.312, 4 is the *units (ones) digit*, 6 is the *tens digit*, 7 is the *hundreds digit*, and 5 is the *thousands digit*. The decimal places have names, too: 3 is the *tenths digit*, 1 is the *hundredths digit*, and 2 is the *thousandths digit*.

➜ **Inequalities.** We use the < symbol for *less than* and the ≤ symbol for *less than or equal to*. Likewise, > means *greater than* and ≥ means *greater than or equal to*. Remember, *least* just means *farthest to the left* on a number line, and *greatest* means *farthest to the right*. On a number line, we represent > and < with open circles (like this: ○), and ≥ and ≤ with closed circles (like this: ●).

⇨ **Special note because I always see kids screw this up:** –11 is *less than* –5, because it's farther to the left on a number line. If you ever have any doubt about an inequality, draw a number line.

➔ **Sets.** A set is really just a group of numbers. You'll sometimes see it spelled out, like "Set A contains the integers 3, 4, and 5." Other times, you'll see a set denoted this way: "Set B = {5, 6, 7}." Occasionally, you may find it useful to visualize the intersection of sets by using a Venn diagram:

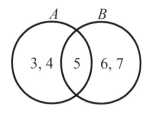

➔ **Other assorted symbols.** There aren't many symbols you need to recognize, but you should know that

⇨ **|x| means *absolute value of x*.** There is a chapter (page 148) in this book discussing specific kinds of common absolute value problems.

⇨ **⊥ means *perpendicular*.** $\overline{AB} \perp \overline{CD}$ means the segment between points A and B forms a right angle with the segment between points C and D.

⇨ **|| means *parallel*.** $\overline{EF} \parallel \overline{GH}$ means segments $\overline{EF}$ and $\overline{GH}$ will never touch, never ever ever, no matter how far they're extended. There is therefore no angle between them.

⇨ **≠ means *not equal to*.** $2 \neq 3$.

➔ **Variables and constants.** A *variable* is a placeholder that can have more than one value. In the line $y = 3x$, y and x are both variables because there are an infinite number of solutions. A *constant* must remain exactly that— constant. It can only ever be one thing. In questions that involve both constants and variables, the SAT will tell you exactly what's what. When the SAT says an equation is "true for all values of x," that means x is a variable.

⇨ It's important to know the difference between variables and constants in polynomials: in the equation $y = ax^2 + bx + c$, x and y are variables and a, b, and c are constants.

→ **Cartesian graphs.** I assume you already understand the basic layout of the Cartesian coordinate plane (also known as the xy-plane). Specifically, I expect that you already know how to find a point given an ordered pair like (3, 4).

⇨ **Intercepts.** A graph's *y-intercept* is the point at which it crosses the y-axis. Since it's understood that the x-coordinate is always zero at the y-intercept, often the y-intercept is given as only the y-coordinate. For example, when a graph has a y-intercept of 5, that means the graph crosses the y-axis at (0, 5). Of course, the same is true for *x-intercepts*: a graph with an x-intercept of 3 crosses the x-axis at (3, 0).

⇨ **Increasing and decreasing.** When a graph is moving up as it goes left to right, we say it's *increasing*. When a graph is moving down as it goes left to right, we say it's *decreasing*. Because the same graph can be increasing and decreasing depending on what part you're looking at, we usually say that a graph is increasing or decreasing over a certain interval. For example, the graph on the right is increasing until $x = -2$, then decreasing from $x = -2$ to $x = 2.5$, then increasing again from $x = 2.5$ on. Note the relationship between the concept of increasing and decreasing graphs and the concept of *slope*: a line with a positive slope is always increasing, and a line with a negative slope is always decreasing. We'll talk much more about slope in the Lines chapter (page 132).

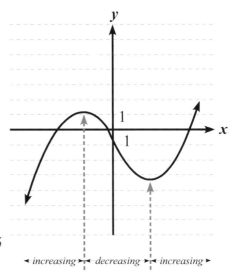

◄ *increasing* ►◄ *decreasing* ►◄ *increasing* ►

General test-taking strategies

When baseball was invented, bunting was not part of the game. Every batter's intention was to hit the ball hard every time. Soon, however, it became apparent that it could be useful to put the ball in play by simply holding the bat over the plate and hitting the ball a few feet once in a while. And thus, the bunt was born. The rules didn't forbid it, and it turned out to be useful, so it became a part of the game.

There are parallels here to the SAT. You need to play the game the way it's played today, not the way it was intended to be played when it was conceived in 1947. You must use the test's design to your advantage, whether its designers meant for you to do so or not. Read on for a few SAT-specific strategies that might help raise your score.

Guessing

I've encountered a lot of misinformation about the SAT in my travels, but the single subject that generates the most confusion and rampant speculation is the guessing. So let's start with the facts.

Every incorrect answer in the multiple choice section[*] costs you one quarter of a raw score point. Every correct answer, of course, gives you a whole raw score point. A blank has no positive or negative effect on your score. Fractional points are rounded to the nearest whole number when scores are compiled. (Half points round up.)

Imagine two ne'er-do-wells, Johnny and Morrissey, are taking a much shorter test with the same scoring scheme. Johnny doesn't give a hoot about the test, and guesses (C) for every question without even looking at it. Morrissey cares even less than Johnny, and just leaves the whole thing blank, opting instead to stare dolefully out the window.

Question #	Johnny's response	Morrissey's response
1	(C)	[blank]
2	(C)	[blank]
3	(C)	[blank]
4	(C)	[blank]
5	(C)	[blank]

When you guess completely randomly, like Johnny did, what are your statistical odds of getting a question right? Well, there are five choices, (A) through (E), so that's a 20% chance (or 1 in 5 odds) that you'll get any particular question correct. Since our test had five questions on it, odds are that Johnny will get one question right, and the other four wrong.

What do the scores of these two rascals look like?

---

[*] You don't lose any points for being wrong on a student produced response (a.k.a. grid-in) question. Why do you think that is?

Question #	Johnny's response	Johnny's score	Morrissey's response	Morrissey's score
1	(C)	1	[blank]	0
2	(C)	−0.25	[blank]	0
3	(C)	−0.25	[blank]	0
4	(C)	−0.25	[blank]	0
5	(C)	−0.25	[blank]	0
TOTAL SCORE		**0**		**0**

When you total up the scores, Johnny's is the same as Morrissey's! Both get a grand total of 0 raw score points. Now, it makes sense that they both would earn a goose egg: they both did about the same amount of work. It would be unfair to give Johnny a better score simply for picking up his pencil and bubbling randomly.*

It might be clear at this point why the SAT's scoring system works the way that it does. It's not to penalize you for wrong answers; it's to prevent unscrupulous test takers from gaining an unfair advantage. Say your proctor calls time at the end of a section that neither you nor the person next to you has finished. You put your pencil down like the obedient student that you are, but your conniving neighbor hurriedly bubbles in random guesses for the last few questions. That person shouldn't have an advantage over you, and the SAT's scoring system (on average) ensures that she doesn't.

So the obvious implication is that random guessing doesn't pay. Why, then, might you consider guessing? In short, because when you guess, you're probably not guessing completely at random. If you're able to correctly eliminate a few choices, you tip the scales in your favor, and you can improve your score a little bit by guessing—*even though you'll get more questions wrong than you get right*.

To illustrate this, let's look one more time at Johnny, but change his strategy a bit. Let's say now that he's still randomly guessing, but before he does so he's putting in a minimal effort and eliminating one choice he knows is wrong (so his

---

* Not that it matters much in the context of this book, but because it doesn't have a guessing penalty, the ACT gives a student like Johnny the upper hand. Crazy, right?

odds of a correct answer become 1 in 4). Let's also say the test got a little longer —it's eight questions now. By the odds, he'll get two questions right and six wrong.

Question #	Johnny's response	Johnny's score
1	(C)	1
2	(C)	−0.25
3	(D)	−0.25
4	(C)	−0.25
5	(C)	−0.25
6	(B)	1
7	(E)	−0.25
8	(A)	−0.25
TOTAL SCORE		**0.5**

When it comes time to calculate final scores, that half point will round up, and Johnny will have—amazingly—improved his score. But not by much.

And that's really the bottom line with guessing. Whether you choose to do it or not will not make a huge difference either way: ideally, you'll be well prepared, so there will be very few questions for which you'll have to choose between guessing and leaving blank. Guessing might get you 10 points on a test, or it might get you none. Since it depends on probabilities that won't play out the same way every time, guessing might even cost you points on a particular test if your luck is worse than average. (Remember, even though statistically you have a 50/50 shot when you flip a coin, sometimes in real life you can flip heads a bunch of times in a row.)

I usually find that my students see small gains when they stop fearing the guessing penalty, so my general recommendation to students is not to leave a question blank if they've taken more than a few seconds to think about it. I make this recommendation because of the small gains it usually produces, and also because it's helpful to have *some* rule in place before the test begins, to avoid any deliberating about guessing strategy during the test. Whether you choose to be a guesser or a leave-it-blanker, you should make that decision before test day.

Try this experiment

So should *you* guess, or not? Are you excited about the potential upside, or are you trepidatious about the potential downside? There's actually a very simple experiment you can perform to help you settle on a guessing strategy that works for you.

Here it is: always, *always*, _always guess_ on practice tests, and make little marks on your answer sheet to remind yourself which choices were guesses. When you're done, score your test twice: once with your guesses in there, and once with all your guesses replaced by blanks.[*]

What you'll probably find is that there isn't much difference either way, but once you've done this on 3 or 4 tests, you'll start to get a sense of how guessing works for you. By the time the real test comes along, you'll be comfortable in your guessing strategy, knowing that it's based not on superstition or blind faith, but *science*.

One last note: guessing is for emergencies only. I include this section because I think it's important to plan ahead for how you're going to deal with uncertainty on test day, because no matter how well you prepare there's always the possibility of some uncertainty on test day. But if you find yourself guessing often, you'd probably benefit more from redoubling your prep efforts than you would from refining your guessing strategy. The only way to improve your score more than a minuscule amount is to learn some techniques to help you actually get the questions right *without* uncertainty. We'll get to those soon.

---

[*] If you want to get really crazy and add a bit of granularity into this, you can. Replace the little mark you were using to signify a guess with a number. Rate your guesses on a scale of 1 (*no idea whatsoever*) to 3 (*got a good feeling about this*), and score your test first with all the guesses, then with only the 3-rated guesses, then with the 3- and 2-rated guesses, etc. You could similarly use numbers to note how many choices (if any) you were able to eliminate before you guessed. I wouldn't go so far down the rabbit hole, but if you want to, you have a lot of options.

The hardest questions are the least important ones

Imagine you're given the task of picking as many apples from a particular apple tree as possible, in a limited amount of time. You know that none of the apples on the tree are any more or less delicious than any of the others, but of course the higher up they are, the harder they are to get.

Are you going to climb right to the top to get the most difficult apples first? Not if you want to pick the most apples! I guess if it's important to you to brag to your friends that you got the highest apple, you might do that. But if that's what you want to brag about to your friends, maybe it's time to look at your life, and look at your choices.

In the SAT math section, the questions go roughly in order from easiest to hardest, but each question carries the same point value. There's no bonus for getting the hardest ones right. So if you're skipping questions early to get to questions late, if you're rushing through the easy ones to get to the hard ones, *you're doing it wrong*. You're spending precious time on questions that are very difficult without giving enough thought to questions that are much easier. If you prioritized your time differently, you might very well see a higher score.

To go back to the apple tree example, skipping early questions or rushing to get to the hard ones faster is like climbing to the top of the tree before you've picked all the easier apples towards the bottom—the ones you can reach from the ground without climbing at all. You're risking your entire day's work by doing so. You might get fired from your apple picking job for being insanely inefficient. How will you afford your Xbox Live subscription without that job?

Let's look at this one more way to really drive the point home. Every test's scoring table is slightly different, but you can usually break 700 with 49 raw score points. There are 54 raw score points available (that's if you get every question right), so you can actually skip 5 questions (or get 4 wrong if you answer everything) and still get your 700.

Do you understand what this means? It means you can get a kick-ass score without ever tackling the hardest question in each math section, and pick two other hard ones to skip! If you stop rushing to get to the hardest questions, laboring through them, and often still getting them wrong, you'll probably make fewer errors on the easier questions. You'll make the test *easier* as you *raise* your score.

This is a subtle point, but it's a huge factor in whether your math score is going to show an impressive improvement. *If you really want your score to go up, start prioritizing the easy points.* Once you're consistently getting all of those—you *never* miss anything of easy or medium difficulty—*then* you can start to worry about the hardest questions.

Is this rubbing you the wrong way? Are you, like, *so* mad at me right now? Don't be obstinate! This is good advice! It's not meant to limit your score; it's meant to maximize it. Unless you're already breaking 700—or whatever your goal score is—getting the easy questions right more often is the easiest way to improve.

On the next page you'll find a handy chart to help you figure out how many questions you can afford to skip on test day and still hit your goal. I've come up with the numbers by averaging the scoring tables from a bunch of previous tests, so they're a pretty good ballpark even though the test you're given on test day might vary a little bit.

Note that these numbers are based on the assumption that you're getting everything you *do* answer right. If you think you're likely to make a few mistakes on the questions you attempt, give yourself a little buffer in your test day game plan.

If you want to score around __…	…you need a raw score of __…	…so you can skip __ questions.
800	54	0 (Duh.)
780	53	1
760	52	2
740	51	3 (one per section)
720	50	4
710	49	5
690	48	6 (two per section)
680	47	7
670	46	8
660	45	9 (three per section)
650	43 or 44	10 or 11
640	42	12 (four per section)
630	41	13
620	40	14
610	39	15 (five per section)
600	38	16
590	37	17
580	36	18 (six per section)
570	34 or 35	19 or 20
560	33	21 (seven per section)
550	32	22
540	31	23
530	30	24 (eight per section)
530	29	25
520	28	26
510	27	27 (nine per section)

As you know, there are three kinds of SAT math sections. On the sections that are completely multiple choice—the 20-question and 16-question sections—you can expect all the hard questions to be at the end. The 18-question grid-in section is a slightly different story. The grid-in section goes from easy to hard twice—once in the first 8 multiple choice questions, and then again in the 10 grid-in questions. This is important information! If you're planning to skip 2 questions per section, you might choose to skip the last two questions in the 20-question and 16-question sections, but skip #8 and #18 in the 18-question section.

In closing, let me repeat myself because this is important: don't worry if you don't finish the hardest question or two in a section if you've made sure you got the easier ones right. That's a good trade-off and it probably improved your score. *You'll increase your score more by getting fewer easy ones wrong than you will by getting more hard ones right.* So slow down, work carefully, and bask in the glow of your score report when it arrives and proves me right.

Be suspicious of "easy" answers to "hard" questions

Since you've been paying such close attention, you know by now that the difficulty of math questions increases as a section progresses. On a 20 question section, you can count on #1 to be super easy, #5 to be bit tougher, #10 to require more than a modicum of thought, and #20 to be a royal pain. Duh, right? You know this. If you've ever taken an SAT or PSAT, it's almost impossible not to have noticed. But have you thought about what it means for you, the intrepid test taker?

This easy-to-hard section structure has two important implications:

→ Easy questions are more important than the hard ones for your score (which we just talked about).

→ You should be leery of "easy" answers to "hard" questions (which we're about to talk about).

When you're faced with a question that's supposed to be more difficult, you should resist the urge to jump on an answer choice that seems immediately obvious. It's probably best to illustrate this with an example.

Example

15. Stephen wins the lottery and decides to donate 30% of his winnings to charity. Then he decides to give 20% of what he has left to his mother. What percent of his winnings does Stephen have left for himself?

(A) 67%
(B) 56%
(C) 54%
(D) 50%
(E) 14%

This question isn't too tough and you might not need my help to solve it, but before we get to the solution I want to ask you something: what choice should you *not even consider*? Well, if this question was just asking you to start with 100%, and subtract 30% and 20% and end up at 50%, it wouldn't be a #15. It would be a #5. So there's *no flippin' way* it's (D). Since we know we're later in the test, there must be something else going on here. And sure enough, we see that Stephen gives 20% of what he has left *after* he's already donated 30% to charity.

I want to be clear: although it's sometimes presented as such, this is *not* a technique for answering a question correctly, and anyone who tells you otherwise hasn't spent enough time learning about the SAT. But it *is* helpful to remember that, once you're about halfway through a math section, the questions are supposed to require some thought, so you shouldn't fall for answers that require no thought at all.

Put another way: *this is not a way to get questions right. This is a way not to get questions wrong.*

To get it right, as we'll often do with percent questions, we're going to **plug in** (We'll talk much more about this technique starting on page 31).

Say Stephen won $100. He gives 30% of that ($30) to charity. Now he's got $70 left, 20% of which he gives to his poor old mother. 20% of 70 is 14, so he gives his mom $14. $70 − $14 = $56, so he's got $56 left for himself. 56% of his original winnings. The answer is (B).

Actually read the question

I'll be honest: I hate that I'm actually devoting pages of this guide to reminding you to read each question very carefully, but I am because I've worked with enough kids to know that errors due to misreading (and *misbubbling*[*]) are unspeakably common.

Rest assured that, if there's a way a question could possibly be misinterpreted by a test taker, the SAT writers have anticipated that error and made it an incorrect answer choice. So if you don't read the question carefully the first time, you'll feel warm and fuzzy about your incorrect answer. You *might* catch your mistake if you finish early and have time to review your answers, but there's also a pretty good chance your warm-and-fuzzy will carry all the way through until you get your score report back and see that you missed #6 and you're all like WTFFFFFF.

Tricks the SAT has been known to pull

➔ Give all the question information in feet, and ask for an answer in inches. Of course, make the same answer in feet an incorrect choice.

➔ Ask testers to solve for x^2, which is 49 (a perfect square—those *monsters*). Make 7 an incorrect answer choice to give the warm-and-fuzzy to everyone who automatically solved for x like they do every other day of the year.

➔ Write a question about John and Susie buying iguana treats or something. Ask how many Susie bought. Make the number John bought a choice too.

So yeah. Just like the aforementioned suspicion of "easy" answers to "hard" questions, this isn't really a strategy so much as it is me *imploring* you to actually put your eyes on the paper and read the question carefully, because the SAT has a long history of humbling those who don't.

---

[*] Misbubbling just gets a footnote. If I gave it its own chapter, I'd probably rip my hair out before I finished writing it. *Triple check* your bubbling. I can't tell you how many *very smart* kids I've worked with who have lost points to bubbling errors on the SAT. It's unbelievable to me. And they always just laugh it off! "Oops, I misbubbled, LOL." "Oops, I threw my shoe at you, LOL. Oops I threw my other one too! LOLLERCOASTER!!!1one"

18. The perimeter of an equilateral triangle with sides of length s is p. What is the perimeter of a square with sides of length $3s$, in terms of p?

(A) p^2
(B) $12p$
(C) $9p$
(D) $4p$
(E) $3p$

Recognize that on a question like this, there's almost always going to be a choice—and often more than one—meant to seem attractive to you when you're rushed and stressed on test day.

On this question, you could breeze through the question too quickly, miss the fact that you're asked about the perimeter of a *square* after you're given information about an *equilateral triangle*, and gravitate towards $3p$. (E) is a classic misread answer.

The other incorrect answers are also designed to look good to someone who's completely panicked (p^2 because you know, *squares*). It's actually a helpful mental exercise to try to figure out how the wrong answers are selected because it gives you insight into the way the test is written. Enough insight like that, and you'll be well on your way to earning your SAT black belt.

The solution, of course, is easiest found by **plugging in** (which, again, we'll discuss at length soon):

Say $s = 2$. An equilateral triangle with sides of length 2 has a perimeter of 6, so $p = 6$. Since $3s = 6$, a square with sides of length 6 has a perimeter of 24. So what's 24 in terms of p when $p = 6$? $4p$, of course! The correct answer is (D).

Read the question carefully. *Always.* You may be laughing now. You won't be when you lose precious points because of careless errors.

Techniques

Let me just say this right up front: *yes, every SAT problem can be solved with some combination of algebra, geometry, and reasoning.* You'll never encounter a question that can't be solved without employing some obscure test prep trickery. Any flesh-hungry zombie can be killed with one's bare hands, too, but it's still probably best, when preparing for a zombie apocalypse, to learn a few more expedient zombie extermination tactics. I hope you see where I'm going with this, because I think I'm doing an awesome job crafting an argument for learning some math-avoidant techniques —*even if you're really good at math.*

The following techniques won't come easily right away if this is the first time you're seeing them, but make no mistake: if you practice plugging in, backsolving, and guesstimating until they're second nature, then you'll be in a much better position to improve your math score than you'd be in if you just drilled yourself on algebra and geometry all day.

Plug in

When I say that *the SAT is not a math test*—which you'll get sick of hearing by the time you're done with this book—this is one of the primary reasons. On the SAT, it's often completely unnecessary to do the math that's been so carefully laid out before you. A lot of the time, and on a lot of the most otherwise onerous problems, all you need to do is make up numbers.

Sounds crazy, right? It's not. It would be crazy to just make up numbers on just about any other number-driven task—for instance, it would be a pretty bad idea just to make up numbers on your taxes—but you'll be dumbstruck by how often doing so works in your favor on the SAT. Of course, you'll have to practice **plugging in** a fair amount before it becomes second nature. That way, when an opportunity to do it on the real test pops up, you don't panic and blow it. This kind of thing is precisely why you and I have come together.

The best way to teach you how to plug in is just to show you how it works, so let's get right into an example that's *begging* to be solved by plugging in.

Example 1

13. If $a + b = c$, which of the following is equal to $a^2 + b^2$?

    (A) $c + 2ab$

    (B) $c(a + b)$

    (C) c^2

    (D) $c^2 - ab$

    (E) $c^2 - 2ab$

Now, maybe you see an algebraic solution here and maybe you don't. For our purposes right at this moment, it doesn't matter. We're going to solve this one by plugging in so that we can do arithmetic, not algebra. Start by assigning values to a and b. I like to keep my numbers small, and it's my book, so let's say $a = 2$ and

$b = 3$. Of course, since the question tells us that c is the sum of a and b, we can't just make up anything I want for c. *When we have an equation, we can't plug in values for both sides; we have to choose one side on which to plug in, and then see what effects our choices have on the other side.* Once I've chosen $a = 2$ and $b = 3$, now I have to say that $c = 5$:

$$a + b = c$$
$$2 + 3 = 5$$

Next, we need to figure out what $a^2 + b^2$ is:

$$a^2 + b^2 = 2^2 + 3^2 = 13$$

From here, all we need to do is plug our values for a, b, and c into each answer choice to see which one gives us 13!

(A) $c + 2ab = 5 + 2(2)(3) = 5 + 12 = 17$ ✗   (too big...)

(B) $c(a + b) = 5(2 + 3) = 5(5) = 25$ ✗   (even bigger...)

(C) $c^2 = 5^2 = 25$ ✗   (good grief...)

(D) $c^2 - ab = 5^2 - (2)(3) = 25 - 6 = 19$ ✗   (warmer...)

(E) $c^2 - 2ab = 5^2 - 2(2)(3) = 25 - 12 = 13$ ✓   (yes!)

Sure enough, only one answer choice works, and we didn't need to do any algebra to figure out which one. Cool, right?

Note that if we'd used different numbers for a and b, we still would have gotten the same answer. That's the beautiful thing about plugging in! Try it yourself: what happens when $a = 11$ and $b = 19$?

Example 2

16. If positive integer constants m and n are divided by 6, the remainders are 4 and 5, respectively. What is the remainder when mn is divided by 6?

(A) 0
(B) 2
(C) 3
(D) 4
(E) 5

What we want to do with a question like this is plug in values for m and n so that we're not dealing with abstract concepts, but rather real values. Of course, there are infinite possibilities for both m and n, but we're just going to pick specific values and stick with them.

Since the problem stipulates that m divided by 6 leaves a remainder of 4, and n divided by 6 leaves a remainder of 5, let's pick $m = 10$ and $n = 11$. (6 goes into 10 once with a remainder of 4; 6 goes into 11 once with a remainder of 5.) That will keep our numbers nice and small, and make the division we'll have to do in the next step less arduous.

Now we just need to find the remainder when mn (or $10 \times 11 = 110$) is divided by 6. I gave you a shortcut for finding remainders in the Introduction to this book, but I include the long division on the right just for nostalgia.

$$
\begin{array}{r}
18\ \text{R}\ 2 \\
6\overline{)110} \\
\underline{-6} \\
50 \\
\underline{-48} \\
2
\end{array}
$$

Bam! Remainder 2. That's choice (B). I feel so *alive* right now.

Again, note that if we picked different numbers for m and n (like, say, 76 and 77), we'd still get the same answer. Try it yourself and see.

How hard would this question have been to solve without plugging in numbers? Pretty darn tricky. A general solution exists, of course, but if you would consider trying to find the general solution under timed conditions on test day, you're probably out of your mind, possibly an evil genius, and definitely in need of SAT guidance.

Let's do one more example together. This one's a little tougher; it might not be obvious right away that you can plug in.

Example 3

17. If k is an integer constant greater than 1, which of the following values of x satisfies the inequality $\frac{x}{3} + 1 \geq k$?

   (A) $k - 3$
   (B) $k - 1$
   (C) k
   (D) $3k - 4$
   (E) $3k - 2$

OK. Forget for a minute that this can be solved with algebra and think about how to solve it by plugging in. Remember, if you don't practice plugging in on problems you know how to do otherwise, you won't be able to plug in well when you come to a problem you don't know how to solve otherwise!

We know k is a positive integer greater than 1, so let's say it's 2. If $k = 2$, then we can do a little manipulation to see that x has to be greater than or equal to 3:

$$\frac{x}{3} + 1 \geq 2$$

$$\frac{x}{3} \geq 1$$

$$x \geq 3$$

Again, note that we don't just make up a number for x! Once we've chosen a value for k, we've constrained the universe of possible values of x.

So, which answer choice, given our plugged in value of $k = 2$, gives us a number greater than or equal to 3 for x?

(A) $k - 3 = 2 - 3 = -1$	✗	(too low...)
(B) $k - 1 = 2 - 1 = 1$	✗	(nah...)
(C) $k = 2$	✗	(nope...)
(D) $3k - 4 = 6 - 4 = 2$	✗	(dude, naw...)
(E) $3k - 2 = 6 - 2 = 4$	✓	**(yes!)**

Rock. On. Note once again that if we had picked a different number for k, we still would have been OK. Try running through this with $k = 10$ to see for yourself.

When to plug in

→ When you see variables in the question *and* the answer, you might want to try plugging in.

→ On percent questions, you'll probably benefit from plugging in (and using 100 as your starting value).

→ In general, if you're plugging in on a geometry question, just make sure that all the angles in your triangles and straight lines add up to 180°. On triangle questions where no angles are given, you might want to try plugging in 60 for all angles.

→ Anytime you're stuck because you don't know something that you think it would be helpful to know, *try making it up*! The worst that can happen is you're no better off than before.

Plug in dos and don'ts

→ As a general rule, ***don't*** plug in 0. When you multiply things by 0, you always get 0, and when you add 0 to anything, it stays the same. I trust you see why this would be bad: too many answer choices will work.

→ Similarly, ***don't*** plug in 1, since when you multiply things by 1, they don't change. Again, this will often make more than one choice seem correct.

→ ***Don't*** plug in random numbers on both sides of an equal sign—equal signs must remain true! Remember back to Example 1: once we plugged in for *a* and *b*, we only had one choice for *c* to keep the equal sign true.

→ ***Do*** try to keep your numbers small. Don't plug in 2545 when 2 will do.

→ ***Do*** think for a minute before picking your numbers. Will the numbers you're choosing result in messy fractions or negative numbers? We plug in to make our lives *easier*, so try to avoid these scenarios! With a little practice, picking good numbers will become second nature.

→ ***Do*** check every single answer choice when you plug in, because there's always a small chance that more than one answer will work. If that happens, *don't panic*...just try new numbers. You can greatly mitigate this risk by adhering to the first two rules above—don't plug in 0 or 1.

Note: *All of these problems can be solved without plugging in, of course, but you're not here to do that right now. You're here to practice plugging in. Don't be intractable in your methods. If you're amenable to change, it's more feasible that you'll improve your scores.*

10. If $r + 9$ is 4 more than s, then $r - 11$ is how much less than s?

    (A) 9
    (B) 11
    (C) 16
    (D) 20
    (E) 24

12. If Brunhilda went to the casino and lost 40% of her money playing Pai Gow poker before doubling her remaining money playing roulette, the amount of money she had after playing roulette is what percent of the amount of money she started with?

    (A) 20%
    (B) 40%
    (C) 80%
    (D) 100%
    (E) 120%

14. If $x^3 = y$, then x^6 is how much greater than x^3, in terms of y?

    (A) y^3
    (B) y^2
    (C) $y(y - 1)$
    (D) $2y - y$
    (E) $y - 1$

Practice questions: Plug in

Remember: Plugging in on the SAT is good. Doing so on your taxes is bad.

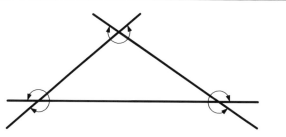

16. What is the sum of the measures of the marked angles in the figure above?

   (A) 1080°
   (B) 900°
   (C) 720°
   (D) 540°
   (E) 360°

20. In a certain office, there are c chairs, d desks, and e employees. Five desks are not occupied, and all other desks are occupied by exactly one employee. All but two of the employees have two chairs at their desks, and all the other desks, whether they are occupied or not, have one chair. If $e > 2$, then which of the following expressions is equal to c?

   (A) $2(d-5)+e$
   (B) $d+e$
   (C) $2(d-e)$
   (D) $2(d-2)$
   (E) $2e+3$

Answers:

10. **(C)**

12. **(E)**

14. **(C)**

16. **(B)**

20. **(E)**

Solutions on page 281.

You can plug in to solve the following Blue Book questions.

Test	§	p	#	Diff.	Test	§	p	#	Diff.
1	3	399	11	3	6	2	701	6	M
1	3	401	20	5	6	2	702	10	M
1	7	414	4	2	6	2	703	13	M
1	8	422	10	3	6	2	705	19	H
1	8	423	12	4	6	4	712	2	E
1	8	424	15	5	6	4	714	7	M
2	2	454	7	2	6	8	731	9	M
2	2	456	14	3	6	8	732	14	H
2	5	464	3	2	6	8	733	15	H
2	5	464	4	2	6	8	733	16	H
2	5	464	5	2	7	3	769	3	E
2	5	465	7	3	7	3	770	7	M
2	5	467	14	3	7	3	773	17	H
2	8	482	4	2	7	7	786	3	E
2	8	483	6	2	7	7	787	9	M
2	8	483	7	3	7	9	796	4	E
2	8	485	13	4	7	9	797	8	M
3	2	516	9	3	7	9	797	9	M
3	2	519	20	5	7	9	797	10	M
3	5	526	3	1	7	9	799	13	M
4	3	581	3	E	8	3	832	8	H
4	3	583	8	M	8	7	848	3	E
4	3	585	18	H	8	7	851	16	M
4	3	586	20	H	8	9	859	7	M
4	6	594	5	M	9	2	887	3	E
4	6	595	8	H	9	2	888	7	H
4	6	597	15	M	9	2	888	8	H
4	9	612	12	M	9	5	905	9	M
4	9	613	13	M	9	5	906	13	M
4	9	613	16	H	9	5	907	15	M
5	2	639	6	E	9	8	916	6	M
5	2	640	8	M	9	8	918	12	M
5	2	641	14	M	10	2	949	6	M
5	2	642	16	M	10	2	952	14	M
5	4	650	1	E	10	5	965	2	E
5	2	640	8	M	10	5	970	20	H
5	8	670	13	M	10	8	979	7	M
5	8	670	14	M	10	8	980	13	M
5	8	671	16	H	10	8	980	14	M
					10	8	981	16	H
					11	3	10	5	3
					11	4	18	17	3
					11	4	19	19	5

Obviously, it's up to you to choose whether to plug in or not on a particular problem, but this table should make it plain to you that you often have the option.

Backsolve

It's important to be ever-cognizant of the fact that on a multiple choice test, one—and *only* one—of the 5 answers has to be right. It's sometimes possible to exploit this aspect of the test's design to answer a question correctly by starting with the answer choices, and working backwards. Most in the prep world call this **backsolving**, and it's so powerful on the SAT because *the SAT will always put numerical answer choices in order*, so it's easy to backsolve efficiently. High difficulty questions are less likely to be vulnerable to backsolving than they are to plugging in, but backsolving is an indispensable technique nonetheless.

As we did in the plug in chapter, let's begin with a fairly simple one.

Example 1

10. Shira keeps both dogs and cats as pets; she has 7 pets in total. A dog eats 4 pounds of food per day, and a cat eats 1 pound of food per day. If Shira uses 16 pounds of food per day to feed her pets, how many dogs does she have?

(A) 2
(B) 3
(C) 4
(D) 5
(E) 6

Alright. So this problem isn't that hard, and I'm sure you could solve it with algebra, but hold off on that for now. I want to talk about backsolving, and if you can't backsolve on an easy question, you're not going to be able to use this technique when it's really useful on a hard question. Instead of trying to write equations, then, let's use the fact that one of the 5 answers has to be right to our advantage. If we start with answer (C), we'll have to try *at most* 3 answers, since

(C) is in the middle and if it's not right we'll know right away whether we need to go higher or lower.

Note that, since we know the total number of pets, we also know how many cats Shira would have in each answer choice. For example, if she has 4 dogs like it says in choice (C), then she has 3 cats to make 7 total pets. We can represent this information in a handy table:

Answer choice	Dogs	Cats
(C)	4	3

But wait. We also know how much food each kind of pet eats. Let's throw that into the table, too! Each dog eats 4 pounds per day, and each cat eats 1.

Answer choice	Dogs	Dog food (lbs per day)	Cats	Cat food (lbs per day)	Total food (lbs per day)
(C)	4	16	3	3	19

Hopefully what you're seeing there is that we're using too much food. The question said we're supposed to use 16 pounds of food per day, but if choice (C) were right, we'd be using 19 pounds. So choice (C) is wrong, and we've got a pretty clear direction to move in: we need to use less food for Shira's 7 pets, so we need fewer dogs (who eat a lot of food) and more cats (who eat less food). So let's try choice (B):

Answer choice	Dogs	Dog food (lbs per day)	Cats	Cat food (lbs per day)	Total food (lbs per day)
~~(C)~~	~~4~~	~~16~~	~~3~~	~~3~~	~~19~~
(B)	**3**	**12**	**4**	**4**	**16**

And there you have it. When there are 3 dogs and 4 cats, Shira uses 16 pounds of food per day, just like the question said. So (B) is the correct answer.

The beauty of this technique is that, while it might take a bit of practice to internalize, it'll eventually feel very intuitive. You start in the middle, and if the middle doesn't work, the question pushes you in the right direction. Again, this was a fairly easy one, and you might not have had any trouble writing equations to solve it, but it's important that you start to look at the SAT a bit differently. Adding a technique like backsolve to your bag of tricks will make you a more formidable test taker, whether you use it all the time or not.

Let's do one more together, shall we? What's that? You want a *harder* one? I suppose I can make that happen.

Example 2

18. Rex is a carnivorous dinosaur who lives on an island that is also inhabited by people. He eats one fourth of the people on his island on Monday, 13 of them on Tuesday, and half as many as he ate on Monday on Wednesday. If there are 22 people left on the island on Thursday, and nobody came to the island or left in a way other than being eaten in that time period, how many people were on the island before Rex's rampage?

(A) 56
(B) 64
(C) 68
(D) 74
(E) 75

As I did for the last question, I'm going to use a table to keep track of what's going on here. When you get comfortable backsolving you might decide you don't need to use a table, but doing so has always been useful to me.* Your call. You just

---

* As you'll see in the back of this book, my handwriting isn't super neat. Tables help me keep things organized, so I can make sense of my work when I go back to check it.

need to pick an answer choice to start with—almost always (C)—and follow the instructions in the question to see whether everything is internally consistent.

Answer choice	People on island before rampage	People eaten Monday ($\frac{1}{4}$ total)	People eaten Tuesday (13)	People eaten Wednesday ($\frac{1}{2}$ eaten Mon)	People left Thursday
(C)	68	−17	−13	−8.5	29.5

As the table above shows, if (C) is true and 68 people were on the island before the carnage, then 17 were eaten Monday. 13 people were eaten Tuesday. Finally, half the number of people who were eaten Monday were eaten Wednesday, which means on Wednesday Rex only ate 8.5 people. We know (C) isn't right if it's going to leave us with a fractional person, but more importantly, $68 - 17 - 13 - 8.5 = 29.5$, which means the number of people left according to (C) is too big! Remember, we're trying to end up with 22 people left on the island, so fewer than 68 people must have started on the island.

Let's try (B) 64 instead:

Answer choice	People on island before rampage	People eaten Monday ($\frac{1}{4}$ total)	People eaten Tuesday (13)	People eaten Wednesday ($\frac{1}{2}$ eaten Mon)	People left Thursday
~~(C)~~	~~68~~	~~−17~~	~~−13~~	~~−8.5~~	~~29.5~~
(B)	64	−16	−13	−8	27

As you can see, 64 doesn't work either, but we're getting closer. At this point, we're pretty confident (A) is our answer, but it also shouldn't take us very much longer to confirm it:

Answer choice	People on island before rampage	People eaten Monday ($\frac{1}{4}$ total)	People eaten Tuesdau (13)	People eaten Wednesday ($\frac{1}{2}$ eaten Mon)	People left Thursday
~~(C)~~	~~68~~	~~−17~~	~~−13~~	~~−8.5~~	~~29.5~~
~~(B)~~	~~64~~	~~−16~~	~~−13~~	~~−8~~	~~27~~
(A)	56	−14	−13	−7	22

Alright. Nice. We've successfully summarized a gruesome scene[*] with a neat and tidy table. High five!

When to try backsolving

→ If the answer choices are numbers (in numerical order—they always will be), there's a decent chance backsolving will work.

→ If the question is a word problem, your chances get even better.

→ Even if neither of these conditions is met, you still might be able to backsolve. Always be on the lookout for chances to work backwards from the answers!

Things to keep in mind while backsolving

→ You're almost always going to want to start with (C), but if a question asks for a least possible value, start with (A) or (E), whichever is least. Same goes, obviously, for questions that ask for greatest possible value.

→ Sometimes it won't be obvious to you which direction to move in if (C) doesn't work. If this happens, don't freak out, just pick a direction and go. Remember, backsolving is supposed to *save* you time, so don't spend all day trying to figure out how to be efficient and not try any extra wrong choices by mistake. You'll spend less time on the question if you just go in the wrong direction first.

→ Practice, of course, will make all this easier, and reveal subtle nuances to the technique that might not be obvious right away. As with any new technique, you'll want to make sure backsolving is second nature for you before you sit down for the real test. So practice it on hard questions *now*, and reap the benefits on test day.

---

[*] This is probably obvious without me saying it, but you'll never see a question so macabre on the SAT. I'm just trying to keep you awake. :)

Note: As was true in the plug in drill, all of these problems have non-backsolve solutions, but you should resist the urge to fall back on your algebra skills. The same old methods you've already been using will just get you the same old score you've already been getting. Use this drill to practice backsolving.

13. Rajesh sells only hats and scarves at his store, for which he charges $13 and $7, respectively. On Monday, he sold 15 items and made $123. How many hats did Rajesh sell on Monday?

    (A) 3
    (B) 4
    (C) 5
    (D) 6
    (E) 7

16. From where he lives, it costs Jared $4 more for a round-trip train ticket to Chaska than it does for one to Waconia. Last month, Jared took round-trips to Chaska 7 times and to Waconia 8 times. If he spent a total of $103 on train tickets, how much does Jared spend on one round-trip ticket to Waconia?

    (A) $12
    (B) $10
    (C) $9
    (D) $7
    (E) $5

$$V(n) = 8100 \left(\frac{7}{6}\right)^n$$

17. A number of years ago, Andy purchased $8,100 worth of stock in PGHH Corporation. The value, in dollars, of his stock n years after purchase is given by the function V, above. If the stock is worth $11,000 now, roughly how many years ago did Andy purchase his stock?

    (A) Five
    (B) Four
    (C) Three
    (D) Two
    (E) One

18. The audience of a reality TV show cast a total of 3.4 million votes, and each vote went to either Brian or Susan. If Susan received 34,000 more votes than Brian, what percent of the votes were cast for Brian?

    (A) 45%
    (B) 49%
    (C) 49.5%
    (D) 49.9%
    (E) 49.95%

19. All the survivors who live in a certain post-apocalyptic settlement spend their miserable days hunting mutant buffalo or growing broccoli, and some do both. If, in total, 45 survivors grow broccoli, 30 hunt, and 37 of them perform only one of those tasks, how many perform both tasks?

    (A) 56
    (B) 38
    (C) 19
    (D) 11
    (E) 9

Answers:

13. **(A)**
16. **(E)**
17. **(D)**
18. **(C)**
19. **(C)**

Solutions on page 283.

You can backsolve the following Blue Book questions.

Test	§	p	#	Diff.	Test	§	p	#	Diff.
1	3	397	3	1	7	7	785	1	E
1	3	398	9	3	7	7	786	6	E
1	7	414	3	2	7	7	789	18	H
1	7	415	8	5	7	9	797	7	M
1	8	424	16	4	7	9	798	12	M
2	2	454	9	2	8	3	831	3	E
2	2	456	16	3	8	3	831	4	E
2	2	457	19	4	8	7	849	7	M
2	8	484	10	3	8	7	849	10	M
3	2	514	1	1	8	7	851	17	H
3	2	517	13	3	8	9	857	1	E
3	2	518	14	3	8	9	858	4	E
3	8	545	7	2	8	9	859	8	M
4	3	581	1	E	9	5	904	6	E
4	3	581	2	E	9	5	908	19	H
4	6	593	1	E	9	8	915	1	E
4	9	609	1	E	9	8	915	2	E
4	9	611	9	M	9	8	916	5	E
5	2	638	1	E	10	2	949	3	E
5	2	638	2	E	10	5	966	4	E
5	2	640	10	M	10	5	966	6	M
5	2	641	13	M	10	5	967	7	M
5	4	651	4	E	10	5	968	12	M
5	8	667	2	E	11	4	15	4	1
6	4	713	4	E	11	4	15	7	2
6	4	714	8	H	11	8	32	1	2
6	8	729	1	E	11	8	34	7	2
6	8	731	8	M	11	8	35	12	4

A bunch of these are very easy. I'm not saying you *must* backsolve the first problem in a section; I'm only saying that you should start to recognize every opportunity.

Guesstimate

All figures on the SAT are drawn to scale unless indicated otherwise. In other words, if it doesn't say "<u>Note:</u> Figure not drawn to scale," underneath a figure then that figure *is* drawn to scale. The majority of figures on the SAT *are* drawn to scale, which means you'll have plenty of opportunities to **guesstimate**.

Guesstimating could mean actively trying to eyeball relative angle measures, areas, or segment lengths, or it could mean sliding pieces of the diagram around in your mind, but either way it means you have to do a bit less math. You might still end up doing some math because guesstimating won't always lead you all the way to an answer, and we'll spend a bunch of time in this book looking at some very mathy geometry, but it's important that you not waste the opportunity when a diagram is drawn to scale to get as far as you can without math. Let's dig right into an example:

Example 1

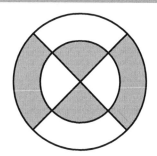

14. The figure above depicts two intersecting diameters of two concentric circles of radius 6 and 10. If the diameters are perpendicular, what is the total area of the shaded regions?

(A) 32π
(B) 50π
(C) 58π
(D) 64π
(E) 74π

Stop doing math! You need almost none of it to solve this problem. How can you guesstimate this? Well, what's the area of the large circle? If its radius is 10, then its area is $\pi(10)^2 = 100\pi$. What's half of that? 50π. Good, the answer is (B).

Why? Glad you asked. What happens if I rearrange the pieces of the puzzle?

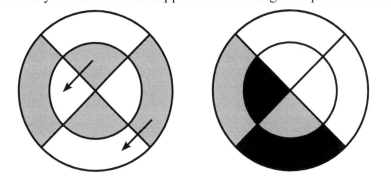

Oh *Hellllll* yes. Look at that. Doesn't that excite you? I love guesstimating so flippin' much.

Note that guesstimating doesn't just apply to shaded regions. You can use it to solve all kinds of geometry questions. As long as a figure is drawn to scale, you should ponder the implications of guesstimating for a few seconds before you start doing any math. *This takes practice*, but I promise you it's worth it when you become proficient.

This one weird trick

Look, I don't want to oversell this. You're not going to see a huge score increase because of it. But if you desperately need to compare the lengths of a few segments, you can make notches in your pencil with your thumbnail, and then use your new makeshift ruler to solve the problem.[*]

Occasionally, a geometry question will appear that asks you to figure out the length of a segment based on information about the lengths of other segments. If the figure is drawn to scale, you and your thumbnail are in business.

---

[*] It's been pointed out to me that one might accomplish the same effect by making marks on the edge of one's answer sheet. I don't like that as much because it involves some amount of paper-shuffling on your desk, which might result in some unwanted attention from your proctor. It's not expressly forbidden to use your answer sheet like that, but that doesn't guarantee a proctor won't give you a hard time about it—or think you were doing something else you weren't supposed to be doing—and if that happens you're at a disadvantage whether you're right or not.

Example 2

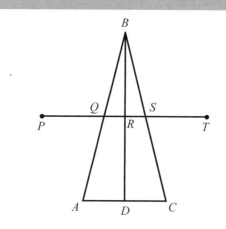

17. In the figure above, $\overline{PT} \parallel \overline{AC}$, R is the midpoint of perpendicular segments $\overline{BD}$ and $\overline{PT}$, and D is the midpoint of $\overline{AC}$. If $AC = 4$, $BD = 8$, and $PQ = 3$, what is the length of $\overline{PT}$?

(A) 6
(B) 8
(C) 10
(D) 10.5
(E) 11

There's a mathematical solution to this, of course, but *since it's drawn to scale* and all we're asked to do is compare the lengths of a couple line segments, I'm going to show you how to do this one the quick and dirty way.

Take a standard wooden #2 pencil. You know, the kind you think of when someone says the word "pencil." The archetype. If you've ever chewed on one of these you know how easy it is to make dents in the wood. Use your thumbnail to make a dent. Go ahead—I'll wait.

Now use the pencil's softness to your advantage. You know $BD = 8$, and since the figure is drawn to scale, you can hold the pencil up to the paper, and carefully use your thumbnails to make two dents in your pencil at each end of $\overline{BD}$. Then you can use this makeshift ruler to compare the length of $\overline{BD}$ to other lengths on the diagram. If you're lucky, you'll be able to eliminate some, or maybe even all, of the answer choices.

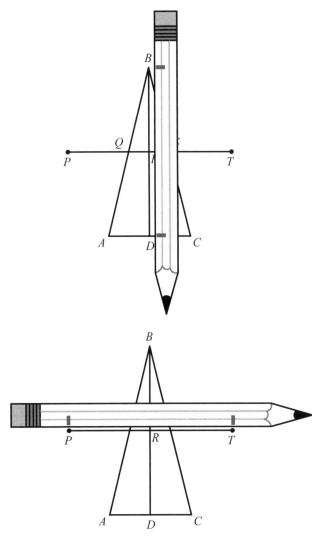

OMG. It looks like $PT = 8$ too! In fact, there aren't any other choices that are close enough to 8 to do any more work. Pick (B) and move right along.

Now, let me repeat what I said above: this pencil-denting trick is not going to win you beaucoup points; you might go through an entire test without an opportunity to use it. But it's one more way to attack a geometry question that's drawn to scale, and it just might help to extricate you from a bind. Keep it in the back of your mind, and look for opportunities to use it as you work through practice tests. Soon you'll be able to recognize when it will work, and when it won't.

Note: The questions in this drill can be solved with math, but your mission is to solve them with guesstimate. Make me proud.

13. The figure above shows an isosceles right triangle with legs of length m. Which of the following has the greatest area?

    (A) Four isosceles right triangles with legs of length m
    (B) A square with sides of length $m\sqrt{2}$
    (C) A square with a diagonal of length $m\sqrt{2}$
    (D) A circle with radius of length m
    (E) It cannot be determined from the information given.

$A \bullet\!\!-\!\!-\!\!-\!\!-\!\!\bullet\quad\quad\bullet\quad\bullet\!\!-\!\!-\!\!-\!\!-\!\!\bullet E$
$\quad\quad B\quad\quad\quad C\quad D$

15. In the figure above, $AB + 1 = BC$, $BE - 6 = BD$, and $DE - 3 = BD - 5$. If $AB = 4$, what is the length of $\overline{CD}$?

    (A) 3
    (B) 4
    (C) 5
    (D) 7
    (E) 8

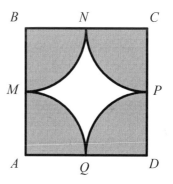

17. In the figure above, $ABCD$ is a square and M, N, P, and Q are midpoints of $\overline{AB}$, $\overline{BC}$, $\overline{CD}$, and $\overline{AD}$, respectively. The arcs shown have centers at A, B, C, and D. If $AB = 6$, what is the area of the shaded regions?

    (A) 36π
    (B) 18π
    (C) 12π
    (D) 9π
    (E) 6π

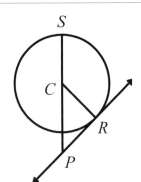

19. In the figure above, the line containing points P and R is tangent to the circle at R, and $\overline{CR}$ is a radius of length 3. If the measure of $\angle RCS$ is 135°, what is SP?

(A) 5
(B) $4\sqrt{2}$ (approximately 5.66)
(C) 6
(D) $3 + 3\sqrt{2}$ (approximately 7.24)
(E) $6\sqrt{2}$ (approximately 8.49)

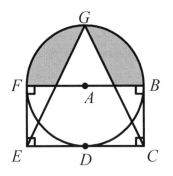

20. In the figure above A is the center of the circle, A and D lie on $\overline{BF}$ and $\overline{CE}$, respectively, and B, D, F, and G lie on the circle. If BC = 3, and $\overline{DG}$ (not shown) bisects $\overline{BF}$, what is the total area of the shaded regions?

(A) $9\pi - 24$

(B) $9\pi - 9$

(C) $\dfrac{9\pi - 9}{2}$

(D) $5\pi - 6$

(E) $\dfrac{3\pi - 3}{2}$

Answers:

13. **(D)**
15. **(A)**
17. **(D)**
19. **(D)**
20. **(C)**

Solutions on page 285.

You might find guesstimating helpful on these Blue Book questions.

Test	§	p	#	Diff.
1	3	400	15	3
2	8	481	2	1
3	2	516	7	2
3	2	518	17	4
3	5	525	2	1
7	7	788	12	M
8	7	852	20	H
9	5	905	8	M
10	2	953	17	H
11	4	19	20	5

Even if you never get comfortable using guesstimate as a primary technique, I *implore* you to use it when a diagram is drawn to scale as a double check to make sure any answer you get with more mathematical methods at least makes sense.

Interlude: Look for trends.

I'm constantly reminding students to look for trends on the SAT, because the key to transcendent scores is a deep understanding of the way the test works. If you want to be a truly adroit test taker, you're going to have to devote yourself to taking every test you take *actively*. You should be looking for trends in the kinds of mistakes you're making, and you should also be making mental (or heck, *physical*) notes of every question you see that strikes you as something new or novel.

Do you play video games? How about poker? Do you ever go outside and play baseball? When I was your age....

True domination in any game comes only after you have internalized the systems in which the game is played. When you start playing a new first person shooter, *even if you're good at FPS games in general*, you have to spend time getting shot in the back right after you spawn until you've really learned the maps. You have to master the trajectories of projectiles that don't go in a straight line (grenades, etc). You must learn the timing of the sniper rifle. You have to learn the game's physics, inside and out, and then you need to start recognizing the common behaviors of other players. For example, you might notice that most guys run right for the rocket launcher when they spawn anywhere near it. Can you use that knowledge to your advantage?

Poker is similar. Decent poker players know how to bet given the hand they have, because they know something about probability. *Good* poker players know what their opponents have based on how their opponents bet. When a good poker player sits down at a new table, she spends time learning about her opponents. Who likes to bluff? Who plays fast, and who plays slow? What are these players' tells?

And then there's baseball. Professional baseball players don't face a pitcher they've never seen before without reading a scouting report to try to learn what pitches they're likely to see in which situations. Ever try to hit a curve ball before? It's really hard to do! But you know what makes it a little easier? *Knowing a curve ball is coming.* Pitchers do the same thing with batters. They know who not to pitch inside and low, for example, and who can't lay off the slider in the dirt.

I've compiled this book to help you identify the most common trends on the SAT, but don't just sit back and allow me to do all the work. As you work through this book and the Blue Book, be on the lookout for familiar themes. When you take ownership of these observations, when you treat the entire SAT like a game of you vs. them, when you start to feel like you know what the SAT is going to throw your way before you even open the test booklet, *that's* when you're ready to PWN it.

Numbers and operations

Don't be lulled into complacency by the fact that you were introduced to the concepts that fall under the "Numbers and Operations" umbrella when you were in elementary school. The writers of the SAT are quite adept at finding ways to test simple concepts with difficult questions.

In this section you'll practice "easy" stuff like percents, ratios, proportions, and some "hard" stuff like counting problems and patterns. Pay close attention to the ways these concepts are tested. This won't be the last time you'll see them done like this, if you know what I mean. (I mean you'll likely see them tested this way on the real thing.)

Percents

First things first: let's make sure you're flawless on simple percent calculations. Different people use different methods to work through simple percent calculations, and if you're comfortable with percents then you might choose to ignore this tip, but here's how I translate sentences describing percents into mathematical notation:

→ The word "what" is a variable to be solved for, like x (or any other variable if x is already in use)

→ The word "is" translates to an equal sign.

→ The word "of" means multiplication.[*]

→ The word "percent" (or the % symbol) means "divided by 100."

So, for example, the sentence "What is 14 percent of 83?" translates to "x equals 14 divided by 100 times 83," or:

$$x = \frac{14}{100} \times 83$$

Solve that for x, and you'd know 14 percent of 83. Here's one more: "12 is 89 percent of what number?" translates to "12 equals 89 divided by 100 times x," or:

$$12 = \frac{89}{100} \times x$$

Cool? How about you try a few, just as a warm up before we get into the fun stuff? (Answers are at the very bottom of the page.)

✎ What is 11 percent of 110?

$(0.11)110 = ?$

✎ 93 is what percent of 31?

$93 = (31)x$

✎ 62 is 16 percent of what?

$62 = (0.16)x$

---

* Sometimes "of" doesn't mean multiplication, like in the phrases "the square root of x," or "f of x." When you're dealing with percents or fractions, though, "of" always means multiplication.

Answers: ● 12.1 ● 300 ● 387.5

OK, so that was fun, right? Of course it was. But unfortunately, the SAT will very rarely ask you to do something so simple. On the SAT, a challenging percent question will look a little more like this.

Example

19. If p is q percent of r, what is r in terms of p and q?

(A) $\dfrac{100p}{q}$

(B) $\dfrac{100q}{p}$

(C) $100pq$

(D) $\dfrac{pq}{100}$

(E) $\dfrac{100}{pq}$

If you've been paying attention, you should be thinking plug in here. Plug in 2 for p, 50 for q, and 4 for r and this question is a piece of cake. 2 is 50% of 4. The question asks for r, which is 4, so which answer choice works out to 4 when $p = 2$ and $q = 50$? Only choice (A).[*]

But of course, there's also an algebraic solution to this question, and I want you to know how to do it both ways. That way, should you see something similar on test day, you'll be able to solve it one way, check your work the other way, and pat yourself on the back for being super duper smart.

What tends to stymie students who struggle to solve this algebraically is the "q percent" part, because they've trained themselves to make quick decimal conversions when presented with percents. They'll calculate 82% of 40, for

---

* If you plugged in 100 for r, p and q would equal each other, so you wouldn't be able to distinguish between choices (A) and (B). When that happens, as you know, you shouldn't panic —just pick new numbers!

example, by moving the decimal point over two spaces to the left and typing "0.82 × 40" into their calculators. But that quick conversion doesn't work here; you can't just move the decimal point over on q.

Of course, when you make that quick decimal conversion in your mind, what you're *really* doing is dividing by 100. And that's why the little translation algorithm I outlined in the beginning of this chapter is useful. Let's apply it: "p is q percent of r" translates to "p equals q divided by 100 times r," or $p = \frac{q}{100}r$. Now just solve for r in terms of p and q:

$$p = \frac{q}{100}r$$

$$100p = qr$$

$$\frac{100p}{q} = r$$

Unsurprisingly, plug in and algebra both lead us to answer choice (A).

Percent change

When I was in high school, I weighed 120 pounds fully clothed and soaking wet. I couldn't do anything to change it, either. That was the worst part. I yearned to play varsity baseball, but at my weight, I just wasn't big enough.

College was mostly the same, although I filled out a little. I'd say my average weight in college reflected the "freshman fifteen," but for me it was a welcome change.

Then I graduated and got a job. I spent a few years living a largely sedentary existence, and eating too much fast food. Before I knew it, I weighed 150 pounds.

So over the years, I put on 30 pounds. What was the percent increase in my weight?

Here's the general formula for this kind of question:

$$\text{Percent Change (Increase or Decrease)} = \frac{\text{Amount of Change}}{\text{Original Value}} \times 100\%$$

Drop my values in:

$$\text{Percent Change}_{\text{Mike's march towards decrepitude}} = \frac{30 \text{ lbs}}{120 \text{ lbs}} \times 100\% = 25\%$$

And would you look at that? My weight increased by 25%! Holy moly. So say then I went on a diet and *lost* 30 pounds, so I'm right back where I started at 120. What will be my percent change then? (If the answer was just going to be 25% again I probably wouldn't be wasting your time with this.)

$$\text{Percent Change}_{\text{Mike's crazy diet}} = \frac{30 \text{ lbs}}{150 \text{ lbs}} \times 100\% = 20\%$$

Whoa. So it was a 25% increase, but now it's only about a 20% decrease? That doesn't seem fair!

An important thing to remember about percents is that the bigger the numbers are, the less difference a difference makes:

➔ If you owe your friend $20, you can reduce your debt by 50% by paying him $10. If you end up taking student loans when you go to college, it will be much harder to reduce your debt by 50%.

➔ The more you weigh, the more pounds you have to gain to increase your weight by 10%.

➔ If you're 16 years old and your little brother is 13, you're about 123% his age. But when you were 4 and he was 1, you were 400% his age. The older you both get, the smaller the percent difference will be, but you'll always be 3 years older than him.

➔ It's socially acceptable if one of your parents is 10 years older than the other, but it would have been *problematic* if they started dating when one of them was your age.

9. When Lucy complained to her boss that she was only making $75 per hour while her coworker Steve was making $100 per hour for the same work, her boss gave her a 25% raise. Lucy's hourly wages are now what percent of Steve's?

(A) 110%
(B) 100%
(C) 93.75%
(D) 75%
(E) 18.75%

15. What is 500% of 45% of 22% of n?

(A) $0.0495n$
(B) $0.099n$
(C) $0.495n$
(D) $0.99n$
(E) $49.5n$

March	$2,000	400
April	$2,400	
May	$3,000	600
June	$3,500	500
July	$4,300	800
August	$5,000	700

14. The table above represents the money Debbie earned, by month, for the last 6 months. When was the percent change in her income the greatest?

(A) From March to April
(B) From April to May
(C) From May to June
(D) From June to July
(E) From July to August

17. There are 30 more boys than girls in Monroe Township's intramural soccer league. If there are g girls in the league, then, in terms of g, what percent of participants in the league are girls?

(A) $\dfrac{g}{g+30}\%$

(B) $\dfrac{g}{2(g+30)}\%$

(C) $\dfrac{g}{100(2g-30)}\%$

(D) $\dfrac{100g}{2g+30}\%$

(E) $\dfrac{100g}{g+30}\%$

20. Arnold had m marbles before he gave some to Sophia, who had n marbles, in a strange and misguided attempt at flirtation. After the exchange, Arnold and Sophia each had 60 marbles and to their amazement, they realized that Sophia's percent gain in marbles was *exactly twice* Arnold's percent loss! What is the value of m?

(A) 77
(B) 80
(C) 90
(D) 103
(E) 119

Answers:

9. **(C)**

14. **(B)**

15. **(C)**

17. **(D)**

20. **(B)**

Solutions on page 287.

The following selected Blue Book questions are examples of this stuff in the wild.

Test	§	p	#	Diff.
1	3	401	20	5
2	8	486	15	5
3	2	517	13	3
3	2	518	15	3
4	3	586	20	H
4	9	613	13	M
5	4	655	16	H
5	8	670	12	M
6	4	716	11	M
6	4	717	16	M
7	9	796	3	E
8	3	834	13	M
8	7	848	5	E
8	9	861	15	H
9	5	908	19	H
11	3	9	4	2

Ratios

So here's the thing with ratios on the SAT: they're really easy. No, seriously, where are you going? Come back! They're easy, I *swear*. All you have to do is keep *very* close track of your units, and you'll be good to go. That means when you set up a proportion, actually *write the units* next to each number. Make sure you've got the same units corresponding to each other before you solve, and you're home free. Pass Go, collect your $200, and spend it all on Lik-M-Aid Fun Dip.

So uh...let's try one?

11. A certain farm has only cows and chickens as livestock. The ratio of cows to chickens is 2 to 7. If there are 63 livestock animals on the farm, how many cows are there?

   (A) 13
   (B) 14
   (C) 16
   (D) 18
   (E) 49

The SAT writers would love for you to set up a simple ratio equation here and solve:

$$\frac{2}{7} = \frac{x}{63}$$

Hooray! $x = 18$! That's answer choice (D)! *Not so fast, Dr. Moreau.*

You just conjured a terrifying hybrid beast, the *COWNIMALKEN*. Let's look at that fraction more carefully, with the units included:

$$\frac{2 \text{ cows}}{7 \text{ chickens}} = \frac{x \text{ cows}}{63 \text{ animals}}$$

So when you casually multiplied by 63 and solved, you solved for a unit that won't do you any good: the $\dfrac{\text{cow} \times \text{animal}}{\text{chicken}}$, or *COWNIMALKEN*. That's terrifying. Nature never intended it to be so. Also, you're getting an easy question wrong. You decide which is worse.

Before we can solve this question, we need to make sure our units line up on both sides of the equal sign. So let's change the denominator on the left to match the one on the right. Get rid of "7 chickens" and replace it with "9 animals." Get it? Because cows count as animals, if there are 2 cows for every 7 chickens, that means there are 2 cows for every 9 animals.

$$\dfrac{2 \text{ cows}}{\textbf{9 animals}} = \dfrac{x \text{ cows}}{63 \text{ animals}}$$

Now, we can solve: $x = 14$. There are 14 cows. That's choice (B). See how the units cancel out nicely when you've properly set up a ratio question? That should make the hairs on your neck stand on end.

Watch out for this trickery as well

But but but! There's one more thing you need to watch out for. Sometimes you'll be given units that aren't quite as easily converted. Like so:

Example 2

15. The ratio of students to teachers at a certain school is 28 to 3. The ratio of teachers to cafeteria workers is 9 to 2. What is the ratio of cafeteria workers to students?

(A) 1 to 42
(B) 2 to 28
(C) 3 to 37
(D) 9 to 56
(E) 3 to 14

Here, we have a few options. First, it's not too hard to find a number of teachers that will work with both ratios. There are 9 teachers in one ratio and 3 in the other. If we just unsimplify the students to teachers ratio, we can get to 9 teachers in both ratios, at which point the teachers become irrelevant.

$$\frac{28 \text{ students}}{3 \text{ teachers}} \times \frac{3}{3} = \frac{84 \text{ students}}{9 \text{ teachers}}$$

If there are 84 students for every 9 teachers, and 2 cafeteria workers for every 9 teachers, then there are 2 cafeteria workers for every 84 students. Simplify that ratio and you've got your answer: 2 to 84 simplifies to 1 to 42. That's choice (A).

Let me also point out that there's a pretty elegant solution here that comes from simply multiplying the two ratios together, essentially solving for the expression we're looking for without the (admittedly minor) manipulation we had to do above. Peep the skillz:

$$\frac{28 \text{ students}}{3 \text{ teachers}} \times \frac{9 \text{ teachers}}{2 \text{ cafeteria workers}}$$

What happens to the teachers? *They cancel!* So multiply, and simplify:

$$\frac{28 \text{ students}}{3 \text{ teachers}} \times \frac{9 \text{ teachers}}{2 \text{ cafeteria workers}} = \frac{252 \text{ students}}{6 \text{ cafeteria workers}} = \frac{42 \text{ students}}{1 \text{ cafeteria worker}}$$

Since the question asked for the ratio of cafeteria workers to students, just flip it and you're done! 1 cafeteria worker to 42 students. That's still choice (A)! Ahh-mazing.

10. In Ms. Picker's 3rd grade class, the ratio of boys to girls is 7 to 5. If there are 14 boys in the class, then how many students are in the class?

   (A) 10
   (B) 20
   (C) 24
   (D) 25
   (E) 36

12. The ratio of pens to pencils in Dore's drawer is 3 to 1. The ratio of sharpened pencils to unsharpened pencils in the drawer is 2 to 1. If there are 18 pens in the drawer, how many pencils in the drawer are sharpened?

   (A) 2
   (B) 4
   (C) 6
   (D) 10
   (E) 15

13. A certain Witch's Brew recipe calls for $1\frac{1}{2}$ cups werewolf hair and 1 eye of newt, and makes enough brew to curse 2 princesses. If Cheryl, who is a witch, wants to make enough Witch's Brew to curse 7 princesses, how many cups of werewolf hair will she need?

   (A) $5\frac{3}{4}$

   (B) $5\frac{1}{4}$

   (C) 5

   (D) $4\frac{3}{4}$

   (E) $3\frac{3}{4}$

16. The ratio of pennies to quarters in Garrett's pocket is 4 to 1. If there are only pennies and quarters in Garrett's pocket, which of the following could be the amount of money in his pocket?

   (A) $0.19
   (B) $0.54
   (C) $1.12
   (D) $1.45
   (E) $1.66

19. Andy and Sean are in a fantasy baseball league. Last month, the players on Andy's team struck out 7 times for every 2 home runs they hit. In the same month, Sean's players hit 9 home runs for every 5 home runs Andy's players hit. If Andy's players struck out 105 times last month, how many home runs did Sean's players hit over the same span of time?

   (A) 39
   (B) 45
   (C) 49
   (D) 54
   (E) 63

Answers:

10. **(C)**

12. **(B)**

13. **(B)**

16. **(D)**

19. **(D)**

Solutions on page 289.

The following selected Blue Book questions are examples of this stuff in the wild.

Test	§	p	#	Diff.
1	7	417	11	2
1	7	417	13	3
2	2	452	2	1
2	5	463	2	1
2	5	464	6	3
3	5	528	9	1
3	5	530	17	4
3	8	545	9	3
4	6	594	6	M
5	2	639	5	E
5	2	641	12	M
5	4	655	15	M
5	8	668	3	E
6	4	715	10	E
7	3	768	1	E
7	7	786	4	E
7	9	796	3	E
7	9	796	5	E
8	7	849	8	M
9	8	916	4	E
9	8	918	11	M
10	2	952	11	M
10	2	953	16	H
11	8	33	3	3

Proportionality

There are two kinds of proportionality[*] that you might see on the SAT: **direct proportionality**, and **inverse proportionality**. I'm going to cover both here since I'm in the business of preparing you for any eventuality, but you should know that the former is more prevalent than the latter. Don't sweat inverse proportionality all that much.

Direct proportionality

There are a few ways to represent direct proportionality mathematically. The Blue Book likes to say that when x and y are directly proportional, $y = kx$ for some nonzero constant k. This definition is correct of course—and you might find it useful sometimes—but since it introduces an extra value into the mix, it doesn't lend itself as easily to the kinds of questions you'll *usually* be asked on the SAT. I much prefer to say that *direct proportionality means the ratio of the two proportional variables will always be the same.*

When x and y are directly proportional:

$$y = kx \quad \text{and} \quad \frac{y_1}{x_1} = \frac{y_2}{x_2}$$

Note that the proportionality constant k remains in the second equation—both fractions equal k—we just don't have to deal with it directly anymore. I like to streamline.

In a direct proportion, as one value gets farther from zero, the other one also gets farther from zero by the same factor. As one gets closer to zero, the other also gets closer to zero by the same factor. If you're dealing with a positive proportionality constant (most of the time), you can say it even more simply: as one gets bigger, the other gets bigger by the same factor. As one gets smaller, the other gets smaller by the same factor.

---

[*] You might be more familiar with terms like *direct variation* and *inverse variation*. They're interchangeable with the terms I'm using in this chapter. Po-tay-to, Po-tah-to.

If p and q are directly proportional:

p	q	What happens?
4	10	Start here.
8	20	p goes UP, so q goes UP.
40	100	p goes UP, so q goes UP.
2	5	p goes DOWN, so q goes DOWN.
1	2.5	p goes DOWN, so q goes DOWN.

One last way you might like to think about direct proportionality if you like graphs: when two variables are in direct proportion with proportionality constant k, they form a line with slope k that passes through the origin. That's right—$y = kx$ and $y = mx + b$ are closely related. Isn't that cool? Don't you roll your eyes at me!

For easy direct proportion questions, all you'll need to do is plug values into the general proportion form, $\dfrac{y_1}{x_1} = \dfrac{y_2}{x_2}$, and solve. And the "hard" direct proportion questions won't actually be much harder.

Example 1

17. If y is directly proportional to x^2, and $y = 8$ when $x = 4$, what is y when $x = 5$?

(A) 5.12
(B) 10
(C) 12.5
(D) 14
(E) 25

What makes this question tricky is that y is proportional to x^2, but we're given values of x. Don't freak out. Just square your x values before you plug them into the proportion. $4^2 = 16$, and $5^2 = 25$. Watch:

$$\frac{y_1}{x^2_1} = \frac{y_2}{x^2_2}$$

$$\frac{8}{16} = \frac{y_2}{25}$$

No big deal, right? Solve that and you should get $y_2 = 12.5$, which is answer choice (C).

At this point, you might be asking yourself: *OK...so what's the difference between solving a direct proportion question and solving a ratio question?* That's a good question, and the answer, honestly, is that there often isn't much of a pragmatic difference: in both cases, we're setting fractions equal to each other, and solving carefully. The difference is mostly in how the question is asked.

Inverse proportionality

Inverse proportionality is much less common on the SAT, but as I said above, it's fair game and so you should know what to do if you actually encounter one. Again, the Blue Book's definition of an inverse proportion ($y = \frac{k}{x}$ for some nonzero constant k) involves a constant and is therefore not always the most expedient definition for test-day deployment. Instead, you might find it helpful to think of it this way: *in inversely proportional relationships, the product of the two variables will always be the same.*

When x and y are inversely proportional:

$$y = \frac{k}{x} \text{ and } x_1 y_1 = x_2 y_2$$

Again, note that k hasn't disappeared in the second equation; k is equal to both sides of the equation. I've just given you one less value to keep track of and have a name for.

In an inverse proportion, one value gets farther from zero as the other gets closer, and vice versa. Assuming your proportionality constant isn't negative (almost always) you can say that as one value gets bigger, the other gets smaller.

If p and q are inversely proportional:

p	q	What happens?
4	10	Start here.
8	5	p goes UP, so q goes DOWN.
10	4	p goes UP, so q goes DOWN.
2	20	p goes DOWN, so q goes UP.
1	40	p goes DOWN, so q goes UP.

Example 2

15. If u and w are inversely proportional, and $u = 11$ when $w = 5$, what is u when $w = 110$?

(A) 242
(B) 50
(C) 5
(D) 1
(E) 0.5

Drop your values into the formula, and you're good to go:

$$u_1 w_1 = u_2 w_2$$

$$11 \times 5 = u_2 \times 110$$

Solve, and you'll find that u_2* is 0.5, so choice (E) is correct. Note that choice (A) is there in case you misread the question and set up a direct proportion instead. Note also that in Example 1 above, which was a question about direct proportions, choice (A) would have been the solution if the question was about inverse proportions instead. I'm not doing that to be a jerk. I'm doing that because the SAT will. Read the question carefully. Every time.

---

* *Unos…dos…tres…CATORCE!*

7. If r and s are directly proportional and $r = 18$ when $s = 15$, what is r when $s = 20$?

    (A) 10
    (B) 13.5
    (C) 18
    (D) 20
    (E) 24

13. If k is a nonzero constant, which of the following does NOT represent a proportional relationship between x and y?

    (A) $y = x + k$

    (B) $ky = kx$

    (C) $\dfrac{y}{x} = k$

    (D) $y = k^2 x$

    (E) $y = \dfrac{x}{k}$

17. Which of the following could represent a directly proportional relationship between x and $f(x)$?

    (A) $f(3) = 5, f(5) = 7, f(15) = 17$
    (B) $f(3) = 6, f(5) = 10, f(15) = 30$
    (C) $f(3) = 9, f(5) = 25, f(15) = 225$
    (D) $f(3) = 5, f(5) = 3, f(15) = 1$
    (E) $f(3) = 10, f(5) = 15, f(15) = 40$

18. If y is inversely proportional to z, and $y = 4$ when $z = 6$, which of the following could NOT equal $y + z$?

    (A) 8
    (B) 11
    (C) 14
    (D) 25
    (E) 48.5

19. If m^{-1} is inversely proportional to n^2, and $m = 2$ when $n = 2$, what is m when $n = \sqrt{2}$?

    (A) 8
    (B) 4
    (C) 2
    (D) $\sqrt{2}$
    (E) 1

Answers:

7. **(E)**
13. **(A)**
17. **(B)**
18. **(A)**
19. **(E)**

Solutions on page 291.

The following selected Blue Book questions are examples of this stuff in the wild.

Test	§	p	#	Diff.
3	5	527	6	3
8	9	858	6	M
9	5	906	12	M
10	2	950	7	M

Yeah...proportionality questions don't happen all that often.

Counting and listing

I'm just gonna say this right up front: *many "counting" problems are really just listing problems*. There aren't really any shortcuts or techniques for listing problems—you solve them simply by listing possibilities. If you've got your Blue Book handy, look at page 468, #16 for an example. No shortcuts there! Just list all the possible "tri-factorable" numbers starting with $1 \times 2 \times 3$, then $2 \times 3 \times 4$, then $3 \times 4 \times 5$, etc. Stop when you list one that works out to a number greater than 1000.

In this chapter, because listing problems are more about following directions than they are about any particular technique, I'm going to focus more on the kinds of counting problems that lend themselves to a few simple, replicable approaches.[*]

Please don't try to shoehorn listing problems into these counting techniques if they don't seem to fit. If you come across a problem that doesn't lend itself nicely to a counting technique, it's a listing problem, so you should just list!

Oh, the possibilities

One kind of counting problem you're likely to see that *is* solvable by technique is what I'll call a "possibilities" problem. It might involve cards (but *not* playing cards—the SAT doesn't like those), or pictures being lined up on a wall in different orders. Your job will be to determine the number of possible outcomes given a particular scenario. Like so:

---

[*] Aside from this footnote, I'm deliberately avoiding the terms "permutation," "combination," and "factorial" in this chapter. That's not because I don't know them; it's because I've found that they create more confusion than they alleviate on the SAT. Remember: *the SAT is not a math test!* If you prefer to solve the questions laid out here by cramming them into nPr and nCr notations in your calculator, be my guest, but don't cry to me when you miss counting questions on the SAT.

Example 1

20. Mike is arranging seven of his various awards and commendations on a shelf in his office. If he insists that his hard-fought Class of 1999 Math Award be placed in the center, in how many different orders could he arrange the seven items?

(A) 60
(B) 72
(C) 120
(D) 720
(E) 1440

The best way to tackle a possibilities problem like this is to draw a bunch of blanks like you're about to play Hangman (best hangman word ever, BTW: "bailiwick"), and then start thinking, methodically, through the choices you have at every step along the way. I'm going to illustrate this process with slightly more thoroughness than you probably will on test day. (You won't need to make up award names, but I will because it's *hilarious*.)

Position	1	2	3	4	5	6	7
Award				Class of 1999 Math Award			
Choices				1			

First, as I did above, you must account for any special conditions or restrictions. The Math Award must go in the middle, so there's only one choice for Position 4.

Position	1	2	3	4	5	6	7
Award	Invisible Man Award			Class of 1999 Math Award			
Choices	6			1			

Once all the restrictions are accounted for, start filling in the rest of the spaces. To fill Position 1, Mike has 6 different awards to choose from. Say, for argument's sake, he chooses the Invisible Man Award next.

Position	1	2	3	4	5	6	7
Award	Invisible Man Award	Acne League – Most Improved	Push Ups Contest – Last Place	Class of 1999 Math Award	Spin the Bottle – Luckiest Player Ever	5th Grade Science Fair – 2nd Place	Shortest Fight in School History – Loser
Choices	6	5	4	1	3	2	1

To fill the next spot, since he used up the Invisible Man Award, he has 5 awards left to choose from. Once he chooses the Acne League – Most Improved award for Position 2, he has 4 choices for Position 3. He continues this process until he's filled all the positions.

To calculate the number of different arrangements Mike could have made, multiply the number of choices he had at every step.

$$6 \times 5 \times 4 \times 1 \times 3 \times 2 \times 1 = 720$$

When solving a possibilities problem, set up the hangman blanks, then imagine yourself actually performing the task described. First take care of special conditions or restrictions, and then take care of everything else. At every step, ask yourself "How many choices do I have?" And then ask yourself "How many choices do I have now?" And then—you guessed it—ask yourself how many choices you have *again*.

Stop when you run out of choices.

Everyone touches everyone (not in a weird way)

Another kind of counting problem you *might* come across is a "matches" problem. A problem like this could involve everyone at a dinner party shaking hands, or a bunch of teams in a league all playing each other. You're going to want to approach problems like this in a different way than we just did. Note that problems like this are pretty rare—I'm really only including this part because the process of solving this kind of problem is so easy to remember that it's worth knowing even though in all likelihood you won't get one of these on your test.

Example 2

18. Each team in a kickball league plays each other team 4 times during the season. If there are 7 teams in the league, how many games are played, in total, during the season?

(A) 28
(B) 56
(C) 84
(D) 112
(E) 116

What you're going to want to do here is draw a diagram. Arrange the letters A-G (representing the 7 teams) in a large circle. Now draw lines connecting each letter to each other letter, *carefully counting as you draw.*[*]

The best way to go about this is to draw every line that you can that originates at A, and then do the same for B, etc. You'll know you're done when you have something that resembles a star with all its outer points connected. Like so:

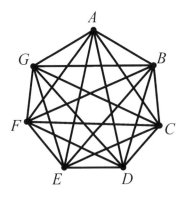

The number of lines you just drew (21, you awesome counter) equals the number of games required for each team to play each other team once. If each

_____

* If you try to count after you're done drawing, you're going to have a pretty difficult time getting an accurate count.

team has to play each other team 4 times, multiply 21 by 4 to get the answer. 84! BAM!

Pretty amazing, right? It's just so…*beautiful*. No, stop crying. It's totally inappropriate for you to be crying right now. I know it's pretty but you need to stop. I refuse to move on until you stop crying.

Of course, if you want to represent the above diagram mathematically, you could say that Team A needs to play all the other teams, so it plays 6 games. Then Team B needs to play all the teams except Team A (since they already played), so that's 5 more games. Follow that line of reasoning until its end and you get:

$$6+5+4+3+2+1=21$$

But I think the star is prettier (and easier to remember).

Counting multiples and factors

Once in a while you'll be asked to count how many positive integers less than a certain number (call it m) are or are not multiples of another certain number (call it n). In this special case, find the highest multiple of n that's less than m, and divide it by n. Then make sure you've read the question carefully and you know whether they want the number of multiples, or the number of positive integers that *aren't* multiples. What, you want an example? OK. Since you asked so nicely.

Example 3 (Grid-in)

17. How many positive integers less than 500 are NOT divisible by 6?

Isn't it nice of me to capitalize "NOT"? The SAT will do that, too. The first thing you should know is that you should treat this kinda like a shaded region[*]

---

[*] We'll get to shaded regions on page 193—consider this a tiny preview.

problem—it's easier to find how many numbers *are* divisible by 6 than it is to find how many *are not*, so let's do that instead.

What's the greatest multiple of 6 that's less than 500? It'll be fastest just to use your calculator here. Just try the even numbers less than 500 until one works. Is 498 divisible by 6? Yes. That was fast.

So what's 498 divided by 6? It's 83. Which means that there are 83 multiples of 6 that are less than 500.

Since the question asked how many positive integers less than 500 are NOT divisible by 6, we have one more step to go. There are 499 positive integers less than 500, so to find our answer we subtract:

$$499 - 83 = 416$$

Boomshakalaka. 416 is the answer.

A little of this, a little of that

One of the dirtiest things the SAT will do is combine the two types of problems we've already discussed into one problem. This is the kind of question test writers will throw into a test if they feel like the rest of the test has somehow been a bit too easy. Almost everyone gets these wrong.

Example 4

18. A science teacher wants to create a lab group consisting of two seniors and one junior. If there are three seniors and five juniors in his class, how many different such groups are possible?

(A) 15
(B) 18
(C) 24
(D) 30
(E) 36

Most students pick (D) for this one. They say "Well, we've got 3 choices for the first senior, 2 choices for the second senior, and 5 choices for the junior: $3 \times 2 \times 5 = 30$. Unfortunately, that's not how this question works.

The problem here is that the order in which the seniors are picked doesn't matter. In other words, if Laura and Michelle are two students in the class, the incorrect solution above considers a selection of *Laura and Michelle*, to be different than one of *Michelle and Laura*. To solve this question correctly, let's make up names for the kids in this class, and then list all the possible groups.

Seniors	Juniors
Laura	Blake
Michelle	Phillip
Cathy	Aaron
	Reed
	Xavier

Possible groupings (by first initial)

LMB	LMP	LMA	LMR	LMX
LCB	LCP	LCA	LCR	LCX
MCB	MCP	MCA	MCR	MCX

The correct answer to the problem is (A) 15. You *could* think of this as a "matching" problem (for the seniors) wrapped up in a "possibilities" problem, but honestly, I'm not sure how helpful that is.

As I said at the beginning of this chapter, the best strategy for non-straightforward counting problems, in all seriousness, is just to make lists. The SAT plays with small numbers, so it won't take you very long, and if you're practiced at listing things methodically, when you get to the end there will be *no* uncertainty about the correct answer. Just sayin'.

13. How many positive integers less than 1000 are NOT divisible by 9?

    (A) 111
    (B) 782
    (C) 841
    (D) 888
    (E) 900

15. After lunch, 6 friends all shake hands with each other before leaving the restaurant. If nobody shakes hands with anybody else more than once, how many handshakes occurred?

    (A) 10
    (B) 11
    (C) 12
    (D) 14
    (E) 15

17. Alicia is arranging photographs of five family members in a row on her refrigerator. If she wants the photograph of her mother and the photograph of her father to be on opposite ends of the row, how many arrangements for the photographs are possible?

    (A) 120
    (B) 60
    (C) 24
    (D) 21
    (E) 12

18. Alex's favorite restaurant is a buffet-style Chinese restaurant downtown. Each time he goes, he chooses two appetizers and one entree. If the restaurant has four appetizers and five entrees to choose from, how many times could Alex go to the restaurant without choosing the same combination of dishes?

  (A) 60
  (B) 48
  (C) 40
  (D) 30
  (E) 18

19. Brady has ten unique cards in his hand. If he is going to line up four of them in a row on his table, how many arrangements are possible?

  (A) 24
  (B) 240
  (C) 1456
  (D) 5040
  (E) 6220

20. How many positive 3-digit integers have a units (ones) digit of 9?

  (A) 50
  (B) 90
  (C) 100
  (D) 111
  (E) 150

Answers:

13. **(D)**

15. **(E)**

17. **(E)**

18. **(D)**

19. **(D)**

20. **(B)**

Solutions on page 293.

The following selected Blue Book questions are examples of this stuff in the wild.

Test	§	p	#	Diff.
1	8	424	14	4
2	5	465	8	4
2	5	468	16	4
3	2	519	18	4
3	8	547	13	4
4	6	598	18	H
5	2	639	3	E
6	8	729	2	E
7	3	773	15	H
7	7	789	15	M
8	7	850	13	M
9	5	904	4	E
10	5	969	14	H
10	8	977	1	E
11	4	16	8	2

Patterns

Pattern questions on the SAT are pretty common, but there are so many different kinds of patterns that could be thrown your way that it's hard to give very specific advice. In fact, the pattern question is one area of the SAT that, ironically, doesn't follow much of a pattern. However, there is one kind of pattern that tends to give people all sorts of difficulty when it (rarely) appears. I'll spend the bulk of this chapter on that. Follow me!

Example

17. A farmer is planting a row of plants. He first plants 2 broccoli plants, then 3 cabbage plants, then 1 apple tree, then 2 orange trees, then 1 dill weed plant. He repeats this pattern over and over again until he's filled up all the land on his (very unorthodox) farm. What kind of plant is the 782nd one he plants?

    (A) cabbage
    (B) apple
    (C) broccoli
    (D) dill weed
    (E) orange

Obviously I take some liberties with the writing style of the test makers, but style aside, this question could totally appear on your SAT. How can you solve it?

Start by writing a few iterations of the pattern on top of each other:

$$B, B, C, C, C, A, O, O, D,$$
$$B, B, C, C, C, A, O, O, D,$$
$$B, B, C, C, C, A, O, O, D, \ldots$$

Now number a few of the terms:

1st term ⟶ B, B, C, C, C, A, O, O, D, ⟵ 9th term
10th term ⟶ B, B, C, C, C, A, O, O, D, ⟵ 18th term
19th term ⟶ B, B, C, C, C, A, O, O, D, .⟵ 27th term

Note that down the *right* side you're basically counting up by multiples of 9. On the *left* side, you're also counting up by 9's, but in a less useful way. The mistake a lot of people make on pattern questions is that they start counting from the beginning of the pattern and get all screwed up. Count from the *end* of the pattern to make this easy on yourself!

When you're counting plants, every multiple of 9 will be a dill weed plant. We want the 782nd plant. 782 ÷ 9 = 86 remainder 8, which means the 782nd plant will be the 8th in our pattern; it'll be an orange tree. That's choice (E).

Another way to think about this: the 783rd plant will be a dill weed plant (because 783 is a multiple of 9), so the 782nd will be one before that: an orange tree. No sweat, right? Isn't this *fun*?

Other kinds of patterns

As I said at the beginning of this chapter, repeating patterns like the one above aren't the only kind of pattern that might get thrown at you, just one kind that's easily solved with a trick.

It's also common for the SAT writers to throw actual mathematical sequences at you, where each term is determined by adding to or multiplying by previous terms. In that case, don't panic! Usually, it's just a test of how well you follow directions. If they're asking about early terms, expand the sequence a little further past the "…", and you'll have your answer. If they're asking for later terms—or about formulas to find n^{th} terms—then it's possible you're dealing with a function question disguised as a pattern question. We'll talk about functions starting on page 114. Hold your horses.

Rule of thumb: if you feel like you have to list 10 or more terms, there's a shortcut you're missing. Otherwise, you're just being tested on whether you can follow directions, so *read the question carefully*, and *follow directions*.

Practice questions: Patterns

I just found out that male pattern awesomeness runs in my family.

8, 11, 14, 17, …

10. In the sequence above, each term after the first term is 3 more than the term before it. The 35th term is how much greater than the 29th term?

    (A) 12
    (B) 15
    (C) 16
    (D) 18
    (E) 21

14. A father decides to set a rule for his 5 children because they're always arguing over the television. Adele gets to decide what to watch on the first night, then Betsy decides what to watch on the second night, Charice decides on the third night, David on the fourth, and Elsie on the fifth. The pattern then begins again. Who gets to decide what to watch on the 38th night after this rule has been set in place?

    (A) Adele
    (B) Betsy
    (C) Charice
    (D) David
    (E) Elsie

3, –9, 27, …

17. The first term in the sequence above is 3, and every term after the first is –3 times the preceding term. How many terms in the sequence are less than 1000?

    (A) 6
    (B) 7
    (C) 8
    (D) 9
    (E) More than 9

Practice questions: Patterns

I just found out that male pattern awesomeness runs in my family.

$$3, 9, 27, 81, \ldots$$

18. Each term in the sequence above is determined by multiplying the previous term by 3. What will be the units (ones) digit of the 1,000,000,000th term?

    (A) 1
    (B) 3
    (C) 6
    (D) 7
    (E) 9

20. Josh goes on a date with Lisette on the first day, Angelique on the second day, Fantasia on the third day, Raquel on the fourth day, Patrice on the fifth day, and Shayla on the sixth day. He begins the patterns again on the seventh day, and repeats it over and over again until he gets hit by a bus. If he was on his way home from a date with Fantasia when he got hit, which of the following could be the number of dates he went on before his accident?

    (A) 19
    (B) 23
    (C) 84
    (D) 173
    (E) 279

Answers:

10. **(D)**
14. **(C)**
17. **(E)**
18. **(A)**
20. **(E)**

Solutions on page 295.

The following selected Blue Book questions are examples of patterns in the wild.

Test	§	p	#	Diff.
1	3	399	13	3
2	2	452	1	1
2	8	486	16	5
3	5	530	16	4
3	8	548	15	4
4	3	583	9	M
4	6	597	14	M
6	8	733	16	H
7	3	769	5	M
8	3	833	10	E
8	7	852	18	M
9	5	903	1	E
10	2	952	13	M
11	3	10	6	3
11	4	16	9	2

Remember to stop and think before you try to apply a shortcut to a pattern for which a shortcut doesn't exist. Sometimes, you're just going to have to follow directions and list a few terms.

Prime factorization and perfect powers

So this isn't a super important thing as far as how often it appears on the SAT, but it does pop up time and again, so if you're shooting for perfection (or close to it) you might want to pay attention. Otherwise, you can get by just fine without this little nugget (but you might as well read it, since you're here anyway).

Do you know what prime factorization is? Basically, the prime factorization of a number is the way you would build that number by multiplying together only prime numbers. To find the prime factorization of a number, divide by 2 as many times as you can. Once you can't do that anymore, try dividing by 3 as many times as you can. Then by 5. Then by 7. Then by 11...you get the idea. Every time you write a prime factor, circle it. You're done when you're left with two prime factors and can therefore factor no more.

Let's try one together, like best friends

Whaddya say we find the prime factorization of 840?

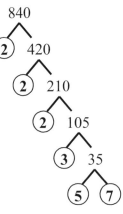

See how, when I couldn't divide by 2 anymore, I went to 3, and then 5? I knew I was done when I had two prime numbers, 5 and 7. If I multiplied all those numbers back together, I'd get 840 again. For serious. Try it:

$$2 \times 2 \times 2 \times 3 \times 5 \times 7 = 840$$

Cool, right? Now try this:

Example 1 (Grid-in)

14. If p is a prime factor of 322, what is the greatest possible value of p?

To solve this, just find the prime factorization of 322!

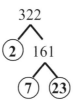

There you go—the greatest prime factor of 322 is 23, so the greatest possible value of p is 23. Pretty easy, huh? If that were all you needed to know about prime factorization, though, I probably wouldn't have devoted a whole chapter to it.

What else is there?

Thanks for asking! Hard SAT questions involving prime factorization might not mention prime factorization at all. Instead, they'll ask about perfect squares. It just so happens that prime factorization is a great tool for finding perfect squares.

The prime factorization of a perfect square will contain *pairs* of each prime number.*

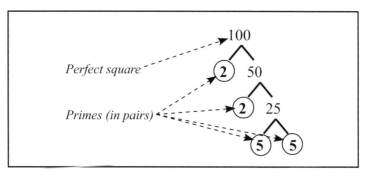

---

* Bonus nerdery: As it turns out, prime factors of positive perfect cubes will come in groups of three, and so on. For positive integers a and n greater than 1, prime factors of a^n will be in groups of n.

Look back at the prime factorization of 840 we did two pages ago. 840 is not a perfect square—its prime factorization contains three 2s, and one each of 3, 5, and 7. If we want to find multiples of 840 that *are* perfect squares, we can use its prime factorization to do so. Let's pretend, for example, that we needed to find the smallest multiple of 840 with an integer square root. In order to get a perfect square, we need to add another 2, another 3, another 5, and another 7 to 840's prime factorization. Yikes. That's gonna be a big number.

$$2 \times 2 \times 2 \times 3 \times 5 \times 7 = 840$$

$$2 \times 2 \times 2 \times \underline{\mathbf{2}} \times 3 \times \underline{\mathbf{3}} \times 5 \times \underline{\mathbf{5}} \times 7 \times \underline{\mathbf{7}} = 176{,}400$$

See the bold underlines? Those are the factors I've added to make sure that every prime factor has a partner. The new product is huge. It's also a perfect square. Seriously.

$$\sqrt{176{,}400} = 420$$

There are no multiples of 840 that are less than 176,400 and are perfect squares. Scout's honor.

What would an SAT question testing this concept look like?

Example 2 (Grid-in)

18. If m is a positive integer and m^2 is divisible by both 9 and 14, what is the least possible value of m?

So...yeah. Start by doing prime factorizations of 9 and 14.

$$9 = 3 \times 3$$
$$14 = 2 \times 7$$

Note that 9 is already a perfect square, but 14 contains one of each of two different prime factors. If we simply find the product of 9 and 14, it won't be a perfect square.

$$9 \times 14 = (3 \times 3) \times (2 \times 7) = 126$$

To make a perfect square, we need another 2 and another 7.

$$3 \times 3 \times 2 \times \mathbf{2} \times 7 \times \mathbf{7} = 1764$$
$$m^2 = 1764$$

Confirm that 1,764 is a multiple of 9 and 14, and also a perfect square:

$$1764 \div 9 = 196$$
$$1764 \div 14 = 126$$
$$\sqrt{1764} = 42$$

Yes, it worked! So $m = 42$. That's your answer.

Note the tempting false shortcut: just multiply 9 by 14 and square the result. But if you do that, you get 15,876 for m^2 and 126 for m. That's not the smallest possible m, as we just showed.

Like I said, you don't see this often on the SAT, but if you're shooting for perfection, you'll want to know this relationship between prime factors and perfect squares.

Note: Because the SAT tests this concept so rarely, I'm doing my best to come up with questions that I think would be fair. Some of these are less inspired by real test questions than I would like, simply because there are so few real test questions to be inspired by. Also, all of these except the first two are grid-ins.

13. If $45b$ is the square of an integer, which of the following could equal $\dfrac{45}{b}$?

   (A) 3
   (B) 5
   (C) 9
   (D) 15
   (E) 45

16. What is the smallest perfect square that is a multiple of both 6 and 10?

15. If n is a prime number, which of the following COULD NOT be a perfect square?

   (A) $13n$

   (B) $32n$

   (C) $3n^2$

   (D) n^4

   (E) $49n^6$

17. What is the smallest multiple of 18 that is the cube of a positive integer?

18. If n is a factor of 5445 and $\sqrt{n}$ is an integer, what is the greatest possible value of n?

Answers:

13. **(C)**

15. **(C)**

16. **900**

17. **216**

18. **1089**

Solutions on page 297.

The following selected Blue Book questions are examples of this stuff in the wild.

Test	§	p	#	Diff.
4	3	585	15	M
6	4	713	6	M
6	4	714	8	H
7	3	773	17	H

Wow—that's not much, is it? Why even include this chapter? Because a few tough questions testing this stuff have appeared on recent exams, and I want you to be ready for anything. You're welcome.

Algebra and functions

Chances are good that you've completed your algebra coursework in school and therefore have the raw skills to do all the questions you'll see in the coming chapters the brute-force math way. However, if you're reading this book, that probably means that you're not happy yet with your SAT math score, so I strongly recommend you resist the urge to use algebra every time you see variables. If you keep taking the test the same old way, you'll keep getting the same old score.

The following chapters cover common question types the SAT will throw at you that fall under the "Algebra and Functions" umbrella. Some of them will require algebra; others will be algebra-optional. How well you distinguish between the two will be a great predictor of your eventual score improvement.

Let's do this.

Solving for expressions

If I were to tell you that today is my birthday and then ask you for a cake, what would you do? (Let's assume, for the moment, that you like me and want me to be happy.) You've got two choices: buy a bunch of ingredients and start baking, or go to a different aisle in the same grocery store and just buy the friggin' cake.

Baking a cake yourself is not only more time consuming than just buying one; it also gives you more opportunities to screw up (for example, if you mistake salt for sugar, you'll bake the grossest cake of all time). Since you know I'm a shameless crybaby who will never let you forget it if you ruin my birthday, you should just buy the cake in the cake aisle, and then use your time to do something more fun than baking.

And so it is with the SAT. What do I mean? *What do I mean???* Read on, young squire.

Example 1

13. If $3x - y = 17$ and $2x - 2y = 6$, what is the value of $x + y$?

    (A) 8
    (B) 9
    (C) 11
    (D) 12
    (E) 14

The SAT is asking you for a cake here. Baking it yourself will still result in a cake, but it will also give you opportunity to screw up, and take longer than just buying one. They don't give a rat turd if you buy the ingredients (x and y), so don't waste time on them! All that matters is the finished cake, (the value of the expression $x + y$), and we should be able to solve for that directly without ever finding x or y individually.

To do so, first stack up the equations we're given and the expression we want:

$$3x - y = 17$$
$$2x - 2y = 6$$
$$x + y = ?$$

Do you see it yet? How about now:

$$3x - y = 17$$
$$\underline{-(2x - 2y = 6)}$$
$$x + y = ?$$

That's right. All we need to do is subtract one equation from the other (I've already distributed the negative here):

$$3x - y = 17$$
$$\underline{-2x + 2y = -6}$$
$$\mathbf{x + y = 11}$$

The answer is (C).

Note that, aside from distributing that negative, there was almost no math at all in that solution. This is not the exception on the SAT; this is *the rule*. **When you're given two equations and asked to solve for an expression, you almost *never* have to do more than a step or two of basic arithmetic.** So instead of jumping into an algebraic quagmire as soon as you see questions like this, ask yourself, "*How do I quickly go from what they gave me to what they want?*" The answer will very often be adding or subtracting whole equations, as we just did in Example 1. When you get nowhere by adding or subtracting, what else might you want to try?

Example 2 (Grid-in)

16. If $(x - y)^2 = 25$ and $xy = 10$, then what is $x^2 + y^2$?

Here, we aren't going to get anywhere by simply adding or subtracting our two equations, but do you see anything else going on? Do you see that you've been provided with all the pieces of a particular puzzle?

Let's start by expanding what we were given (FOIL works here of course, but you should really make an effort to memorize the contents of the table on the right—the binomial squares and difference of two squares—to save you time on the test; they all show up frequently):

> **Binomial squares:**
>
> $$(x + y)^2 = x^2 + 2xy + y^2$$
> $$(x - y)^2 = x^2 - 2xy + y^2$$
>
> **Difference of two squares:**
>
> $$(x + y)(x - y) = x^2 - y^2$$

$$(x - y)^2 = 25$$
$$x^2 - 2xy + y^2 = 25$$

And would you look at that! We're pretty much already done. Just substitute the value you were given for xy, and do a little subtraction:

$$x^2 - 2(10) + y^2 = 25$$
$$x^2 - 20 + y^2 = 25$$
$$\mathbf{x^2 + y^2 = 45}$$

Note again that we didn't need to solve for x or y individually to find this solution; all we needed to do was move some puzzle pieces around. Note also that actually solving for the individual variables would have been a *huge* pain.

Again, your mantra: *"How do I quickly go from what they gave me to what they want?"*

Practice questions: Solving for expressions

How will you get from where you are to where you want to be?

13. $3x + 7y = 22$ and $2x + 6y = 12$, what is $13x + 13y$?

  (A) 34
  (B) 58
  (C) 72
  (D) 130
  (E) 156

16. If $a + b = -8$ and $a^2 + b^2 = 50$, what is ab?

  (A) 14
  (B) 10
  (C) 9
  (D) 8
  (E) 7

15. If $p^2 - r^2 = 18$ and $p - r = 2$, what is $p + r$?

  (A) 5
  (B) 9
  (C) 13
  (D) 16
  (E) 18

Practice questions: Solving for expressions

How will you get from where you are to where you want to be?

$$x + 2y - 3z = 92$$
$$2x - y + z = 36$$
$$4x - y + 2z = 12$$

19. Based on the system of equations above, what is the value of x?

   (A) 11
   (B) 20
   (C) –40
   (D) –42
   (E) It cannot be determined from the information given.

20. If $x + y = m$ and $x - y = n$, then what is $x^2 + y^2$, in terms of m and n?

   (A) mn

   (B) $\dfrac{m^2 + n^2}{2}$

   (C) $(m - n)^2$

   (D) $(m + n)^2$

   (E) $\dfrac{m^2 - n^2}{2}$

Answers:

13. **(D)**

15. **(B)**

16. **(E)**

19. **(B)**

20. **(B)**

Solutions on page 299.

The following selected Blue Book questions are examples of this stuff in the wild.

Test	§	p	#	Diff.
1	3	398	7	2
1	3	399	14	3
1	3	400	16	3
2	5	467	12	4
2	8	484	10	3
3	2	516	6	2
3	8	544	5	2
4	6	597	12	M
4	9	613	14	M
6	2	700	3	E
6	4	716	14	M
6	8	730	5	E
8	3	835	15	H
8	7	847	2	E
9	5	903	2	E
10	2	950	8	H
10	5	969	15	M
11	4	14	1	1
11	8	33	4	2

Exponents

You can be sure that you're going to encounter exponents on the SAT. Hopefully, once you've been through this book, you'll look forward to the opportunity to spank these questions like they deserve to be spanked. Look at them, mocking you. They're totally asking for it. Show no mercy.

Basic exponent rules

Rule	Example
Don't forget what a regular integer exponent means![*]	$x^4 = xxxx$
Anything to the first power equals itself.	$y^1 = y$
Anything raised to the zero power equals 1.[**]	$m^0 = 1$
When you multiply like bases, you *add* their exponents.	$p^3 p^5 = p^{3+5} = p^8$
When you divide like bases, you *subtract* their exponents.	$\dfrac{r^9}{r^4} = r^{9-4} = r^5$
When you apply one exponent to another, you *multiply* the exponents.	$\left(z^3\right)^7 = z^{3\times7} = z^{21}$
When you apply an exponent to a single term in parentheses, you can *distribute* the exponent. Be careful, though! You *cannot distribute* an exponent to multiple terms (i.e. terms separated by + or – sign) in parentheses.	$(xy)^7 = x^7 y^7$ $(x+y)^7 \neq x^7 + y^7$
When you're adding or subtracting like bases with different exponents, you can factor if that would be helpful but otherwise *you can't do JACK.*	$y^4 + y^3 = y^3(y+1)$ $y^4 + y^3 \neq y^7$

That last one is important: there's no simplifying when exponents are separated by a + or – sign. If you make the mistake of adding or subtracting exponents when you shouldn't, people will laugh at you. It'll be like that

---

* Don't be ashamed to do this when you're stuck. You'll be amazed how often doing so will unstick you. All the rules that follow are derived directly from this basic principle.

** Except zero. There's some debate about what 0^0 equals. Some people say it equals 1, others say it's undefined. You needn't worry about this for the SAT. I've never seen 0^0 appear there.

nightmare where you somehow went to school in only your underwear, only it'll be worse and it'll be real. Don't do it.

Before we go further, let's make sure you've got the above. Try simplifying the following. (Answers at the bottom of the page.)

✎ $t^9 t^2 =$

✎ $\dfrac{3^n}{3^2} =$

✎ $(xy^3)(x^5 y) =$

✎ $(8^m)^2 =$

✎ $(3x)^3 =$

✎ $r^{16} - r^{12} =$

Fractional and negative exponents

Honestly, these appear pretty rarely on the SAT. I'm including them for completeness's sake, but don't sweat them too much.

Here's what you need to know about **fractional exponents**:

⇨ The numerator of the exponent is the *power*

⇨ The denominator of the exponent is the *root*

⇨ The power can go inside or outside the radical symbol

⇨ Like so:

$$y^{\frac{3}{5}} = \sqrt[5]{y^3} = \left(\sqrt[5]{y}\right)^3 \qquad r^{\frac{5}{11}} = \sqrt[11]{r^5} = \left(\sqrt[11]{r}\right)^5$$

And here's what you need to know about **negative exponents**:

⇨ An expression with a negative exponent is the reciprocal of the corresponding expression with a positive exponent

⇨ Like so:

$$p^{-5} = \frac{1}{p^5} \qquad y^{-\frac{3}{5}} = \frac{1}{y^{\frac{3}{5}}} = \frac{1}{\sqrt[5]{y^3}}$$

What's nice is that even though these rules might be a bit more confusing, fractional and negative exponents follow the same rules as integer exponents. Stare at these for a minute to see what I mean:

$$\frac{m^4}{m^{\frac{1}{2}}} = m^{\frac{7}{2}} \qquad \frac{2^x}{2^{-y}} = 2^{x-(-y)} = 2^{x+y} \qquad \frac{1}{p^5} = \frac{p^0}{p^5} = p^{-5}$$

Example 1

19. If $x^{\frac{3}{5}} = m$ and $y^{-\frac{3}{5}} = n^{-1}$, which of the following is equal to xy?

(A) $(mn)^{\frac{3}{5}}$

(B) $(mn)^{\frac{9}{25}}$

(C) $m^{\frac{5}{3}} n^{-\frac{5}{3}}$

(D) $(mn)^{\frac{5}{3}}$

(E) $\dfrac{n}{m}$

Well, you have two options. You could plug in, or you could work through this using the exponent rules. Since this is the exponent chapter, I'm going to use the exponent rules, but you should solve this by plugging in, too, just for the extra practice.

The first thing to do is get rid of those pesky negatives in the second equation. Remember that as long as you do the same thing to both sides of an equation, it's cool, man. Nobody gets hurt. So raise both sides of that equation to the -1 power. Remember what the rule says about raising exponents to other exponents? You *multiply* them.

$$\left(y^{-\frac{3}{5}}\right)^{-1} = \left(n^{-1}\right)^{-1}$$

$$y^{\frac{3}{5}} = n$$

That's better, right? Now let's do the real work. This is, at its core, a solve-for-the-expression (remember back from page 100?) question. Look at what you've got, and ask yourself how on earth you're going to transform that into what you want.

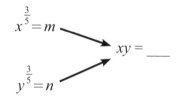

Looks to me like our first step has to be multiplication. Let's combine the two equations by multiplying the left and right sides of each together.

$$x^{\frac{3}{5}} y^{\frac{3}{5}} = mn$$

$$(xy)^{\frac{3}{5}} = mn$$

Almost there now, right? We'll get rid of that pesky $\frac{3}{5}$ the same way we got rid of the -1: we'll raise both sides to a clever exponent that will leave us with what we want. What do I multiply $\frac{3}{5}$ by to make it go away? Yep. $\frac{5}{3}$. I *knew* you had it in you.

$$\left(\left(xy\right)^{\frac{3}{5}}\right)^{\frac{5}{3}}=\left(mn\right)^{\frac{5}{3}}$$

$$xy=\left(mn\right)^{\frac{5}{3}}$$

So the answer is (D). Whew! That was beautiful. I got chills.

Exponential growth and shrinkage

Quit giggling. What are you, five? Once in a while, the SAT will throw a question at you that requires you to understand how different kinds of numbers will react when raised to powers. You should know, for example, that numbers between 0 and 1 will shrink when raised to a positive power: $0.5^2 = 0.25$. You should also know that negative numbers will turn positive when raised to even powers, but stay negative when raised to odd powers: $(-2)^2 = 4$, $(-2)^3 = -8$.

Example 2

16. Each of the following inequalities is true for some value of a EXCEPT

(A) $a^3 < a < a^2$
(B) $a < a^3 < a^2$
(C) $a < a^2 < a^3$
(D) $a^3 < a^2 < a$
(E) $a^2 < a^3 < a$

The best way to avoid careless errors on questions like this is to plug in. Pro tip: use values for a that are greater than 1, between 0 and 1, between -1 and 0, and less than -1. Here's a little table I whipped up:

a	a^2	a^3	Order	Eliminate
2	4	8	$a < a^2 < a^3$	(C)
0.5	0.25	0.125	$a^3 < a^2 < a$	(D)
-0.5	0.25	-0.125	$a < a^3 < a^2$	(B)
-2	4	-8	$a^3 < a < a^2$	(A)

That eliminates everything except for (E), so (E) is the answer. No sweat.

Note: _The last problem in the following drill is a grid-in._

$$\frac{x^4 x^6}{x^8} = 81$$

10. According to the equation above, which of the following could equal x^2?

   (A) 81
   (B) 72
   (C) 18
   (D) 9
   (E) 3

13. If $x^6 = 60$ and $w^{10} = 20$, what is $x^{12} w^{-10}$?

   (A) 36
   (B) 60
   (C) 120
   (D) 180
   (E) 360

14. If $a^2 = b$, what is a^4 in terms of b?

   (A) $2b$
   (B) $b + 2$
   (C) $2b + 2$
   (D) b^2
   (E) $4b$

17. If z, p, and q are each positive integers, which of the following is equivalent to z^q?

(A) $z^{pq} - z^p$

(B) $\sqrt[q]{z^{2q}}$

(C) $\dfrac{z^{pq}}{z^p}$

(D) $\dfrac{z^p}{z^{p-q}}$

(E) $2z^{\frac{q}{2}}$

18. If $(m+n)^2 = m^2 + n^2$, what is $(3^m)^n$?

Answers:

10. **(A)**

13. **(D)**

14. **(D)**

17. **(D)**

18. **1**

Solutions on page 301.

The following selected Blue Book questions are examples of this stuff in the wild.

Test	§	p	#	Diff.
1	3	400	18	4
1	8	422	8	3
2	2	456	14	3
2	8	485	13	4
3	5	529	11	2
4	3	581	2	E
4	9	611	7	M
5	4	652	6	M
5	8	669	7	M
6	4	714	8	H
7	7	788	11	M
7	7	790	19	H
8	3	831	5	M
9	2	891	15	M
10	8	980	11	M
11	3	10	8	4
11	4	15	4	1

Functions

Think of a function question like you think of a car wash. Not like a bikini car wash where you pay $20 and your car isn't even that clean at the end—*WHAT IS THE POINT?*—but an automatic car wash. If I drive my bird-poop-covered silver Toyota Yaris up to the car wash, what's going to happen? First it'll get sprayed with water, then with soap, then it'll get to the spinning brushes, then those dangly-slappy things that don't seem to serve much of a purpose, then the rinse, then the biggest hairdryer of all time will blow it dry. What comes out on the other end? A clean silver Yaris. *Not* a clean blue Honda; that'd be crazy. However, if a dirty blue Honda went in after my Yaris, then all the same stuff would happen to it as happened to my car, and then a clean blue Honda *would* come out.

The point is that you can always predict what's going to come out of a car wash based on what goes into it. Functions are the same way.

You've probably been working with the $f(x)$ notation in school for some time now, but let's review some of the things you'll see over and over again on the SAT.

Interpreting function notation

One thing you're definitely going to need to be able to do is interpret function notation. For some questions, it's enough to remember that saying $f(x) = x^3$, for example, is basically the same as saying $y = x^3$.

For other questions, you're going to need to take that a bit further and identify points on a graph using function notation. Here's a quick cheat for you: **when you have $f(x) = y$, that's the same as an ordered pair (x, y).** For example, if you know that $f(4) = 5$, then you know that the graph of the function f contains the point $(4, 5)$. Likewise, if you know that $h(c) = p$, you know that the graph of function h contains the point (c, p). And so on.

$$f(x) = y$$
$$\downarrow \quad \downarrow$$
$$(x, \ y)$$

Basically, whatever is inside the parentheses is your *x*-value, and whatever's across the equal sign is your *y*-value. This is important. If you don't understand yet, read it over and over until you do. Might help to write it down. Just sayin'.

To make sure you've got this, think about what the following things mean (answers at the bottom of the page).

✎ $f(0) = 3$

✎ $p(12) = 0$

✎ $s(3) = r(3)$

Nested functions (functions in functions)

Have you ever seen those dolls where you open them up and there are smaller ones inside? They're called Russian nesting dolls. Google them sometime.

Anyway, sometimes the SAT will put a function inside another function to try to bamboozle you. Don't let yourself get stymied here. All you need to do is follow the instructions, same as you do with all other function questions.

Example 1

18. If $f(x) = x^2 - 10$ and $g(x) = 2f(x) + 3$, what is $g(\sqrt{2})$?
    (A) 7
    (B) 5
    (C) −5
    (D) −7
    (E) −13

Let's just take this one step at a time. First, let's take the $\sqrt{2}$ we're given and put it in for every x we see in $g(x)$.

$$g(\sqrt{2}) = 2f(\sqrt{2}) + 3$$

Not too bad, right? Now let's replace the $f(\sqrt{2})$ with an expression we can actually work with. Remember that $f(x) = x^2 - 10$, so we write:

$$g(\sqrt{2}) = 2((\sqrt{2})^2 - 10) + 3$$

See how this is working? Now just simplify to arrive at choice (E):

$$g(\sqrt{2}) = 2(-8) + 3$$
$$g(\sqrt{2}) = -13$$

Tables and function notation

Now that you're good with function notation by itself, it's time to talk about how functions can be represented in table form. It's pretty common for the SAT to present a function to you this way:

x	2	3	4	5	6
$f(x)$	13	18	25	34	45

We can use this table to find points. For example, $f(5) = 34$. See if you can do the following questions(answers at the bottom, natch):

✎ If $f(p) = 18$, what is one possible value for p?[*]

✎ What is $f(6 - 4)$?

✎ What is $f(6) - f(4)$?

✎ Holy crap those are different?

---

* The function f here turns out to be quadratic, and there are 2 values that could produce 18, one of which is 3. In a function, each input can only have one output, but multiple inputs can have the same output. To go back to the car wash example, a blue Honda (input) that goes through can *only* result in a clean blue Honda (output). However, there are many blue Hondas in the world, so multiple inputs can produce the same output.

Answers: ● p could equal 3 ● $f(2) = 13$ ● $45 - 25 = 20$ ● ...yup.

Graphs and function notation

Now that you're good with tables, let's talk about function notation as it pertains to graphs. Using function notation to interpret graphs is one of the most common bugaboos of SAT math students. If you're willing to put in a few minutes of focused practice here, however, you'll laugh in the face of these dangerous questions.

Example 2

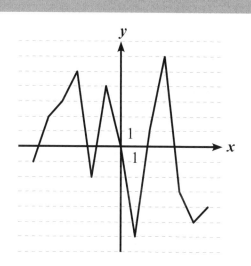

15. The figure above shows the graph of $f(x)$ from $x = -6$ to $x = 6$. If $f(3) = p$, what is $f(p)$?

    (A) −4
    (B) −2
    (C) 2
    (D) 3
    (E) 6

The first thing I want to point out, since I've found it to be a sticking point for a lot of students, is that you don't need to know the equation for $f(x)$. All the information you need to know is in the figure! To solve a question like this, you must remember a simple but important fact that we've already discussed: that "$f(a) = b$" is just shorthand for saying "the function f contains the point (a, b)." So when this question tells you that $f(3) = p$, it's telling you that the function f

contains the point (3, *p*). All you need to do is go to the graph and see where it is when *x* = 3.

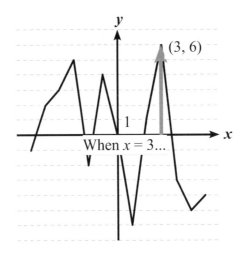

When *x* = 3, the graph of the function is at (3, 6). So *f*(3) = 6, and therefore *p* = 6. And now you're almost done! To finish up, just go to the graph one more time to find *f*(*p*), which you now know is really just *f*(6).

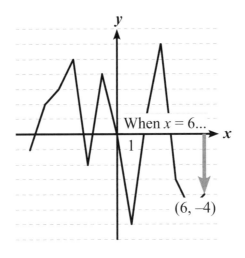

And there you have it. When *x* = 6, the graph of the function is at (6, –4). This means that *f*(6) = –4, so (A) is your answer.

Becoming deft with questions like this simply requires practice. So...you should do some practice. Let's use the same graph, and I'll ask you some more questions, increasing the complexity as I go.

The answers to these questions are at the bottom of the page.

✎ What is the *y*-intercept of *f*(*x*)? *0*

✎ When, in the given interval, is *f*(*x*) greatest?   *f(3)=6*

✎ If *f*(4) = *a*, what is *f*(*a*)?

   5

✎ If *f*(−2) = *b*, what is *f*(*b*)?

   -2

✎ If *f*(−1) = *e*, what is *f*(*e*) − 6?

   -9

✎ If *f*(1) = *g*, what is *f*(−*g*)?

   -4

✎ If *f*(5) = *c*, what is *f*(*c* + 1)?

   (-4+1)   3

✎ If *f*(*s*) = 0, how many possible values are there for *s* in the given interval?

   6

✎ If *f*(2) = *d*, what is 2*f*(2*d*)?

   d=1   2·1=2

✎ If *f*(6) = *m* and *f*(2) = *n*, what is 3*f*(*m* − *n*)?

   m=-4   n=1   (-4-1)   6
                        (-5)

✎ If *f*(−3) = *r*, what is *f*(*f*(*r*))?

   r=5   2

These are super fun, right?

_____

Answers: ● 0 ● *f*(3) = 6 ● 5 ● −2 ● −9 ● −4

● *f*(5) = −5, so *f*(−5 + 1) = *f*(−4) = 3

● 6 (*f*(*x*) = 0 means an *x*-intercept, and there are 6 of those)

● *f*(2) = 1, so *d* = 1 and 2*d* = 2. 2*f*(2) = 2 × 1 = 2

● *f*(6) = −4 and *f*(2) = 1, so *f*(*m* − *n*) = *f*(−5). 3*f*(−5) = 3 × 2 = 6

● *f*(−3) = 5, so *f*(*f*(*r*)) = *f*(*f*(5)) = *f*(−5) = 2

Graph translation, reflection, and amplification

Sometimes the SAT likes to test you on whether you can figure out how a graph will react to some manipulation of its equation. Usually, though, they won't give you the equation. They'll draw some crappy squiggly line, call it $g(x)$, and then ask what will happen to $g(x + 1)$.

I'm including the rules for common manipulations, but I *strongly* recommend that you remind yourself of them with your calculator if you should need them on your SAT. It's very easy to set a simple function (like $f(x) = x^2$, which you've seen a million times) as your starting point and experiment with your graphing calculator to see how the graph reacts when the function is modified:

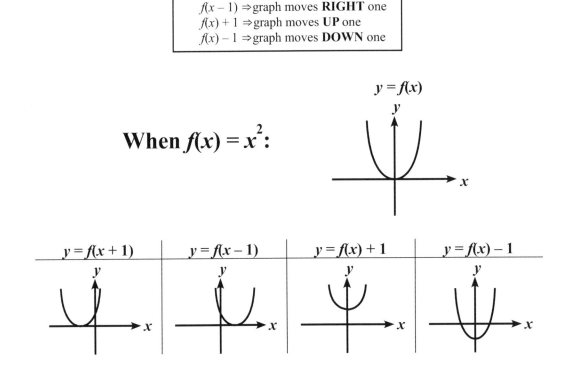

Note that the graph does just what you expect it to when the operation is outside the function (+ means up, – means down) but behaves differently when it's inside the function (+ means *left*, – means *right*).

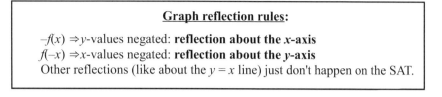

Graph reflection rules:

$-f(x) \Rightarrow y$-values negated: **reflection about the x-axis**
$f(-x) \Rightarrow x$-values negated: **reflection about the y-axis**
Other reflections (like about the $y = x$ line) just don't happen on the SAT.

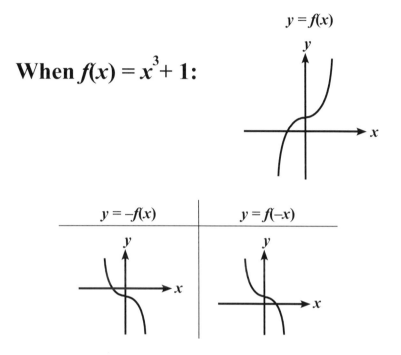

When $f(x) = x^3 + 1$:

$y = f(x)$

$y = -f(x)$ $y = f(-x)$

Notice that when you have a reflection about the x-axis (as you do on the left), the x-intercept remains the same. When you have a reflection about the y-axis, the y-intercept likewise remains the same. The intercepts that don't remain the same are negated. Makes sense, right? Math is awesome.

I'm going to repeat this on page 134, but when you reflect a line over *either* axis, the slope is negated. If you reflect it over the y-axis, the y-intercept stays the same. If you reflect it across the x-axis, the y-intercept and slope are both negated. For example, consider the line $y = 3x + 2$, with a slope of 3 and a y-intercept of 2. Its reflection across the y-axis will be $y = -3x + 2$ (slope negated), and its reflection across the x-axis will be $y = -3x - 2$ (slope and y-intercept negated).

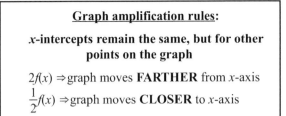

When $f(x) = x^2$:

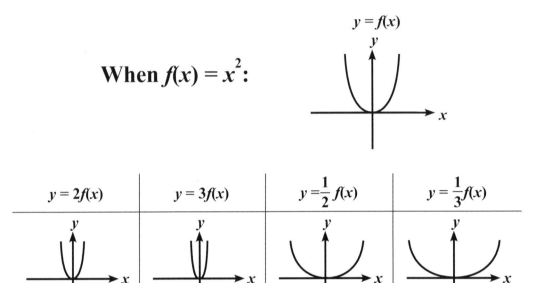

As you can see above, when a parabola is amplified by a coefficient greater than 1, it gets skinnier. When it's amplified by a coefficient between 0 and 1, it gets fatter.

It's not a bad idea for you to see this effect on a function that has more than one x-intercept. You'll *never* see trigonometry on the SAT, but just for your own edification, use your graphing calculator right now to see the difference between the graphs of $y = \sin x$, $y = 2\sin x$, and $y = \frac{1}{2}\sin x$. Go ahead...I'll wait.

12. If $f(x) = 2x - 1$, what is $f(10) - f(5)$?

(A) 5
(B) 9
(C) 10
(D) 11
(E) 19

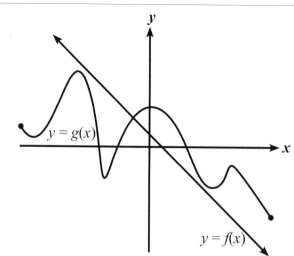

16. The figure above shows the graphs of $f(x)$ and $g(x)$. If $f(b) = g(b)$, which of the following could be the value of b?

(A) −3
(B) 0
(C) 1
(D) 7
(E) 10

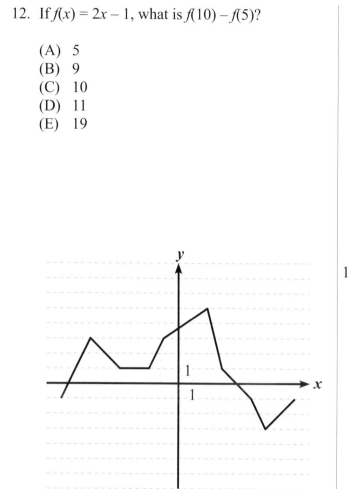

14. The figure above shows the graph of $y = f(x)$. If $f(-1) = k$, what is $2f(k)$?

(A) −3
(B) 2
(C) 4
(D) 6
(E) 8

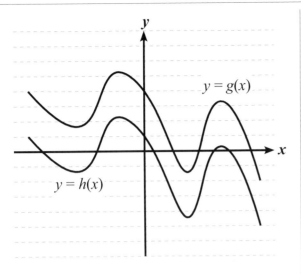

x	1	3	5	7	9
$g(x)$	-2	15	6	-3	-10

20. The table above gives values of the function g for selected values of x. If $f(x) = |g(x)|$, and $f(7) = t$, what is $f(t)$?

    (A) -2
    (B) 15
    (C) 6
    (D) -3
    (E) -10

18. The figure above shows the graphs of $y = g(x)$ and $y = h(x)$. Which of the following could be an expression of $h(x)$ in terms of $g(x)$?

    (A) $h(x) = g(x + 3)$
    (B) $h(x) = g(x - 3)$
    (C) $h(x) = g(x) + 3$
    (D) $h(x) = g(x - 1) - 2$
    (E) $h(x) = g(x) - 3$

Answers:

12. **(C)**
14. **(B)**
16. **(A)**
18. **(E)**
20. **(B)**

Solutions on page 303.

The following selected Blue Book questions are examples of this stuff in the wild.

Test	§	p	#	Diff.	Test	§	p	#	Diff.
1	3	400	18	4	6	2	702	9	M
1	7	418	18	5	6	2	704	17	M
1	8	422	9	3	6	8	731	8	M
1	8	424	16	4	6	8	732	13	M
2	5	465	7	3	7	3	773	18	H
2	5	467	14	3	7	7	790	20	H
2	8	482	3	1	7	9	798	11	M
2	8	484	9	2	8	7	849	11	M
3	2	517	10	3	8	9	861	13	M
3	2	518	16	4	8	9	861	14	H
3	2	519	19	4	9	2	891	18	H
3	8	547	14	3	9	5	906	14	M
4	3	583	10	M	9	5	908	19	H
4	6	594	4	E	10	2	948	2	E
4	6	597	16	H	10	5	970	19	M
4	9	610	5	E	10	8	979	9	M
5	2	639	4	E	11	3	5	11	4
5	2	641	13	M					
5	4	654	13	M					
5	8	669	6	M					
5	8	671	15	H					

Yeah...the SAT tests functions a lot.

Symbol functions

One of the SAT's most nefarious tricks is the symbol function. That doesn't mean you should be intimidated, though. In fact, symbol functions are some of the easiest hard questions on the test. *These questions are rated as "hard" because kids do poorly on them, not necessarily because they're actually difficult.* That's an important distinction. People panic when they see something unfamiliar used as a mathematical symbol, so a bunch of test takers get these questions wrong, despite the fact that if you just stay calm and follow directions, they're really not so bad.

Say the function $a \, \S \, b$ is defined for all integers a and b as:

$$a \, \S \, b = a^2 + 2ab$$

Oh noes! That's a symbol we've never seen before! But take a deep breath— it's really just there to illustrate a relationship. Just like the car wash in the last chapter, we can predict what will come out of the $\S$ function based on what went into it. For example, it's easy to figure out $x \, \S \, y$ based on the definition we have:

$$x \, \S \, y = x^2 + 2xy$$

No sweat. Just put x every place there was an a in the definition, and do the same for y every time there was a b! Again, a function's output is always predictable based on its input. And this is true no matter how crazy you get. To illustrate, let's see if we can simplify $[x \, \S \, (y + z)] - [x \, \S \, (y - z)]$. Don't freak out! We'll hold hands.

$$
\begin{aligned}
x \, \S \, (y + z) \ &= x^2 + 2x(y + z) \\
&= \mathbf{x^2 + 2xy + 2xz}
\end{aligned}
$$

$$
\begin{aligned}
x \, \S \, (y - z) \ &= x^2 + 2x(y - z) \\
&= \mathbf{x^2 + 2xy - 2xz}
\end{aligned}
$$

$$
\begin{array}{r}
x^2 + 2xy + 2xz \\
- (x^2 + 2xy - 2xz) \\
\hline
\mathbf{4xz}
\end{array}
$$

I want to make two points about what we just did. First, note that we can

check our work easily by plugging in. If $x = 2$, $y = 5$, and $z = 3$, the problem

simplifies to $(2 \, \S \, 8) - (2 \, \S \, 2)$. According to our work, that should resolve to $4xz$,

or $4(2)(3) = 24$. Does it?

$$(2 \, \S \, 8) - (2 \, \S \, 2)$$
$$= 2^2 + 2(2)(8) - (2^2 + 2(2)(2))$$
$$= 4 + 32 - (4 + 8)$$
$$= 36 - 12$$
$$= 24$$

Second, and perhaps more importantly, symbol functions are nothing to be

afraid of—you'll be fine as long as you follow directions. Here, try some.

If $a \, \S \, b = a^2 + 2ab$ (answers below):

✎ What is $3 \, \S \, 2$?

$$3^2 + 2(3)(2)$$
$$9 + 12$$
$$\boxed{= 21}$$

✎ What is $p \, \S \, 5$?

$$p^2 + 2(p)(5)$$
$$\boxed{p^2 + 10p}$$
$$p(p + 10)$$

✎ What is $4 \, \S \, (a + b)$?

$$4^2 + 2(a+b)(4)$$
$$16 + 8a + 8b$$

✎ If $4 \, \S \, x = 96$, find x.

$$4^2 + 2(4)x = 96 \qquad \boxed{x = 10}$$
$$16 + 8x = 96$$

Notes about symbol functions

→ **It doesn't matter what the symbol is.** All that matters is what
relationship it defines. The symbol could be an arrow, or a happy face, or
one of those Calvins peeing on stuff that people put on their trucks. It
could be *ANYTHING*. Doesn't matter. All you need to do is understand the
relationship, and then follow the directions.

Answers: ● 21 ● $p^2 + 10p$ ● $16 + 8a + 8b$ ● $x = 10$

➔ **There are *no* shortcuts!** Since these functions usually denote multiple operations, there are no shortcuts, only wrongcuts. You can't, for example, see ⊕6 – ⊕2 and assume that's the same as ⊕4, because it's almost definitely not.

Example

17. Let the ✸ operation be defined such that ✸$n = |n - 5|$ for all real numbers n. What is the greatest possible value of x such that ✸$x = 6$?

   (A) –11
   (B) –1
   (C) 1
   (D) 6
   (E) 11

OK, this one is so easy it's almost insulting. The test writers want you to panic and give up easy points here, but as long as you don't allow yourself to be spooked by the (intentionally spooky) spider web function, you're golden.

You can solve this with algebra if you like, but I'm just going to backsolve. Since the question is looking for the *greatest* possible x, I'm going to start with (E).

What happens when I make $x = 11$?

$$|11 - 5| = 6$$

Oh. Wow. That *was* easy. Since 11 is the largest of my options, and it works, I'm done already.

So uh…anybody know any good jokes? Ooh, I have one! What did the zero say to the eight?[*]

---

[*]   Nice belt!

Practice questions: Symbol functions

Look at all the cool crap I found in my computer's font library!

15. For all integers x, let $\lozenge x = x^{x+2}$. What is $\lozenge 4$?

   (A) 16
   (B) 64
   (C) 256
   (D) 4096
   (E) 65536

18. If $\supset 3 = 24$ and $\supset 5 = 38$, which of the following could be the definition of $\supset x$ for all positive integers x?

   (A) $\supset x = 8x$
   (B) $\supset x = 8x - 2$
   (C) $\supset x = x^2 + 13$
   (D) $\supset x = 7x + 3$ ✓
   (E) $\supset x = 10x - 6$

16. For all integers r and s, let $r \clubsuit s$ be defined as $r \clubsuit s = 4r + 7s$. If $3 \clubsuit p = 33$, which of the following is equal to p?

   (A) $3 \clubsuit 21$
   (B) $3 \clubsuit 3$
   (C) $(-1) \clubsuit 1$
   (D) $1 \clubsuit 3$
   (E) $7 \clubsuit 4$

19. Let the ⊶ symbol be defined such that b⊶ equals the sum of the greatest two integer factors of positive integer b. For example, the greatest two integer factors of 8 are 4 and 8, so 8⊶ $= 4 + 8 = 12$. Which of the following has the greatest value?

    (A) 46⊶
    (B) 49⊶
    (C) 50⊶
    (D) 53⊶
    (E) 55⊶

20. For all integers m, let ♣m be defined to be $m^2 + 10$. Which of the following equals ♣(♣2)?

    (A) ♣10
    (B) $2($♣$10) - 14$
    (C) (♣4) $+ 200$
    (D) ♣196
    (E) ♣206

Answers:

15. **(D)**

16. **(C)**

18. **(D)**

19. **(C)**

20. **(B)**

Solutions on page 305.

The following selected Blue Book questions are examples of this stuff in the wild.

Test	§	p	#	Diff.
1	2	420	3	1
2	2	456	15	4
3	8	543	2	2
4	3	585	17	M
5	8	670	11	M
6	2	705	20	H
7	9	800	16	H
8	3	835	17	H
9	2	890	11	E
10	5	967	10	M
11	4	16	10	3

As you can see, you can expect about one symbol function question per test.

Lines

We'll get into the mathy math in a minute, but before we do I want you to try to remember the first time a math teacher introduced the concept of slope to you. Chances are you were taught that the slope of a line is a ratio that tells you how steep the line is by telling you how much it "rises" for every unit it "runs." In those halcyon days, your mantra might very well have been "rise over run." I don't want to belabor this point because if you're reading this you've likely been working with slope for quite some time. I simply bring it up because questions about lines and slopes are some of the easiest questions to overcomplicate. Make a conscious effort to keep line questions as simple as possible, and you might save yourself a good deal of aggravation.

11. Line j has a slope of $\dfrac{1}{3}$ and passes through the point (1, 1). Which of the following points is NOT on line j?

(A) (−5, −1)
(B) (−2, 0)
(C) (0, −3)
(D) (4, 2)
(E) (7, 3)

Don't even *think* of writing an equation here! Just apply the first thing you ever learned about slope: that it's the **rise** (up and down) over the **run** (left and right). You can easily list other points on the line simply by adding 1 to the y-value for every 3 you add to the x-value. In the following graph, I've drawn the line by starting at (1, 1) and figuring out one more point based on the slope. Specifically, I added 1 to the y-value and 3 to the x-value to get (4, 2). That means we can eliminate (D) right away, of course, but it should be enough to eliminate *every* incorrect choice.

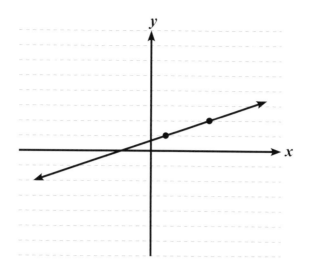

Which answer choice doesn't fall on the graph? Choice (C) is nowhere close: (0, –3) is very far from the line. So (C) has to be your answer! All of the other points clearly fall on the graph.

OK, on to the mathy math

If you're going to do algebra, you're going to want to use **slope-intercept form** whenever possible. If you're given the equation of a line and it's *not* in slope-intercept form already, your first step is to get it there. Many questions will consist of nothing more than comparing the slopes of numerous lines, so make sure you know this:

<u>Slope-intercept form of a line</u>

$y = mx + b$

(m is your slope, b is your y-intercept)

Some times you won't be given a line equation at all, just two points. In that case, you can calculate the slope using this formula:

<u>Slope formula</u>

$$\text{slope} = m = \frac{y_2 - y_1}{x_2 - x_1}$$

(given (x_1, y_1) and (x_2, y_2) as two points on a line)

Know the slope formula and the slope-intercept form of a line, and you're well on your way.

Other facts to know cold

→ Parallel lines have the same slope.

→ Perpendicular lines have *negative reciprocal* slopes (so if one line has a slope of 2, a perpendicular line has a slope of $-\frac{1}{2}$; if one has a slope of $-\frac{16}{5}$, the other has a slope of $\frac{5}{16}$).

→ The *x*-intercept of a line is the *x*-value of the equation when $y = 0$.

→ The *y*-intercept of a line (*b* in the slope-intercept form) is the *y*-value of the equation when $x = 0$.

→ When you reflect a line over *either axis*, the slope is negated. If you reflect a line over the *x*-axis, its *y*-intercept is also negated. If you reflect a line over the *y*-axis, its *y*-intercept stays the same. Consider the implications for the slope-intercept form of a line. The reflection of $y = 3x + 2$ over the *x*-axis is $y = -3x - 2$; the reflection of $y = 3x + 2$ over the *y*-axis is $y = -3x + 2$. (More on reflections and other graph manipulations on page 120.)

One other reminder that deserves its own heading

When you are told that a particular point is on a line, that's the same as being told that the equation of the line works out when that point is plugged into the equation for *x* and *y*. In other words, (4, 6) is on the line $y = x + 2$ because $6 = 4 + 2$. When a question gives you a point and an equation, *put the point into the equation*.

Variants of the following question are fairly common. Let's see if, given what we know about lines, we can figure it out.

Example 2

15. Line p has a slope of $-\dfrac{2}{3}$ and a positive y-intercept.

Line q passes through the origin, is perpendicular to

line p, and intersects line p at the point $(c, c + 1)$. What

is the value of c?

(A) 1
(B) 2
(C) 3
(D) 4
(E) 6

With only a cursory glance, it might seem like we don't have much to work with here. Look closer. Note that the question states that line q passes through the origin. *This is very important.* It's common for the SAT writers to tell you that, and it's also common for students to completely breeze by it. When a line passes through the origin, that means we have the y-intercept (zero). It also, more generally, means we have a *point*, which ends up being the key to solving lots of questions.

So we know the y-intercept of line q is 0, and we can easily calculate the slope. Line q is perpendicular to line p, so its slope has to be the negative reciprocal of p's slope. Since the slope of p is $-\dfrac{2}{3}$, the slope of q is $\dfrac{3}{2}$.

$$y\text{-intercept} = b = 0$$

$$\text{slope} = m = \dfrac{3}{2}$$

We can write the equation of the line:

$$y = mx + b$$

$$y = \frac{3}{2}x + 0$$

$$y = \frac{3}{2}x$$

Then we can drop the point $(c, c + 1)$ into that equation, and solve:

$$c + 1 = \frac{3}{2}c$$

$$2(c + 1) = 3c$$

$$2c + 2 = 3c$$

$$\mathbf{2 = c}$$

The answer is (B).

The SAT writers are adept at writing difficult line questions, and as I said above, questions like this one are not uncommon. Make sure you understand what's going on here, because it's a good bet that you'll see one like this again.

6. What is the *x*-intercept of $y = 5x - 20$?

   (A) −20
   (B) −4
   (C) 4
   (D) 5
   (E) 15

10. Which of the following is the equation of a line that is perpendicular to $y + 3 = 3x - 8$?

   (A) $3y + x = 26$
   (B) $3y - 3x = -8$
   (C) $9y - 6x = 18$
   (D) $y + 3x = 9$
   (E) $y - 3x = 10$

14. If a line has a slope of −2 and it passes through the point (−3, 2), what is its *y*-intercept?

   (A) 8
   (B) 6
   (C) 0
   (D) −4
   (E) −6

16. Which of the following sets of points forms a line that is parallel to $3y = 2x + 11$?

    (A) $(-1, 3)$ and $(3, -1)$
    (B) $(12, 4)$ and $(3, -2)$
    (C) $(6, 2)$ and $(8, 5)$
    (D) $(11, 2)$ and $(11, 3)$
    (E) $(7, 4)$ and $(5, 7)$

19. Line l has the equation $y = 3x + c$ and line m has the equation $4y - 3x = 11 - d$, for some constants c and d. If lines l and m intersect at $(-3, -2)$, what is the sum of c and d?

    (A) -3
    (B) -7
    (C) 7
    (D) 10
    (E) 17

Answers:

6. **(C)**
10. **(A)**
14. **(D)**
16. **(B)**
19. **(E)**

Solutions on page 307.

The following selected Blue Book questions are examples of this stuff in the wild.

Test	§	p	#	Diff.
1	7	415	6	3
2	2	455	11	2
2	2	457	20	5
2	8	482	3	1
3	5	529	12	3
3	8	546	10	3
4	3	584	12	M
4	3	585	16	M
4	9	609	2	E
5	2	642	17	M
5	8	671	15	H
6	2	703	14	M
6	8	731	7	M
7	7	788	12	M
7	9	798	11	M
8	7	850	14	M
8	9	859	9	M
9	2	887	4	M
9	8	918	13	M
10	2	948	2	E
10	2	951	10	E
10	2	953	17	H
11	3	10	7	3
11	3	11	10	2

Parabolas

The parabola is actually a hugely important mathematical concept with tons of forms, properties, and even its own history. It can open up, down, left, right, or any other direction. It can be used to graph the flight trajectory of the last AT&T cell phone I threw in a lake when it dropped one too many calls. But if you're interested in that stuff, you should go to the Wikipedia article about parabolas. On the SAT, there's actually not much you need to know about them. Let's keep things simple.

Parabolas are symmetrical

This is the most important thing to remember about parabolas, because this is the key that will unlock the SAT's most difficult parabola questions. The awesome thing is that you probably already knew this. The not awesome thing is that the SAT still finds ways to make you miss these questions.

When presented with a parabola on the SAT (especially when it's not accompanied by an equation), your first step should be to draw the line of symmetry down the middle of it. Find the minimum or maximum, and draw a vertical line[*] cutting the parabola right in two. Each point to the left of that line will have a point exactly mirroring it on the right.

---

[*] Horizontal parabolas are so rare on the SAT that I'm not mentioning them here—because they're not functions, I guess?—but obviously if you had a horizontal parabola your line of symmetry would be horizontal.

Example 1

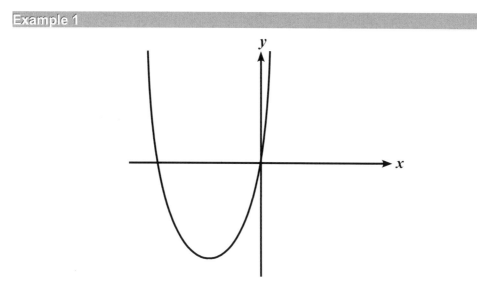

18. The graph above represents the quadratic function $f(x)$.
    If the function's minimum is at $f(-3)$, and $f(0) = 0$,
    which of the following is equal to 0?

    (A) $f(3)$
    (B) $f(-1)$
    (C) $f(-4)$
    (D) $f(-5)$
    (E) $f(-6)$

Right. So let's translate this into English first. What they're saying here is that the line of symmetry for this parabola is at $x = -3$, and that the function goes right through the origin: $f(0) = 0$ means that this graph contains the point $(0, 0)$. They're basically asking us to find the other x-intercept.

Here's where the whole symmetry thing really comes in. If we know the line of symmetry, and we know one of the x-intercepts, it's a piece of cake to find the other. Put very simply, they each have to be the exact same distance from the line of symmetry. Since $(0, 0)$ is a distance of 3 from the line of symmetry at $x = -3$, our other x-intercept has to be a distance of 3 away from the line of symmetry too!

So we're looking for the point (−6,0). Choice (E) is the one that does that for us: $f(−6) = 0$.

Can they find ways to make symmetry questions difficult? You bet. Will you be ready for them? I'd say so.

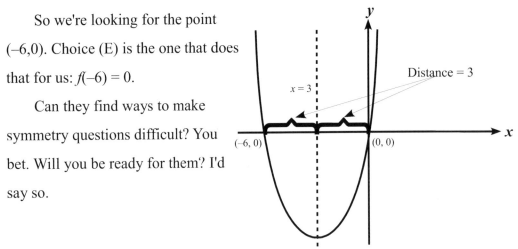

The equation of a parabola

There are a number of forms for a parabola equation; you probably already know a few. But one is by far the most important for the SAT. Know the form below, and what its coefficients signify, and you're good to go.

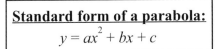

> **Standard form of a parabola:**
> $$y = ax^2 + bx + c$$

➜ The constant **a** tells you whether the parabola opens up or down. If a is positive, the parabola's a smiley face. If a is negative, it's a frowny face. Easy to remember, no?

➜ The constant **b** is not important, at least as far as the SAT is concerned.[*]

➜ The constant **c** is your y-intercept. If there is no c, that means your parabola has a y-intercept of 0. In other words, it goes through the origin.

When you're tested on this equation, it'll often be as simple as being given an equation, and having to match it to the correct parabola graph. If your equation has a positive a, eliminate the parabolas that open down. Then focus on y-intercepts. If your equation has a positive c, only one remaining choice will have a positive y-intercept. It'll be that simple.

---

*   There are some who point out that b is important because $−b/2a$ will give you the x-coordinate of the parabola's vertex, and therefore the parabola's line of symmetry. But as cool as it is, I've never seen an SAT question that requires this knowledge, so I'm relegating it to a footnote.

The other form of a parabola that you'll *probably not need*, but that has appeared on the SAT occasionally, is the vertex form of a parabola:

Vertex form of a parabola:
$$y = a(x - h)^2 + k$$

➔ The constant **a** still tells you whether the parabola opens up or down, just like it does in the general form.

➔ The constants **h** and **k** tell you the vertex of the parabola—the vertex is at (h, k).

⇨ Note that this is just an application of the graph translation rules we discussed in the Functions chapter on page 120. If $f(x) = ax^2$, which would have a vertex at $(0, 0)$, then $f(x - h) + k = a(x - h)^2 + k$ would move the vertex to (h, k).

⇨ Also note the negative inside the parentheses, which is the trickiest thing about the vertex form of a parabola. The parabola with equation $y = 3(x + 4)^2 + 1$ will have its vertex at $(-4, 1)$, not $(4, 1)$!

I want to stress the limited utility of this form for SAT purposes, especially if you have a graphing calculator. I'm including it to be super-thorough, but it really appears *very* rarely.

Example 2 (Grid-in)

$$y = 2(x + 1)^2 + 3$$

17. What is the slope of the line that contains the vertex and the *y*-intercept of the parabola with the equation above?

To solve this, first we must note that the parabola is given in vertex form.[*] So we know the vertex is (−1, 3).

Now we need to foil everything out to put the parabola in general form and find the *y*-intercept.

$$y = 2(x + 1)^2 + 3$$
$$y = 2(x^2 + 2x + 1) + 3$$
$$y = 2x^2 + 4x + 5$$

So the *y*-intercept of the parabola is 5, meaning the other point on the line for which we're finding the slope is (0, 5).

All we need to do now is calculate the slope!

$$\text{slope} = \frac{5 - 3}{0 - (-1)}$$

$$\text{slope} = \frac{2}{1}$$

$$\text{slope} = 2$$

And there you have it. Not so bad, right?

---

[*] If you ever have to deal with vertex form on your SAT, this is probably how it'll happen—you'll be given the parabola in that form.

$$g(x) = -6x^2 + 3x$$

15. Which of the following is true about the graph of the function g defined above?

    I.   It passes through the origin.
    II. It is increasing from $x = 1$ to $x = 6$.
    III. $g(-6)$ is negative.

(A) I only
(B) II only
(C) III only
(D) I and III only
(E) I, II, and III

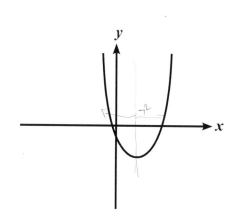

16. The parabola in the figure above has its minimum at $x = 2$. Which of the following could be an x-intercept of the parabola?

(A) 2.5
(B) 3
(C) 3.5
(D) 4
(E) 4.5

17. If a parabola passes through the points (0, 3) and (8, 3), and has its minimum at $(p, -2)$, what is p?

(A) -2
(B) 0
(C) 4
(D) 5
(E) 8

18. If a and b are constants, and the graph of $g(x) = (x - a)^2 + b$ has its minimum at $g(6)$, which of the following pairs of points could also be on the graph of $g(x)$?

    (A) (5, –9) and (8, –9)
    (B) (0, 6) and (10, 10)
    (C) (5, 6) and (7, 8)
    (D) (2, –5) and (10, –5)
    (E) (–2, 0) and (14, 2)

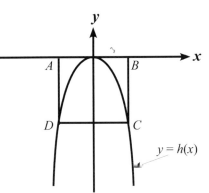

Note: Figure not drawn to scale.

20. In the figure above, $ABCD$ is a square that intersects the graph of $h(x)$ at points C and D. A and B lie on the x-axis. If the area of $ABCD$ is 36 and $h(x) = kx^2$, what is k?

    (A) 3

    (B) $\dfrac{1}{3}$

    (C) $-\dfrac{1}{6}$

    (D) $-\dfrac{1}{3}$

    (E) $-\dfrac{2}{3}$

PWN the SAT

Answers:

15. **(D)**
16. **(E)**
17. **(C)**
18. **(D)**
20. **(E)**

Solutions on page 309.

The following selected Blue Book questions are examples of this stuff in the wild.

Test	§	p	#	Diff.
3	5	530	18	4
4	9	611	8	M
4	9	612	11	M
5	4	652	8	H
7	3	772	12	M
7	9	799	14	M
10	5	969	16	M
11	3	13	15	3

Note that #8 on page 611 does not actually contain a parabola. I'm including it here anyway because it's a symmetry question, much like the kind we discussed in this chapter. Part of SAT prep is taking specific things you've learned and applying them to slightly new situations, so apply what you know about parabolas and symmetry to the semicircle—which is also symmetrical—in that question. Note also that, although there are not many parabola questions in the Blue Book, I still think it's super important that you know how to deal with them.

Absolute value

I trust you already know the very basics of absolute value: that $|5| = 5$, and $|-5| = 5$, etc. Taking the absolute value of a positive number has no effect on the number. Taking the absolute value of a negative number makes it positive. This applies, of course, to variables and expressions as well. The absolute value of x is just plain old x when x is positive, and it's $-x$ when x is negative.

When $x < 0$	When $x \geq 0$
$|x| = -x$	$|x| = x$

You might also find it helpful to think about absolute value as it relates to a number line.

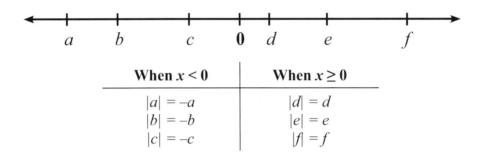

When $x < 0$	When $x \geq 0$
$|a| = -a$	$|d| = d$
$|b| = -b$	$|e| = e$
$|c| = -c$	$|f| = f$

If you don't know whether something is positive or negative, *you must account for both possibilities*. When the $|x| = 5$, then either $x = 5$, or $x = -5$.

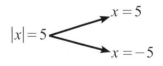

Is this bending your brain a bit? Or is it like *duh*? Stick around, please, either way, because now it's time to talk about the ways this stuff will appear on the SAT.

Absolute value and inequalities

Interesting things start happening when absolute values are combined with inequalities, so one of the SAT writers' favorite things to do is to kill two birds with one stone and test absolute value and inequalities concomitantly. Remember that $|x| = 5$ means that $x = 5$, or $x = -5$. You can draw similarly simple conclusions with inequalities.

If I told you that $|y| < 3$, and y is an integer, then what are the possible values for y? There aren't many: y could equal 2, 1, 0, –1, or –2. In other words, y has to be less than 3, *and* greater than –3. You can get rid of the absolute value brackets in $|y| < 3$ by translating the expression into a range: $-3 < y < 3$.

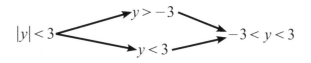

Example 1

19. In order to be considered "good for eating" by the La'Urthg Orcs of Kranranul, a human must weigh between 143 and 181 pounds. Which of the following inequalities gives all the possible weights, w, that a human in Kranranul should NOT want to be?

(A) $|w - 143| < 38$
(B) $|w - 162| < 19$
(C) $|w + 38| < 181$
(D) $|w - 181| < 22$
(E) $|w - 162| < 24$

First of all, it's possible to plug in here, although it matters greatly what numbers you choose. Picking a number right in the middle of the range (like 165) probably won't help you out much. To plug in successfully, choose weights that should *just barely* be within the range (like 144 or 180) and then, if you still haven't eliminated all the answers, choose weights that should *just barely* be outside the range (like 142 or 182). Be careful with this second part! You're looking to eliminate any choices that *work* when you know you picked a number that *shouldn't work*.

Let's start with $w = 144$ and see what happens. A person who weighs 144 pounds should try to lose weight, pronto, lest he become a meal for the orcs. Right now, he's in the "good for eating" range! Since 144 is in the range, we're looking for choices that will give us *true* inequalities when we plug it in.

(A) $|144 - 143| < 38$
     $|1| < 38$
     $1 < 38$

(B) $|144 - 162| < 19$
     $|-18| < 19$
     $18 < 19$

(C) $|144 + 38| < 181$
     $|182| < 181$
     $182 < 181$

(D) $|144 - 181| < 22$
     $|-37| < 22$
     $37 < 22$

(E) $|144 - 162| < 24$
     $|-18| < 24$
     $18 < 24$

So, bummer. Our first plug-in only eliminated 2 out of 5 choices. What happens when we plug in a number that shouldn't work, like 141? Remember, now we're looking to eliminate anything that gives us a *true* inequality, because a 141 pound person is NOT considered on the menu by the orcs. Note that I'm not bothering with (C) and (D) since we've already eliminated them.

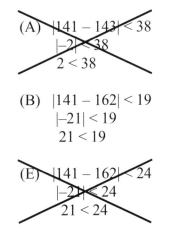

(A) $|141 - 143| < 38$
     $|-2| < 38$
     $2 < 38$

(B) $|141 - 162| < 19$
     $|-21| < 19$
     $21 < 19$

(E) $|141 - 162| < 24$
     $|-21| < 24$
     $21 < 24$

Only (B) was true when we needed it to be true, and false when we needed it to be false, so that's our answer. But if plugging in here seems cumbersome to you, you're not alone. I actually prefer to do questions like this another way.

Let's have a look at (B), our correct answer, and convert it like we did at the beginning of the chapter:

$$|w - 162| < 19 \longrightarrow -19 < w - 162 < 19$$

Now things are about to get crazy. Add 162 to each side to get w by itself:

$$-19 + 162 < w - 162 + 162 < 19 + 162$$
$$\mathbf{143 < w < 181}$$

Wow, that's exactly what we were looking for. I mean, I knew that was coming, and I'm *still* amazed. I can't even imagine how you must feel.

So on a question like this, you can just convert every answer choice in this way to see which one gives you what you want, or you can even take it one step further. If and when you get a question like this, the correct answer will look like this:

To say that a variable falls into a particular range:

|variable – middle of range| < distance from middle to ends of range

---

This formula tells you how far from a central value you can get before being outside of the desired range. Let's look at how it applies to the question we just answered:

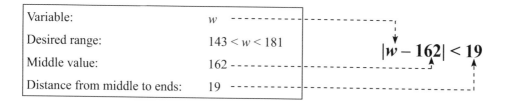

Variable:	w	
Desired range:	$143 < w < 181$	$\|w - 162\| < 19$
Middle value:	162	
Distance from middle to ends:	19	

Not bad, right? What $|w - 162| < 19$ is really saying is that the ideal eating weight of a human, w, is less than 19 pounds away from 162.

Absolute value and functions

As you hopefully know, order of operations dictates that you don't apply absolute value brackets until you've completed all the operations inside the brackets:

$$\textbf{GOOD: } |-8 + 5| = |-3| = 3$$
$$\textbf{BAD: } |-8 + 5| = 8 + 5 = 13$$

Seriously, don't do that second one. *Don't.*

The same is true if you have absolute value brackets around a function, like $|f(x)|$. The order of operations is such that the absolute value brackets don't take effect until the function has done its thing inside. If the function comes out positive on its own, the brackets have no effect. If the function comes out negative, it becomes positive:

x	$f(x)$	$|f(x)|$
1	−8	8
2	−3	3
3	−1	1
4	4	4
5	6	6

See? Now here's the important part: what happens to the *graph* of a function when you take the absolute value of the function? Well, when the function is positive, as we see in the table above *nothing at all happens to it*. When the function is negative, it reflects off the *x*-axis. In other words, it bounces. BOING!

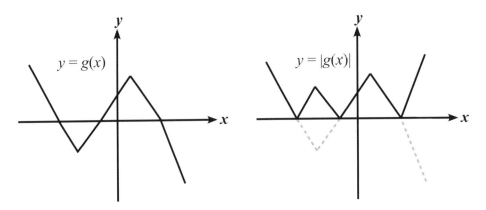

Cool, right? Don't forget: the graph of $|g(x)|$ is identical to the graph of $g(x)$ whenever $g(x)$ is positive. The only changes occur when $g(x)$ is negative.

Practice questions: Absolute value

Strengthen your core! (Get it? Because "absolute" has "abs" in it? High five!)

13. If $|a| + |b| = 7$ and a and b are integers, which of the following could NOT equal $a + b$?

    (A) 7
    (B) 5
    (C) 0
    (D) −3
    (E) −7

14. If $h(x) = 2x - 10$, which of the following is NOT true?

    (A) $h(3) < |h(3)|$
    (B) $h(1) = |h(1)|$
    (C) $h(10) = |h(10)|$
    (D) $h(10) = |h(0)|$
    (E) $-h(10) = h(0)$

17. All the bowlers on Robbie's bowling team, Strike Force, have average scores between 215 and 251. Which of the following inequalities can be used to determine whether a bowler with an average score of s could be on the team?

    (A) $|s - 233| < 36$
    (B) $|s - 251| < 215$
    (C) $|s - 18| < 233$
    (D) $|s - 233| < 18$
    (E) $|s - 223| < 18$

x	g(x)
3	−3
5	8
9	12
13	−11
17	15

18. The table above shows a few values for the function g. According to the table, which of the following statements is NOT true?

(A) $|g(3)| = 3$
(B) $|g(5)| > g(5)$
(C) $g(17) - g(9) = |g(3)|$
(D) $|g(13)| < g(9)$
(E) $|g(17)| = g(17)$

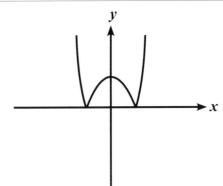

19. Which of the following could be the equation of the graph above?

(A) $y = |-x^2 + 4|$
(B) $y = |x^2| - 4$
(C) $y = |x^2 + 4|$
(D) $y = -|x^2 - 4|$
(E) $y = |-x^2 - 4|$

Answers:

13. **(C)**
14. **(B)**
17. **(D)**
18. **(B)**
19. **(A)**

Solutions on page 311.

The following selected Blue Book questions are examples of this stuff in the wild.

Test	§	p	#	Diff.
1	7	418	15	3
2	2	456	17	3
2	5	467	14	3
3	8	545	7	2
5	4	653	10	E
5	8	669	9	M
6	2	701	6	M
7	9	797	8	M
8	9	860	10	M
9	8	917	9	M
10	2	949	4	E
11	4	17	12	3

Corresponding coefficients in equivalent polynomials

This isn't tested on the SAT all that often, but it *has* appeared, and I've had more students tell me they don't remember learning this in school than just about any other concept I've covered with them as a tutor:

When two polynomials equal each other for all values of *x*, the polynomials are equivalent and their corresponding coefficients are equal.

For nonzero constants a, b, c, p, q, and r,

IF: $ax^2 + bx + c = px^2 + qx + r$, for all values of x,

THEN: $a = p$, $b = q$, and $c = r$

$$ax^2 + bx + c$$
$$= px^2 + qx + r$$

To me, the easiest way to understand why this is true is to think about two parabolas. (Quadratics are the polynomials you'll probably see tested if you see this concept tested at all.) If two parabolas intersect once, then their polynomials are equal for *one* value of *x*. The polynomials are only equal for *all* values of *x* if the parabolas are right on top of each other—they're the same parabola!

You might find it useful, when you're presented with equivalent polynomials, to stack them on top of each other just like I did in the box above and put circles around the corresponding coefficients. *I* find it useful to do that, anyway.

Example (Grid-in)

$$(x + 9)(x + k) = x^2 + 4kx + p$$

20. In the equation above, k and p are constants. If the equation is true for all values of x, what is the value of p?

To solve this, first FOIL the left hand side:

$$(x + 9)(x + k)$$
$$= x^2 + 9x + kx + 9k$$

Let's factor x out of those middle terms:

$$= x^2 + (9 + k)x + 9k$$

Pay close attention to what just happened there. If we're going to compare coefficients of x in two equivalent polynomials, then we need *one* coefficient of x on each side of the equation. Factoring $(9 + k)$ out accomplishes this for us. Now stack up the two sides, and see what equals what:

$$x^2 + (\mathbf{9 + k})x + \mathbf{9k}$$
$$= x^2 + (\mathbf{4k})x + \mathbf{p}$$

So we know two things:

$$9 + k = 4k$$
$$9k = p$$

From here, this is cake, no?

$$9 + k = 4k$$
$$9 = 3k$$
$$3 = k$$

$$9(3) = p$$
$$27 = p$$

There—that wasn't so bad. This kind of problem can really throw you for a loop the first time you see one, but you can get very good very quickly once you understand the process. And that, my friend, is what good SAT prep is all about!

Don't let these questions FOIL you.

Note: The final two questions in this drill are grid-ins.

10. If $(a + b)x^3 = cx^3$ for all values of x, which of the following must be true about constants a, b, and c?

(A) $b - a = c$
(B) $a - b = c$
(C) $b - c = a$
(D) $a - c = b$
(E) $c - a = b$

$$(x - 5)(x - 7) = x^2 + mx + n$$

13. The equation above is true for all values of x; m and n are constants. Which of the following equals $n - m$?

(A) 2
(B) 12
(C) 23
(D) 30
(E) 47

$$ax^2 - bx + c = rx^2 + sx + t$$

16. If the equation above is true for all values of x, and a, b, c, r, s, and t are nonzero constants, which of the following is FALSE?

(A) $b = s$
(B) $c = t$
(C) $b^2 = s^2$
(D) $a + c = r + t$
(E) $a + b = r - s$

$$(x - 3)(x - d) = x^2 - 2dx + m$$

17. In the equation above, d and m are constants. If the equation is true for all values of x, what is the value of dm?

18. If a and b are positive integer constants, and $x^2 + ax + bx + 40$ is equivalent to $(x + 8)(x + 5)$, what is the greatest possible value of a?

Answers:

10. **(E)**

13. **(E)**

16. **(A)**

17. **27**

18. **12**

Solutions on page 313.

The following selected Blue Book questions are examples of this stuff in the wild.

Test	§	p	#	Diff.
3	5	527	8	5
3	8	546	11	3
10	5	969	17	H

Much like prime factorization problems, corresponding coefficients problems occur on the SAT pretty rarely. I included this short chapter in the guide because a little practice goes a long way on this very specific problem type, and I want you to be as thoroughly prepped as possible. Hopefully, after working through this chapter, you're *eager* for a corresponding coefficients problem to rear its head on test day.

Interlude: Be nimble.

There's a question I love to throw at students early on in the tutoring process:

If $\dfrac{4^{999} + 4^{998}}{5} = 4^x$, what is x?

It's a beautiful question because no matter what, it's going to show me something about the kid with whom I'm working. Almost everyone goes to the calculator first. Once it becomes clear that the calculator won't help I see a few divergent paths, all illuminating:

1. If my student says it can't be done, I know one kind of question on which I'm going to have to drill her repeatedly.

2. If my student says $x = 1997$, then I know he just added the exponents in the numerator and completely ignored the denominator, so we're going to need to review the exponent rules and get his vision checked.

3. If my student factors 4^{998} out of the numerator to see that everything else cancels out and $x = 998$, then I know I'm going to have to really challenge her to get her score higher than it already is (full solution explained below).

4. If my student starts wrestling with other, more manageable numbers to try to get a foothold on the problem, I know I'm dealing with a kid who knows how to struggle and who doesn't back down from tough questions.

This fourth student might, for example, write the following:

$$\dfrac{4^3 + 4^2}{5} = 16 = 4^2 \text{ , and } \dfrac{4^4 + 4^3}{5} = 64 = 4^3 \text{ , so } \dfrac{4^{999} + 4^{998}}{5} = 4^{998}$$

Let's be clear here: it's fantastic to know how to do this question the right way, like the third student. She has a strong base of mathematical knowledge and has seen enough similar problems not to succumb to the pitfall of misusing exponent rules, and is creative enough to try pulling out the greatest common factor to see if anything good happens (and it does). As her tutor, this fills me with confidence and pride, but I'm also aware that I still don't know how she's going to react when she gets to a problem that's unlike any she's seen before (and on the SAT, that will indubitably happen, probably when it counts). So I'm going to keep watching her closely until I get to see what she does when a question makes her squirm.

The fourth student, though, is one who finds a way to claw out the correct answer even when faced with an intimidating problem that his tools seem at first not to be able to solve. He might not be as well-versed in math as the third student, but in the eyes of the SAT, she and he are exactly the same on that question. Because he's scrappy. He's nimble. And that will take him far.

In sports, you'll often hear a commentator say, "That's why you play the game," after an underdog team wins a game it wasn't expected to. It doesn't matter who looks better on paper. It matters who performs on game day. I've got faith in student #4 on game day.

If you want to take your place in the pantheon of great test takers, you're going to have to be nimble. You're going to have to grapple with tough problems sometimes. You're going to have to make mistakes, learn from them, and try not to repeat them. You're going to have to be flexible, and willing to try more than one approach.

This is, in a nutshell, why I want you to know how to plug in and backsolve, but I also want you to be able to do the math. Once in a while, no matter how good you are, the first thing you try isn't going to work. The best test takers, the most nimble, don't get frustrated when this happens. They always have one or two more approaches in reserve.

This, above all else, is the skill I'm trying to help you develop with this book

Solution

$$\frac{4^{999} + 4^{998}}{5} = 4^x$$

$$\frac{4^{998}(4+1)}{5} = 4^x$$

$$\frac{4^{998}(5)}{5} = 4^x$$

$$4^{998} = 4^x$$

$$998 = x$$

Geometry and measurement

This is the part of the SAT prep experience where you're all like "Geometry? I *hate* geometry." And then I'm all like "Whaaat?" Because seriously, geometry on the SAT is not the geometry you learned to hate[*] in school—far from it. You'll come across some tough questions in this section, but even the toughest of them can be solved with careful application of a surprisingly short list of rules.

So come along on an adventure of the mind! We're gonna see shapes and stuff.

---

[*] If you love geometry, that's awesome! Me too. Let's start a club.

Angles and triangles

Before we get into triangles, we need to take a very quick look at the ingredients of a triangle: line segments and angles. I'm betting you already know this stuff:

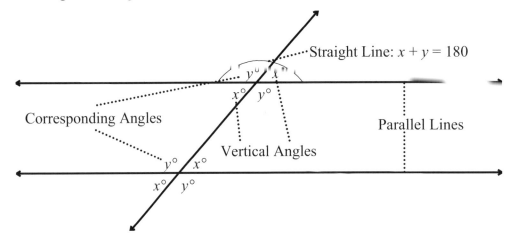

→ The degree measure of a straight line is 180°.

→ Angles directly across an intersection of two lines from each other are called *vertical angles* and they're congruent.

→ When two lines are parallel, and a third line (called a *transversal*) intersects both of them, the angles created at one intersection correspond to the angles at the other, like in the figure above.

→ If you have a transversal between two parallel lines and you know one angle, you can figure out all the rest using corresponding angles, vertical angles, and the fact that a straight line measures 180°.

Oh, and one more thing just to make sure our bases are covered: **all angles on the SAT are measured in degrees.** Leave everything you know about radians at the door.

Example 1

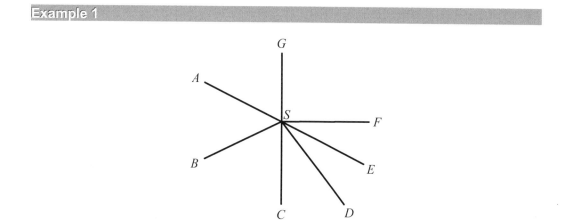

8. In the figure above, $\overline{AE}$, $\overline{BS}$, $\overline{CG}$, $\overline{DS}$, and $\overline{FS}$ intersect at point S. Which of the following pairs of angles must be congruent?

(A) $\angle ASF$ and $\angle BSF$
(B) $\angle ASG$ and $\angle CSE$
(C) $\angle ASG$ and $\angle FSG$
(D) $\angle ASB$ and $\angle ASG$
(E) $\angle ASC$ and $\angle BSE$

What to do, what to do? It's often possible to guesstimate on a question like this. They're asking you which angles are congruent, and the diagram is drawn to scale, so *look at the thing*. Enough choices look plausible here that we can't eliminate many on looks alone, but we can use guesstimate to eliminate (C).

Which angles are vertical angles? We know that all these segments meet at point S, but which ones actually go through it? $\overline{AE}$ and $\overline{CG}$ both go all the way through, so they'll create a set of vertical angles: $\angle ASG$ and $\angle CSE$. We know vertical angles are always congruent, so (B) is the answer. You're really going to want to make sure you're solid on this kind of question.

Now let's talk triangles

There are only a few things you need to know about angles and triangles for the SAT, many of which are given to you at the beginning of each math section. This chapter is going to be long (I know what you're thinking: *It's already long!*)

because there are a lot of different kinds of questions you might be asked and I want you to see all of them, but don't be daunted by its length; I'm willing to bet you already know pretty much everything you need to know.

Now, as always, you just need to study the scouting report: know what the SAT will throw at you, and you'll have a better chance of knocking it out of the park. Note also that for now, I'm only going to cover non-right triangles. I'll devote the next chapter to the special case of right triangles (and the double-special cases therein).

→ **The sum of the measures of the angles in a triangle is 180°:**

→ **The area of a triangle can be found with $A = \dfrac{1}{2} bh$:**

→ **In an isosceles triangle, the angles across from the equal sides are also equal:**

→ **In an equilateral triangle, all the angles are 60°, and all the sides are of equal length:**

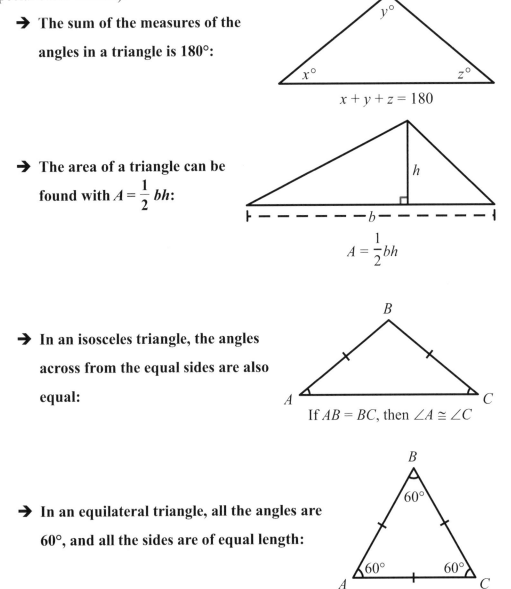

$$x + y + z = 180$$

$$A = \frac{1}{2}bh$$

If $AB = BC$, then $\angle A \cong \angle C$

→ **The bigger the angle, the bigger its opposite side:**

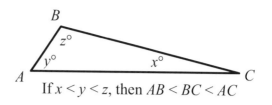

If $x < y < z$, then $AB < BC < AC$

→ **No side of a triangle can be as long as or longer than the sum of the lengths of the other two sides:**

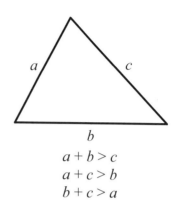

$$a + b > c$$
$$a + c > b$$
$$b + c > a$$

This last one is called the *Triangle Inequality Theorem*. The basic thrust: if the length of one side were equal to the sum of the lengths of the other two, would you have a triangle? No, you'd just have a straight line segment. And if one side were *longer* than the other two put together, then how would those two shorter ones connect to form the triangle? As hard as they might try, those poor little guys couldn't reach each other. They'd create a sadness gap. You don't want to make them make a sadness gap, do you?

To drive this home: imagine your forearms (apologies to my armless friends) are two sides of a triangle, and the imaginary line that connects your elbows is the third side. If you touch your fingertips together and pull your elbows apart, eventually your fingertips have to disconnect...that's when the length between your elbows is longer than the sum of the lengths of your forearms. Neat, huh?

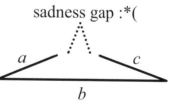

Similarity and congruence

When triangles are *similar*, they have all the same angles, and their corresponding sides are proportional to each other.[*] At the top of the next page, triangles *ABC*

---

* Fun fact: because every equilateral triangle has three 60° angles, all equilateral triangles are similar to each other.

and *DEF* are similar—their
angles are all the same and the
corresponding sides of *DEF*
are twice the length of the
corresponding sides of *ABC*.

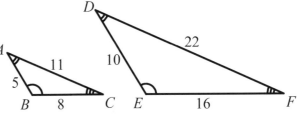

You probably remember the similarity rules from your geometry class, but let's quickly review them here.

→ **AA (Angle-Angle).** If two triangles have two pairs of congruent angles, then the triangles are similar. (You might know this one as AAA—same thing.)

→ **SAS (Side-Angle-Side).** If two triangles have corresponding sides that are proportional in length, and the angles between those sides are congruent, then the triangles are similar.

→ **SSS (Side-Side-Side).** If all the sides of one triangle are each proportional in length to the sides of another triangle, then the triangles are similar.

It's a good idea for you to be able to recognize common similar triangle configurations quickly. Have a look at the two figures below.

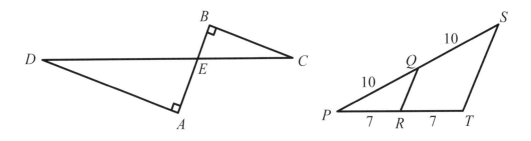

Look at the figure on the left first. ∠*A* and ∠*B* are right angles, so obviously those are congruent. Because ∠*BEC* and ∠*AED* are vertical angles, they are also congruent. Therefore, AA says you can bet your bottom dollar that △*BEC* is similar to △*AED*!

On the right, note that $PQ = 10$, and $PS = 20$. Likewise, $PR = 7$, and $PT = 14$. So two sides of △*PQR* are proportional in length to two sides of △*PST*. Because the angle between those sides is ∠*P* for both triangles, and ∠*P* is congruent to itself, $\triangle PQR$ is similar to $\triangle PST$ by SAS. Because in this case you know the ratio of the sides of $\triangle PQR$ to the sides of $\triangle PST$, you know that $\overline{ST}$ will be twice the length of $\overline{QR}$. Easy, right?

When the sides of similar triangles are in a 1:1 ratio—in other words, their sides are exactly the same—we say the triangles are *congruent*. That's right: **triangle congruence is really just a special case of triangle similarity**. You'll probably remember that there are a bunch of special geometry theorems that can be used to prove triangle congruency,[*] but for SAT purposes, you don't really need to memorize them. If you know the conditions of triangle similarity well, and you know that congruence is when triangles are similar and their sides are in a 1:1 ratio, then you need not over-clutter your brain with a bunch of special case congruency rules.

Example 2

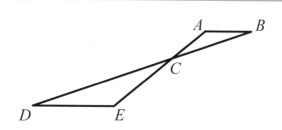

Note: Figure not drawn to scale.

14. In the figure above, the perimeter of $\triangle ABC$ is 15, and $\overline{AB} \parallel \overline{DE}$. If the ratio of AC to AE is 1:3, what is the perimeter of $\triangle EDC$?

(A) 60
(B) 45
▸(C) 30
(D) 15
(E) 5

---

[*] Angle-Side-Angle (ASA), Angle-Angle-Side (AAS), Side-Angle-Side (SAS), Side-Side-Side (SSS)

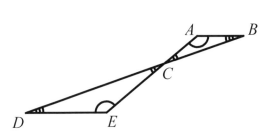

OK, so the first thing you need to recognize is that you've got similar triangles here. Because $\overline{AB}$ and $\overline{DE}$ are parallel, angles A and E are congruent, and angles B and D are congruent. Of course, the angles in each triangle at point C are congruent because they're vertical.

Once you've got that bit down, you need to deal with the ratio. If $\dfrac{AC}{AE}=\dfrac{1}{3}$, then $\dfrac{AC}{CE}=\dfrac{1}{2}$. WHAAAT!? I'm throwing tricky ratio conversions at you in a triangle question!? What am I, some kind of sadist? No, silly. I'm just trying to prepare you for a test that is famous for testing multiple concepts at once.

If the ratio of AC to CE is 1:2, then the ratios of all the sides of $\triangle ABC$ to their corresponding sides in $\triangle EDC$ will be 1:2. Therefore, if the perimeter of $\triangle ABC$ is 15, the perimeter of $\triangle EDC$ will be 30. That's choice (C).

Everything else

There's an awful lot to know about triangles if you're doing regular school math, but on the SAT, the preceding basically covers it. You will *never* need trigonometry of any kind, nor will you need any knowledge about things like circumcenters or orthocenters of triangles. (Google them if you want a reminder, you lunatic.)

There are some who think you need to know things like the external angle rule, or rules about alternate interior angles and opposite exterior angles in transversals. I say that if you know a straight line measures 180° and you know a triangle's angles add up to 180°, you already know them! Why over-complicate your life with overlapping rules?

I'm in the business of preparing you for a very specific test. The above is, in my 2400-scoring opinion, the salient stuff. Isn't it awesome how little there is?

Example 3

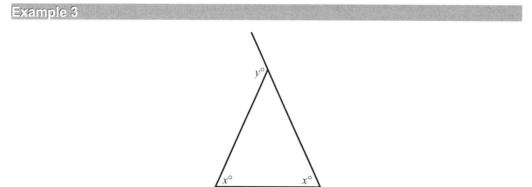

Note: Figure not drawn to scale.

17. If $y = 180 - x$ and all lengths are integers, which of the following could be the perimeter of the triangle in the figure above?

(A) 19
(B) 22
(C) 23
(D) 24
(E) 26

Wait, what? We don't know anything about any of the lengths, how are we supposed to figure out anything about the perimeter? Relax, friend. We'll get through this.

We know $y = 180 - x$. How can we use that? Note that the arc in the image to the right denotes a straight line, which means we have 180°. Therefore, the unlabeled angle in our original figure must be equal to $180 - y$. Do a little algebra now:

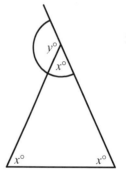

$$[\text{unmarked angle measure}] = 180 - y$$
$$[\text{unmarked angle measure}] = 180 - (180 - x)$$
$$[\text{unmarked angle measure}] = x$$

It doesn't look like it (that's what "not drawn to scale" means!) but we've got an equilateral triangle on our hands. All the angles inside it are equal so they must all be 60°! If all our lengths are integers, then, the perimeter must be a multiple of 3. Only one of our choices is: (D) 24.

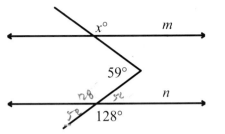

Note: Figure not drawn to scale.

13. In the figure above, *m* ∥ *n*. What is *x*?

- (A) 128
- (B) 159
- (C) 167
- (D) 171
- (E) 173

17. If △*RST* is isosceles, *RS* = 9, and *RT* and *ST* are integers, then which of the following is NOT a possible perimeter of △*RST*?

- (A) 15
- (B) 19
- (C) 22
- (D) 33
- (E) 69

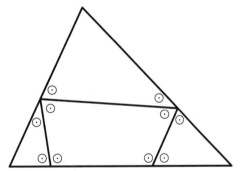

16. What is the sum of the measures of the marked (⊙) angles in the figure above?

- (A) 360°
- (B) 720°
- (C) 900°
- (D) 1080°
- (E) 1200°

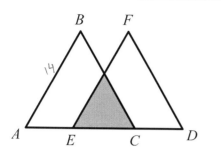

Note: Figure not drawn to scale.

18. In the figure above, $\triangle ABC$ and $\triangle DEF$ are congruent equilateral triangles. If E is the midpoint of $\overline{AC}$, and $AB = 14$, what is the perimeter of the shaded region?

- (A) 7

- (B) 14

- (C) 21

- (D) 28

- (E) $\dfrac{49\sqrt{3}}{2}$

20. In $\triangle PQR$, $PQ > PR$. Which of the following MUST be true?

  I. $PQ - QR < PR$
  II. The measure of $\angle PRQ$ is greater than the measure of $\angle PQR$
  III. $2PR > PQ$

- (A) I only
- (B) II only
- (C) III only
- (D) I and II only
- (E) II and III only

Answers:

13. **(E)**
16. **(B)**
17. **(A)**
18. **(C)**
20. **(D)**

Solutions on page 315.

The following selected Blue Book questions are examples of this stuff in the wild.

Test	§	p	#	Diff.	Test	§	p	#	Diff.
1	3	398	10	2	6	2	704	18	H
1	7	413	2	1	6	4	713	5	M
1	7	415	7	3	6	4	714	7	M
1	7	418	17	4	6	8	730	6	E
1	8	419	2	1	6	8	733	15	H
1	8	421	6	3	7	3	769	6	M
2	2	455	10	3	7	7	787	7	E
2	5	466	10	3	7	9	795	2	E
2	8	482	5	2	7	9	799	13	M
2	8	485	14	5	8	3	831	3	E
3	2	515	5	2	8	3	832	7	M
3	5	530	15	4	8	7	848	4	E
3	8	545	6	2	8	9	858	3	E
4	3	584	11	M	8	9	859	7	M
4	3	584	14	M	8	9	860	12	M
4	6	593	2	E	9	5	907	16	H
4	6	595	8	H	9	8	916	3	E
4	6	597	11	M	10	2	952	12	M
4	6	597	15	M	10	5	966	3	E
4	9	610	6	M	10	5	968	11	M
5	2	640	9	M	10	8	980	12	M
5	2	642	15	M	10	8	980	14	M
5	4	651	5	M	11	3	12	11	2
5	4	654	11	M	11	3	13	16	3
5	4	654	14	M	11	8	3	2	1
5	8	668	4	E					

Right triangles

So now that we've covered angles, and triangles in general, let's have a look at a special case. Right triangles get a chapter all to themselves because they're special, and have rules of their very own. Like that one friend of yours whose parents let him get away with everything.

Ancient Greece was awesome

First, let's *briefly* discuss the **Pythagorean theorem**. You know this, yes? It is, after all, basically the most important thing to have come out of Ancient Greece.[*] Basically it says that the sum of the squares of the legs (short sides) of a right triangle are equal to the square of the hypotenuse (longest side, across from the right angle). Oh, you know it? OK, good.

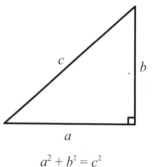

$$a^2 + b^2 = c^2$$

Example

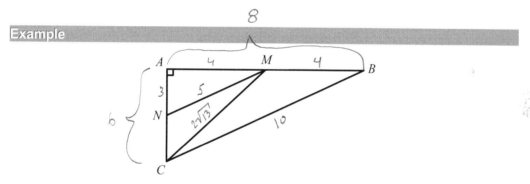

Note: Figure not drawn to scale.

16. In the figure above, $AC = 6$, $BC = 10$, and $CM = 2\sqrt{13}$. If N is the midpoint of $\overline{AC}$, what is $BM + MN$?

    (A) $3 + \sqrt{13}$
    (B) 7
    (C) $5 + 3\sqrt{2}$
    (D) 9
    (E) $4 + 5\sqrt{3}$

---

[*]   There was also, like, democracy and stuff.

Let's start by filling in what we know, which is how you should start basically every geometry problem you ever do. This diagram just contains what we're given. The slightly thicker lines, of course, are what we're trying to find.

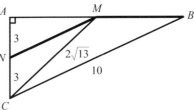

Note that we have 2 out of 3 sides of two different right triangles: $\triangle ABC$ and $\triangle ACM$. Let's Pythagorize (not a word) them both:

$$\triangle ABC: 6^2 + AB^2 = 10^2$$
$$36 + AB^2 = 100$$
$$AB^2 = 64$$
$$\mathbf{AB = 8}$$

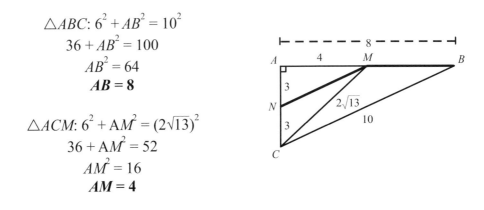

$$\triangle ACM: 6^2 + AM^2 = (2\sqrt{13})^2$$
$$36 + AM^2 = 52$$
$$AM^2 = 16$$
$$\mathbf{AM = 4}$$

OK, we've got BM now…it's $8 - 4 = 4$. Easy. How do we find MN? Help us Pythagoras, you're our only hope!

$$3^2 + 4^2 = MN^2$$
$$9 + 16 = MN^2$$
$$25 = MN^2$$
$$\mathbf{5 = MN}$$

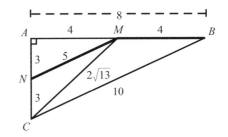

So our answer is $5 + 4 = 9$. That's choice (D). Ain't no thang.

Special right triangles

Now, are you ready for some amazing news? Even though you should absolutely know the Pythagorean theorem inside out, you actually don't have to use it very often on the SAT provided you know the 5 special right triangles. *Five!? But they only give me two at the beginning of each section!* I know. I'mma give you some extra ones. You're welcome.

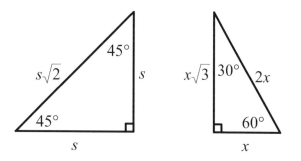

Above are the two special rights you're given at the beginning of every math section: the 45°-45°-90° (his friends call him "isosceles right") and the 30°-60°-90° triangles. Know the ratios of their sides cold…you'll need them often.

You should also know how to deal with a common SAT special right triangle trick: providing a whole number for the side that's usually associated with a radical. For example, the SAT might try to throw you by giving you a 45°-45°-90° with a hypotenuse of 20. Don't panic if this happens. Just divide the hypotenuse by $\sqrt{2}$ to find the legs. $\frac{20}{\sqrt{2}} = 10\sqrt{2}$, so the legs of a 45°-45°-90° triangle with a hypotenuse of 20 are each $10\sqrt{2}$.

Pythagorean triples

Below are three common right triangles that you *aren't* given in the beginning of each section, but nonetheless appear on the SAT—the first one quite often.

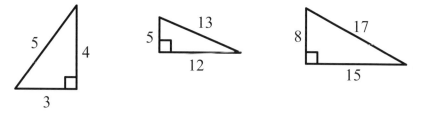

There's nothing worth saying about the angles; what's important are the sides. Here's the deal: because the SAT aims to be a "calculator optional" test, its writers have a *strong* predilection for "easy" numbers. There aren't that many sets of integers that work nicely with each other in the Pythagorean theorem, but these three (and all their multiples) do.[*]

These are called **Pythagorean Triples**, and you'll be seeing a bunch of them as you prep for the SAT. Note that we saw the 3-4-5 (and its big brother the 6-8-10) in the example problem a few pages ago.

It's not *necessary* to know these, but quick recognition of them will save you 30 seconds of old-Greek-guy work. This is the kind of trend recognition that will pay off in small increments for you as you continue on your quest for SAT hegemony. Here are the few Pythagorean Triples I recommend you memorize (in convenient table form!):

3-4-5	5-12-13	8-15-17
6-8-10	10-24-26	16-30-34
9-12-15		
12-16-20		
15-20-25		

One more important note on right triangles

Remember that every part of an SAT problem (even the answer choices) might contain clues about the solution. If you see $\sqrt{2}$, $\sqrt{3}$, or any other radical in the answer choices for a hard question, that's a clue! There's a pretty good chance that a right triangle is involved—even if you don't see one in the figure provided. More on this when we get to working in 3-D on page 199.

---

[*] There are actually a whole bunch of Pythagorean triples, including (7-24-25), (9-40-41), (11-60-61), (12-35-37), (13-84-85), etc. You get the point. For the purposes of the calculator optional SAT, you needn't worry about all of these. I've noted the ones that appear on the test commonly above.

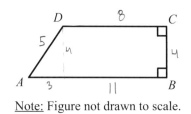

Note: Figure not drawn to scale.

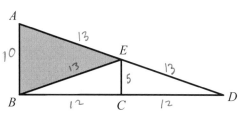

Note: Figure not drawn to scale.

12. In the figure above, $AB = 11$, $AD = 5$, and $DC = 8$. What is the perimeter of quadrilateral $ABCD$?

  (A) 24
  (B) 28
  (C) 29
  (D) 30
  (E) 33

15. In the figure above, $\overline{AB} \perp \overline{BD}$, $\overline{EC} \perp \overline{BD}$ and $\overline{EC}$ bisects both $\overline{BD}$ and $\overline{AD}$. If $ED = 13$ and $EC = 5$, what is the area of the shaded region?

  (A) 120
  (B) 90
  (C) 60
  (D) 40
  (E) 12

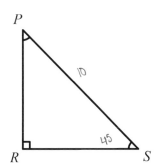

13. In the figure above, $\angle RPS$ and $\angle RSP$ each measure $45°$. If $PS = 10$, what is RS?

  (A) $5\sqrt{2}$
  (B) $5\sqrt{3}$
  (C) 7
  (D) 10
  (E) $10\sqrt{2}$

$$\frac{10}{\sqrt{2}} = 5\sqrt{2}$$

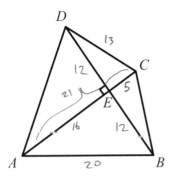

Note: Figure not drawn to scale.

17. In the figure above, point E is the midpoint of $\overline{BD}$. If $CD = 13$, $BD = 24$, and $AC = 21$, what is AB?

   (A) $13\sqrt{2}$
   (B) $10\sqrt{5}$
   (C) 20
   (D) 21
   (E) 22

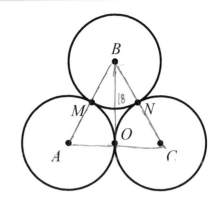

20. In the figure above, three congruent circles with centers A, B, and C are tangent to each other at M, N, and O. If $BO = 18$, what is the area of one of the circles?

   (A) $18\pi\sqrt{3}$
   (B) $36\pi\sqrt{2}$
   (C) 72π
   (D) 81π
   (E) 108π

Answers:

12. **(B)**
13. **(A)**
15. **(C)**
17. **(C)**
20. **(E)**

Solutions on page 317.

The following selected Blue Book questions are examples of this stuff in the wild.

Test	§	p	#	Diff.
1	3	400	17	4
2	8	481	2	1
3	5	526	5	4
3	8	545	8	2
4	9	613	15	M
5	2	643	19	H
5	4	652	7	M
5	4	655	18	H
7	7	789	16	M
8	3	832	7	M
8	3	835	16	M
9	2	888	5	M
9	5	908	20	H
10	2	953	15	H
10	5	969	15	M
10	5	970	18	H
11	4	19	20	5
11	8	35	13	4

Circles

Circles can be difficult to deal with, especially if you're approaching them from a very mathy perspective. Approach them with the swagger of someone who grasps that *the SAT is not a math test*, and you're going to have a much easier time.

Much of what you've learned (to hate?) about circles don't really apply on the SAT. To wit: polar coordinates, radians, circle equations (Cartesian or otherwise), and trigonometry are all forbidden ground for the test writers. So you might as well forget those things. They will only cause you problems. When you over-complicate things, you obfuscate easy solutions.

On the SAT, you only need to know a few things about circles. Here are the basics, which you're told in the beginning of every section. For radius r and diameter d:

➔ The area of a circle can be calculated using $A = \pi r^2$.

➔ The circumference of a circle can be calculated using $C = 2\pi r$ (or $C = \pi d$).

➔ The number of degrees of arc in a circle is 360.

I trust you have little problem with the facts above, but please remember that you don't need to be a memory hero—they're given to you in the beginning of each math section and there's no shame in checking your formulas.

But that's not all

There are a few other circle facts that you're not given, but that you might be tested on. You should also keep the following in mind:

➔ A line that is *tangent* to a circle (a line that intersects a circle at exactly one point) is perpendicular to the radius that goes to that point.

➔ When a wheel is rolling, it makes one revolution for every one circumference traveled, and vice versa.

Let's explore these with a couple grid-ins.

Example 1 (Grid-in)

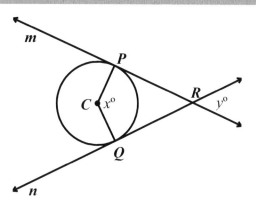

15. In the figure above, lines *m* and *n* are tangent to the circle at points *P* and *Q*, respectively, and *C* is the center of the circle. If *x* = 130, what is *y*?

This one isn't so bad at all if you know the rule about tangents being perpendicular to radii. Those tangent lines make 90° angles with $\overline{CP}$ and $\overline{CQ}$, and we know the measure of ∠*PCQ* is 130°. So we know 3 of the 4 angles in a quadrilateral. Since the angles in a quadrilateral add up to 360°*, we can easily calculate the fourth:

$$360° - 130° - 90° - 90° = 50°$$

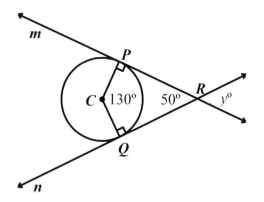

Since the angle marked *y*° is vertical to ∠*PRQ*, which measures 50°, *y* = 50.

---

* This is an extension of a rule you know: that the angles in a triangle add up to 180°. A quadrilateral is just two triangles mashed together! To see this, draw segment $\overline{CR}$.

Example 2 (Grid-in)

14. A certain wheel has a radius of $\frac{1}{4\pi}$ meters. If the wheel rolls in a straight line without slipping for 10 meters, how many revolutions does it make?

Remember that a wheel makes one complete revolution when it travels a distance of one circumference. So if we can figure out how many circumferences go into 10 meters, we're good to go.

The circumference of a wheel with a radius of $\frac{1}{4\pi}$ meters is:

$$C = 2\pi r$$

$$C = 2\pi\left(\frac{1}{4\pi}\right)$$

$$C = \frac{1}{2} \text{, or } 0.5$$

Now that we know the wheel has a circumference of 0.5 meters, we can calculate how many revolutions it makes when it travels 10 meters by dividing.

$$\frac{10 \text{ meters}}{0.5 \text{ meters per revolution}} = 20 \text{ revolutions}$$

Not too shabby, right? Now let's get into my favorite kind of circle questions.

Sector areas and arc lengths

All of the above is well and good (and important), but if you want to be invincible on SAT circle questions, there's something else you have to know: many of the scariest SAT circle problems are actually ratio problems in disguise!

Let me 'splain. Picture a circle with radius 4. It'll have an area of $\pi(4)^2 = 16\pi$. Now, if I asked you for half of its area, that's easy, right? 8π. What about a 25% of its area? Still easy: 4π. What about the area of a 45° sector* of that circle? Hmm...

Wait a minute. Isn't this still easy? 45° is $\frac{1}{8}$ of 360°, is it not? So wouldn't the area of that sector simply be $\frac{1}{8}$ of 16π, or 2π? Yes, indeed it would. And in fact, finding the area of a sector (or the length of an arc) will *always* be this easy, as long as you know its central angle and its radius.

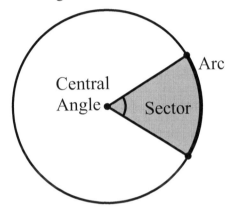

We can solve for the various parts of this circle with the following ratio:

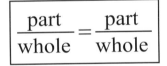

Which can be expanded out into a more battle-ready form:

$$\frac{\text{Degree Measure of Central Angle}}{360°} = \frac{\text{Arc Length}}{\text{Circumference}} = \frac{\text{Area of Sector}\left(A_{sector}\right)}{\text{Area of Whole}\left(A_{whole}\right)}$$

If you can complete just one of these fractions (for example, if you know the ratio of arc length to circumference), you can figure out everything else. Often, all you'll get will be the radius and a central angle, but as you're about to see, that's *plenty.*

---

* A sector is a part of a circle enclosed by two radii and their intercepted arc. But that's awfully technical. Most people I know just call it a pizza slice—see the diagram on the next page.

Let's use these ratios to find the area and perimeter of PacMan.

First, calculate the area and circumference of the whole circle (PacMan with his mouth closed):

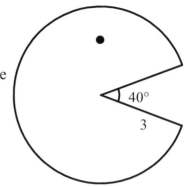

40°

3

$$A_{whole} = \pi(3)^2$$
$$A_{whole} = 9\pi$$

$$C = 2\pi(3)$$
$$C = 6\pi$$

Now we can use the angle of PacMan's gaping maw to find what we're looking for. Note that since PacMan's mouth is open at a 40° angle (which is empty space), we're actually looking for the part of the circle that is 320°. Let's tackle his area first:

$$\frac{320°}{360°} = \frac{A_{PacMan}}{A_{whole}}$$

Substitute in our value for A_{whole}:

$$\frac{320°}{360°} = \frac{A_{PacMan}}{9\pi}$$

Simplify the fraction on the left:

$$\frac{8}{9} = \frac{A_{PacMan}}{9\pi}$$

So we've solved for PacMan's area:

$$8\pi = A_{PacMan}$$

The process for his perimeter is very similar. Now, instead of looking for a part of the whole area of the circle, though, we're looking for a part of its circumference:

$$\frac{320°}{360°} = \frac{\text{Arc Length}_{PacMan}}{C}$$

Substitute, simplify, and solve:

$$\frac{8}{9} = \frac{\text{Arc Length}_{PacMan}}{6\pi}$$

$$\frac{16}{3}\pi = \text{Arc Length}_{PacMan}$$

But wait! We're not *quite* done yet. That's just the arc length around PacMan. To find his perimeter, we have to add the top and bottom of his mouth, too.

$$\frac{16}{3}\pi + 6 = P_{PacMan}$$

There we go. Arc length and sector area questions: not so bad, right? Don't panic, just work with the ratios.

I want to spend a *little* more time on arc length.

Example 3

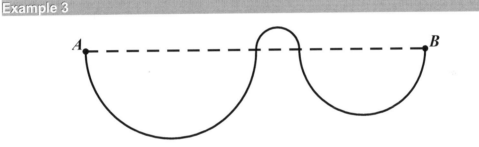

17. In the figure above, three semicircles with centers on $\overline{AB}$ form a continuous path from point A to point B. If the straight line distance between A and B is 26, what is the length of the path?

   (A) 13π
   (B) 18π
   (C) 26π
   (D) 51π
   (E) It cannot be determined from the information given.

Before you jump for (E), consider plugging in. Say the diameters of the semicircles, from left to right, are 14, 2, and 10. That way, they add up to 26, just like they're supposed to.

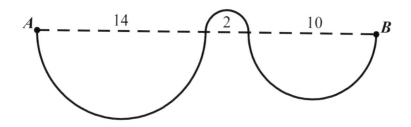

So your radii, then, are 7, 1, and 5, respectively. If you had full circles, you'd have circumferences of 14π, 2π, and 10π, respectively.

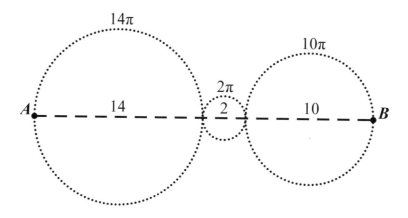

But you *don't* have full circles—you've got half circles. So your arc lengths are all half of their respective full circumferences, or 7π, π, and 5π, respectively. Sum those up and you get 13π, your total arc length. The answer is (A).

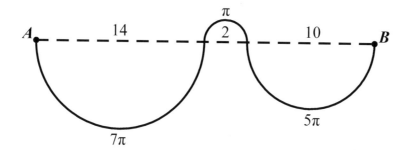

But wait a minute—we just plugged in random numbers! No way we're allowed to do that! Au contraire, mi amigo. We are *totally* allowed to do that. Try it again with different numbers. Say now our original diameters are 20, 2, and 4. You'll get the same answer: $10\pi + \pi + 2\pi = 13\pi$. Diameters of 17, 1, and 8, will give you $8.5\pi + 0.5\pi + 4\pi = 13\pi$. As long as your diameters add up to 26, you'll get 13π as your answer.

In fact—and this is *really* cool—when semicircles[*] connect to form a continuous path between two points that lie on the same line as the semicircles' centers, like they do in this question, the arc lengths of the semicircles add up to the length of a single semicircular arc connecting the same two points.

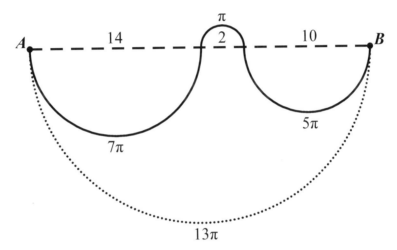

So there. Now you have something to impress your friends with at the next party you go to.

_____

[*]   Remember: A semicircle is exactly half a circle, not just part of a circle.

16. If a circle is divided evenly into 12 arcs, each measuring 3 cm long, what is the degree measure of an arc on the same circle that measures 8 cm long?

    (A) 64°
    (B) 72°
    (C) 80°
    (D) 96°
    (E) 112°

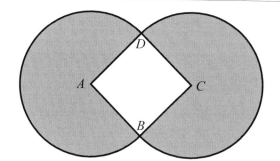

18. In the figure above, *ABCD* is a square, and *A* and *C* are the centers of the circles. If *AB* = 2, what is the total area of the shaded regions?

    (A) 3π
    (B) 6π
    (C) 8π
    (D) 8π − 4
    (E) 9π − 4

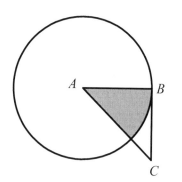

17. In the figure above, *A* is the center of the circle, $\overline{BC}$ is tangent to the circle at *B*, and *AB* = *BC*. If *AC* = 8, what is the area of the shaded region?

    (A) 4π
    (B) 8π
    (C) 10π
    (D) 16π
    (E) 24π

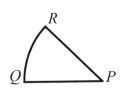

Note: Figure not drawn to scale.

19. In the figure above, P is the center of a circle, and Q and R lie on the circle. If the length of arc QR is π and $PQ = 6$, what is the measure of $\angle RPQ$?

(A) 15°
(B) 20°
(C) 30°
(D) 45°
(E) 80°

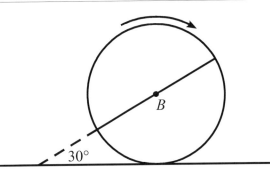

20. In the figure above, a wheel with center B and a radius of 12 cm is resting on a flat surface. A diameter is painted on the wheel as shown. If the wheel begins to rotate in a clockwise direction and rolls along the surface without slipping, how far will B travel before the painted diameter is perpendicular to the surface for the first time?

(A) 2π cm
(B) 4π cm
(C) 8π cm
(D) 12π cm
(E) 16π cm

Answers:

16. **(C)**
17. **(A)**
18. **(B)**
19. **(C)**
20. **(C)**

Solutions on page 319.

The following selected Blue Book questions are examples of this stuff in the wild.

Test	§	p	#	Diff.
1	3	398	8	2
1	7	414	5	3
1	8	419	2	1
2	2	453	4	3
2	5	463	2	1
3	2	518	17	4
3	5	525	2	1
3	5	528	10	2
4	3	586	19	H
4	6	597	13	M
5	2	641	11	M
5	2	643	19	H
6	2	703	16	M
6	4	713	5	M
6	4	717	15	M
7	3	773	16	H
7	7	789	17	M
8	3	834	14	M
8	7	852	20	H
9	5	906	11	M
9	5	907	18	H
10	2	949	3	E
10	8	979	8	M
11	8	34	9	3

Shaded regions

Anyone who's ever taken an SAT has come across shaded region questions. Although they're actually not that prevalent, they're among the most iconic question types on the test, so much so that you may find that the memory of them remains with you long after your SAT taking days have passed. True story: I had a roommate in college that used to talk in his sleep sometimes, and one time I woke up in the middle of the night to hear him plaintively moaning about shaded regions.

Should you let yourself get intimidated by a shaded region question? *Absolutely not.*

Say I told you that the area of the entire blob shape in the figure to the right (which is not drawn to scale) was 15, and then asked you for the area of the unmarked region. It'd be cake, right?

If I know you like I think I do, you'd probably say something like: "Thank you for insulting my intelligence with this asinine question; it's 5."

All you did was recognize that areas just add up: you know the total area and the sum of the marked areas, so the unmarked bit must make up the rest. If the total area is 15, and the marked part is 10, then the unmarked part has to be 5. Easy, yes?

So it is with many tricky shaded region questions:

$$A_{whole} - A_{unshaded} = A_{shaded}$$

Let's try one.

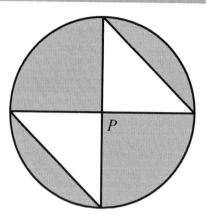

15. In the figure above, P is the center of the circle and also a vertex of both of the two right triangles. If the radius of the circle is 3, what is the area of the shaded region?

(A) π

(B) 6π

(C) $9\pi - 9$

(D) $9\pi - 6$

(E) $9\pi - 3$

In order to solve for the shaded region, we need to find A_{whole} and $A_{unshaded}$. The area of a circle is πr^2, so $A_{whole} = \pi(3)^2 = 9\pi$.

What's the area of the unshaded bits? Note that they're both right triangles, and that each leg is a radius. In other words, we know the base and height of both triangles are 3. The area of one of the triangles is $\frac{1}{2}bh = \frac{1}{2}(3)(3) = \frac{9}{2}$ Since there are two of the triangles, $A_{unshaded} = 9$.

So far so good? Now we can solve:

$$
\begin{array}{rcl}
A_{whole} & = & 9\pi \\
- A_{unshaded} & = & -9 \\
\hline
A_{shaded} & = & 9\pi - 9
\end{array}
$$

That's choice (C). Easy, right? Just remember $A_{whole} - A_{unshaded} = A_{shaded}$ and you'll be fine.

I know this seems painfully obvious, but it's important to remember that the SAT specializes in making it tricky to deal with concepts that are, on the surface, obvious.

Are you familiar with Rubin's Vase? It's there on the right of this paragraph. If I had told you before showing you the image that I was about to show you a picture of a vase, it's likely that you'd see exactly that when shown the image. But had I told you that I was about to show you a picture of two faces and then presented you with *the same image*, you'd probably see the faces. Pretty cool, right?

Credit:
http://commons.wikimedia.org/wiki/User:Bryan_Derksen

The writers of the SAT, of course, know this. So when they ask you to find the area of a shaded region, they're often trying to make you focus on the most difficult thing to find directly (and sometimes, an *impossible* thing to find directly). That's why it's important to always keep the aforementioned shaded region procedure at the front of your mind. If you don't, you'll likely find yourself choking down a dish of geometrical futility, drizzled with a balsamic disgruntlement reduction and served with a side of anguish fries. It can happen.

Just remember that SAT writers *love* to misdirect—they'll try to make you focus on the part of a diagram that's difficult to solve for, instead of the part that isn't. But since you're so thoroughly steeped in their methods, you're not going to fall for it. You know that the SAT likes to make it difficult to solve directly for the shaded regions, so you're going to solve for everything else instead. You know the curve ball is coming, so you're in the best possible position to hit it out of the park.

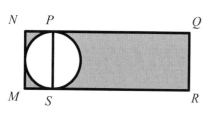

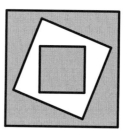

Note: Figure not drawn to scale.

10. In the figure above, a circle with diameter $\overline{PS}$ is tangent to rectangle *MNQR* on three sides. If *MN* = 6 and *MR* = 8, what is the total area of the shaded regions?

    (A) $14 + \pi$
    (B) $20 + 3\pi$
    (C) $40 - \pi$
    (D) $48 - 6\pi$
    (E) $48 - 9\pi$

13. In the figure above, three squares have sides of length 6, 10, and 15. What is the total area of the shaded regions?

    (A) 289
    (B) 225
    (C) 189
    (D) 161
    (E) 89

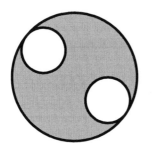

Note: Figure not drawn to scale.

11. In the figure above, the smaller circles both have a radius of 3 and are tangent to the larger circle. If the larger circle has a radius of 7, what is the area of the shaded region?

    (A) 18π
    (B) 31π
    (C) 40π
    (D) 49π
    (E) 64π

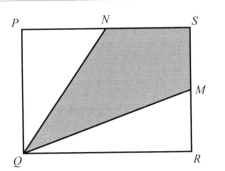

16. In the figure above, *PQRS* is a rectangle, *M* is the midpoint of $\overline{SR}$, and *N* is the midpoint of $\overline{PS}$. If $NS + SM = 12$ and $QR = 14$, what is the area of the shaded region?

(A) 35
(B) 45
(C) 70
(D) 85
(E) 115

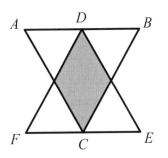

20. In the figure above, $\triangle ABC$ and $\triangle DEF$ are both equilateral triangles with perimeters of 24, and $\overline{AB} \parallel \overline{EF}$. If $\overline{DC}$ (not shown) bisects both $\overline{AB}$ and $\overline{EF}$, what is the area of the shaded region?

(A) $32\sqrt{3} - 4$
(B) $28\sqrt{3}$
(C) $16\sqrt{3}$
(D) $8\sqrt{3}$
(E) $4\sqrt{3}$

Answers:

10. **(E)**
11. **(B)**
13. **(D)**
16. **(C)**
20. **(D)**

Solutions on page 321.

The following selected Blue Book questions are examples of this stuff in the wild.

Test	§	p	#	Diff.
3	2	518	17	4
7	3	773	16	H
8	3	835	16	M
11	8	34	9	3

There are a few more shaded regions in the Blue Book than I list here, but most of those questions either don't ask for the area of the shaded region (they ask for the perimeter or something else instead) or they're circle questions and the methods in that chapter (page 182) obviate the need for the technique in this chapter. Still, I wouldn't have gone to the trouble to write this chapter—drawing these diagrams took forever—if I didn't think your SAT prep would be incomplete without a treatment of shaded region area problems. As is the case with all of the tips in this book, practice will help you to identify appropriate times to to apply this technique.

Working in three dimensions

It's not uncommon for a question or two involving three-dimensional shapes to appear on the SAT. Luckily, most of the time these questions either deal directly with the simple properties of three-dimensional shapes (like surface area and volume), or are just 2-D questions in disguise. It's pretty rare to come across a truly difficult 3-D question, but of course I'll provide some here.

Volume

Generally speaking, the SAT will give you every volume formula that you need, either in the beginning of the section (rectangular solid: $V = lwh$; right circular cylinder: $V = \pi r^2 h$) or in the question itself in the (exceedingly) rare case where you'll have to deal with the volume of a different kind of solid. It's worth mentioning, though, that the volume of *any* right prism[*] can be calculated by finding the area of its base, and multiplying that by its height.

For example, if you needed to calculate the volume of a prism with an equilateral triangle base, you'd find the area of an equilateral triangle:

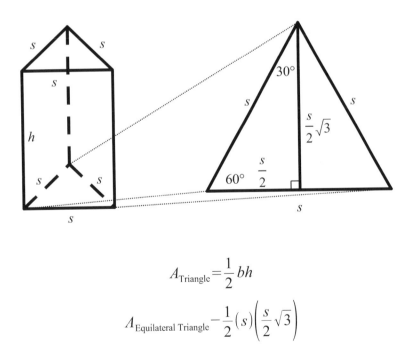

$$A_{\text{Triangle}} = \frac{1}{2}\,bh$$

$$A_{\text{Equilateral Triangle}} = \frac{1}{2}(s)\left(\frac{s}{2}\sqrt{3}\right)$$

---

[*]   Right circular cylinders and rectangular solids are both special cases of right prisms: a right prism is any prism whose top lines up directly above its bottom.

$$A_{\text{Equilateral Triangle}} = \frac{s^2 \sqrt{3}}{4}$$

And multiply that by the height of the prism:

$$V_{\text{Equilateral Triangular Right Prism}} = \frac{s^2 \sqrt{3}}{4} h$$

You almost definitely won't need this particular formula on the SAT, but it's nice to know how to find the volume of a right prism in general: just find the area of the base, and multiply it by the height.

$$\boxed{V_{\text{Right Prism}} = A_{\text{base}} \times \text{height}}$$

The SAT will often require you to maneuver between the volume of a solid and its dimensions. Let's try one.

Example 1

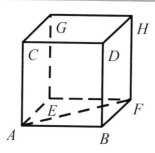

16. If the volume of the cube in the figure above is 27, what is the length of $\overline{AF}$?

(A) 3
(B) $3\sqrt{2}$
(C) $3\sqrt{3}$
(D) $3\sqrt{5}$
(E) 6

Remember that a cube is the special case of rectangular solid where all the edges are equal, so the volume of a cube is the length of one edge CUBED:

$$V = 27 = s^3$$
$$s = 3$$

So far, so good, right? Now it's time to do the thing that you're going to find yourself doing for almost every single 3-D question you come across: work with one piece of the 3-D figure in 2-D.

The segment we're interested in is the diagonal of the square base of the cube. If we look at it in 2 dimensions, it looks like this:

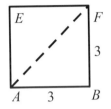

The diagonal of a square is the hypotenuse of an isosceles right triangle, so we can actually skip the Pythagorean Theorem here since we're so attuned to special right triangles. $\overline{AF} = 3\sqrt{2}$. That's choice (B).

Note that after the fairly trivial step of figuring out the dimensions of the solid from its volume, this was basically a right triangle question. Most difficult 3-D questions, it turns out, end up being right triangle questions. More on this in a bit.

Surface area

The surface area of a solid is simply the sum of the areas of each of its faces. Easy surface area problems are really easy. Trickier surface area problems will often also involve volume. Have a go at this one:

Example 2

18. The volume of a certain cube is v cubic inches, and its surface area is a square inches. If $v = 8p^3$, which of the following is NOT a value of p for which $a > v$?

(A) 0.5
(B) 1
(C) 2
(D) 2.25
(E) 4

Yuuuuck. What to do? Well, to find the surface area of a cube, you need to know the areas of its faces. To find those areas, you need to know the lengths of the cube's edges. Luckily for us, it's pretty easy to find the lengths of the edges of this cube, since we know that the volume is $8p^3$. Let's call the length of one edge of the cube s. We know that $v = s^3$, so we can find s in terms of p:

$$v = s^3 = 8p^3$$
$$s = \sqrt[3]{8p^3}$$
$$s = 2p$$

If an edge of the cube is $2p$, then the area of one face of the cube is $(2p)^2$, or $4p^2$. There are 6 faces on a cube, so the surface area of the cube is found thusly:

$$a = 6 \times 4p^2$$
$$a = 24p^2$$

From here, it's trivial to either backsolve—try that on your own for practice—or solve the inequality spelled out in the question:

$$a > v$$
$$24p^2 > 8p^3$$
$$3p^2 > p^3$$
$$3 > p$$

The answer must be (E), the one choice for which the inequality is *not* true.

A little more about right triangles

Since almost every solid you're going to be dealing with on the SAT is a right prism, *almost every solid you're going to be dealing with is going to contain right angles, and thus, right triangles.* The most difficult 3-D questions might require you to use the Pythagorean Theorem twice: once in the plane of one of the sides of the solid (usually the base), and once cutting through the solid. This will feel atrociously complicated the first few times you do it, but if you practice this enough for it to become second nature to you, you'll be unstoppable on tough 3-D problems.

Example 3

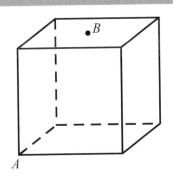

19. Point B is the center of the top face of a cube, and A is at one of the cube's vertices, as shown in the figure above. If each edge of the cube has a length of 3, what is the distance between A and B?

(A) $\dfrac{3\sqrt{3}}{2}$

(B) $\dfrac{3\sqrt{6}}{2}$

(C) $\dfrac{3\sqrt{2}}{5}$

(D) $3\sqrt{3}$

(E) $3\sqrt{2}$

Yikes. In order to find the distance between A and B, we're going to have to work with the right triangle formed by the dotted lines and the edge of the cube in the drawing on the right. And in order to do *that*, we're going to have to deal first with just one face of the cube. Let's look at the top face by itself.

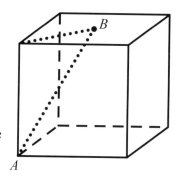

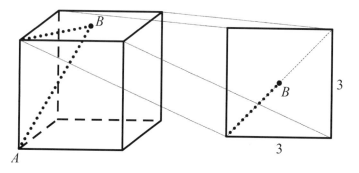

Of course, any face of a cube is a square. Note that *B* lies at the midpoint of the square's diagonal. If the sides of the square have a length of 3, then the diagonal must be $3\sqrt{2}$. So the distance from the corner to *B* must be half that: $\frac{3\sqrt{2}}{2}$.

Now let's have a look at our triangle, drawn in its own plane for clarity's sake. We can find the distance between A and B using the Pythagorean Theorem:

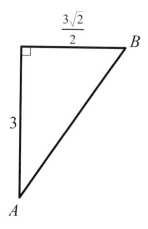

$$3^2 + \left(\frac{3\sqrt{2}}{2}\right)^2 = AB^2$$

$$9 + \frac{18}{4} = AB^2$$

$$\frac{27}{2} = AB^2$$

$$\sqrt{\frac{27}{2}} = AB$$

$$\frac{3\sqrt{3}}{\sqrt{2}} = AB$$

Since that's not an answer choice, rationalize by multiplying top and bottom by $\sqrt{2}$:

$$\frac{3\sqrt{3}}{\sqrt{2}} \times \frac{\sqrt{2}}{\sqrt{2}} = AB$$

$$\frac{3\sqrt{6}}{2} = AB$$

Bam! We've arrived at choice (B).

Once you get accustomed to their patterns, you'll be able to rip through these double-Pythagorean 3-D questions with ninja-efficiency. Your friends are going to flip out so hard!

Let's try one more together before I set you loose on a drill.

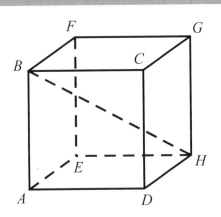

17. In the figure above, $\overline{BH}$ connects vertices of a cube with edges of length 8. What is the length of $\overline{BH}$?

(A) $8\sqrt{2}$
(B) $8\sqrt{3}$
(C) $8\sqrt{5}$
(D) $8\sqrt{7}$
(E) $8\sqrt{11}$

Before we get into the solution, a bit of terminology that I might as well mention: $\overline{BH}$ is what's called the *long diagonal* of the cube. Other long diagonals in this cube (not shown) are $\overline{DF}$ and $\overline{AG}$. The reason we have the term long diagonal is to contrast it with the *short diagonal*, or side diagonal, like $\overline{AH}$, which runs along a face of the cube, instead of cutting through it.

Anyway, just like we did before, we're going to solve this with right triangles. $\overline{BH}$ is the hypotenuse of right triangle ABH. We know $AB = 8$, so we just need to find AH, and then Pythagorize.

If you've been paying attention to this chapter so far, finding AH should be no problem. If you haven't been paying attention, turn down the Skrillex or whatever and note that short diagonal $\overline{AH}$ is the diagonal of square $AEHD$. The diagonal of a square always cuts the square into two 45°-45°-90° triangles, so it will always be the length of the square's sides times $\sqrt{2}$. The sides of $AEHD$ have a length of 8, so $AH = 8\sqrt{2}$.

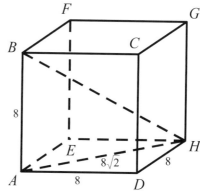

Now drop your values into the Pythagorean theorem to solve for BH:

$$AB^2 + AH^2 = BH^2$$
$$8^2 + (8\sqrt{2})^2 = BH^2$$
$$64 + 128 = BH^2$$
$$192 = BH^2$$
$$\sqrt{192} = BH$$
$$8\sqrt{3} = BH$$

So there you go—the answer is (B).

Major shortcut

It turns out that the long diagonal of a cube with edges of length s will always have a length of $s\sqrt{3}$. *This only applies to long diagonals of cubes!* If you're not dealing with that very special case, you have to solve the "long way," with right triangles, like we did above.

---

13. What is the surface area of a cube with a volume of 27?

    (A) 54
    (B) 36
    (C) 27
    (D) 18
    (E) 9

18. Xorgar H'ghargh is building a pyramid to honor himself on the planet Geometrox. If the pyramid has a square base with edges 50 meters long, and its other four sides are equilateral triangles, how tall will the pyramid be, in meters?

    (A) $50\sqrt{5}$
    (B) $50\sqrt{3}$
    (C) $50\sqrt{2}$
    (D) $25\sqrt{3}$
    (E) $25\sqrt{2}$

17. John is a weird kid who likes math and plays with bugs. He is holding a cylindrical cardboard tube in his hand, and two ants are crawling around on it. If the cylinder is 12 inches long and has a radius of 2.5 inches, what is the farthest the two ants could possibly be from each other and still both be on the tube?

    (A) 12 inches
    (B) 12.25 inches
    (C) 13 inches
    (D) 14.5 inches
    (E) $12\sqrt{2}$ inches

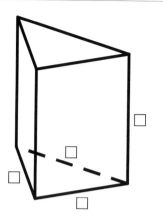

19. In the figure above, each empty box (□) is to be filled by the value of the length of one edge of the right triangular prism. If four unique constants, *a*, *b*, *c*, and *d*, are needed to fill the squares, and if the surface area of the prism equals *ab* + *ad* + *bd* + *cd*, then which constant represents the length of the longest edge of the prism's base?

(A) *a*
(B) *b*
(C) *c*
(D) *d*
(E) It cannot be determined from the information given.

20. What is the volume of the largest cube that can be contained by a sphere of radius 4?

(A) 16

(B) $64\sqrt{3}$

(C) $\dfrac{64}{3}$

(D) $512\sqrt{2}$

(E) $\dfrac{512\sqrt{3}}{9}$

Answers:

13. **(A)**

17. **(C)**

18. **(E)**

19. **(C)**

20. **(E)**

Solutions on page 323.

The following selected Blue Book questions are examples of this stuff in the wild.

Test	§	p	#	Diff.
1	3	401	19	5
1	8	423	11	3
2	2	457	18	4
3	8	548	16	5
5	8	669	10	M
6	2	702	12	M
7	9	800	15	H
8	7	851	15	M
9	5	904	5	E
9	8	919	15	M
10	8	979	10	M

3-D questions are fairly rare—difficult ones doubly so—so you shouldn't be pulling your hair out trying to perfect your 3-D techniques until you've got the more common concepts down pat.

Data analysis, statistics, and probability

I'm not going to sugar-coat this: these questions can be a total bear. Not all of them, mind you. Some will be easy. Many others will follow very predictable patterns and you'll pump your non-writing fist in the air as you bubble in your correct answer because all your hard work paid off. But a few of these will be the kinds of questions that wake you up in the middle of the night, cold sweat soaking your sheets, the horrible voices of the probability demons from your nightmares still echoing in your newly awakened head. Only a few, though. Only a very few. Shhh...go back to sleep now, little lamb. In the morning, there will be PWNing to do.

Average, median, and mode

Average (arithmetic mean),[*] median, and mode are useful properties of a set of numbers and can give statisticians great at-a-glance insights into copious data. When the SAT gets its hands on them, though, they are usually stripped of any analytical utility and instead used as a framework in which to ask tricky reasoning questions. So I'll leave it to your college stats class to elucidate the myriad ways average, median, and mode are useful in real life, and just show you what you need to know to PWN them when they appear on the SAT (fairly often for average, less so for median and pretty rarely for mode).

Average, weighted average, and average speed

As is true of many of the concepts in this book, the SAT can and will ask you about averages in a number of different ways. Some questions will be pretty straightforward and require only some simple algebra—or maybe a fancy technique—to solve. We'll have a look at one of those to warm up.

Example 1

11. If the average (arithmetic mean) of four consecutive even integers is 25, what is the greatest of those integers?

(A) 24
(B) 25
(C) 26
(D) 28
(E) 30

---

[*]   On the SAT, you'll always see it written thusly: "...the average (arithmetic mean) of..." *unless* you're dealing with average speed. More on that shortly.

First of all, I hope you're noticing right away that this can be backsolved. Start with (C). If the largest of the consecutive even integers was 26, then our numbers would be 20, 22, 24, and 26. To find the average of those four numbers, add them up and divide by 4. You know this.

$$\frac{20+22+24+26}{4}=\frac{92}{4}=23$$

Oops, too small! Try (D) instead. If your largest even integer is 28, then your four consecutive even integers would be 22, 24, 26, and 28. Get their average:

$$\frac{22+24+26+28}{4}=\frac{100}{4}=25$$

Bingo. (D)'s the answer.

But, of course, backsolving isn't the only way to skin this cat. You can also just do a little algebra. Say the largest of your consecutive even integers is x. Then the others would be $x-2$, $x-4$, and $x-6$. Set up an equation that says their average is 25, and solve for x:

$$\frac{(x-6)+(x-4)+(x-2)+(x)}{4}=25$$

$$(x-6)+(x-4)+(x-2)+(x)=100$$

$$4x-12=100$$

$$4x=112$$

$$x=28$$

Boom. Answer's still (D). Easy, right? *So* easy.

But average questions won't always be that easy, so now I'd like to address a particular kind of question about weighted averages that I see on the test all the time and that you need to know how to deal with.

Weighted averages can be pretty confusing without a nice, easy way to organize your information. Enter **The Average Table**. KNEEL WHEN IT ENTERS THE ROOM, KNAVE! Seriously, this thing rocks.

This nifty little table is derived from the way averages are generally calculated:

$$\text{Average of Values} = \frac{\text{Sum of Values}}{\text{Number of Values}}$$

Now watch what happens when we multiply both sides of that equation by the Number of Values:

$$\boxed{\text{Number of Values} \times \text{Average of Values} = \text{Sum of Values}}$$

A table with these elements as headings will help you solve even the hairiest weighted average questions. I'll illustrate with a particularly gnarly example.

Example 2

19. A delivery truck is loaded with seven packages weighing an average (arithmetic mean) of 30 pounds. At his first stop, the delivery man drops off three packages weighing a total of 60 pounds. He also picks up one package weighing 15 pounds. He makes one more stop to deliver two more packages, which weigh 42 and 48 pounds. What is the average weight, in pounds, of the packages that remain on the truck?

(A) 15
(B) 17
(C) 19
(D) 25
(E) 30

Yikes, right? There's a lot of information in there, which is why it's going to be so nice to be able to organize it all neatly. Here's what the average table looks like with this question's information:

Num of Values	× Avg of Values	= Sum of Values
7 packages	30 pounds	
−3 packages		−60 pounds
+1 package		+15 pounds
−2 packages		−90 pounds

See where everything comes from? When we have an average (30 pounds for the initial 7 packages) we put it in the average column. When we have a sum, we put it in the sum column. We keep track of whether the packages are being delivered or picked up with + and − signs. Now let's fill in the rest of the table just to see how everything works together (calculated values are in bold type...make sure you understand where they come from):

Num of Values	× Avg of Values	= Sum of Values
7 packages	30 pounds	**210 pounds**
−3 packages	**20 pounds**	−60 pounds
+1 package	**15 pounds**	+15 pounds
−2 packages	**45 pounds**	−90 pounds

So we know the driver started with a total weight in the truck of 210 pounds. He dropped off 3 packages weighing 60 pounds, picked up 1 package weighing 15 pounds, and dropped off 2 more weighing 90 pounds. Using the table, we can easily see that the number of packages left on the truck is $7 - 3 + 1 - 2 = 3$. We can also calculate the total weight left on the truck: $210 - 60 + 15 - 90 = 75$.

Num of Values	× Avg of Values	= Sum of Values
7 packages	30 pounds	210 pounds
−3 packages	20 pounds	−60 pounds
+1 package	15 pounds	+15 pounds
−2 packages	45 pounds	−90 pounds
= 3 packages	_**25 pounds**_	**= 75 pounds**

If there are 3 packages left on the truck, and they weigh a total of 75 pounds, it's trivial to calculate the average: $75 \div 3 = 25$. That's choice (D)!

Before we move on, let me just say a few more things about the average table I love so much.

→ You can only add or subtract up and down the *outer* columns. Try adding and subtracting averages and you'll get all screwed up. The middle column can only be used for 1) calculating the sum of the values by multiplying the number of them by their average, or 2) calculating the average by dividing the sum by the number of values.

→ This table works with questions that have variables instead of numbers, although you might decide to plug in real numbers to make your life easier.

There's one more kind of average question that, although pretty rare, you might see: **average speed** questions. On an average speed question you won't see the word average followed by the parenthetical "(arithmetic mean)" because average speed is not an arithmetic mean! To find average speed, all you need is the total distance traveled, and the total time it took to travel it:

$$\text{Average Speed} = \frac{\text{Total Distance Traveled}}{\text{Total Travel Time}}$$

I see students struggle mightily with average speed questions, but if you remember that all you want are those two things, you'll do just fine. Let's do one.

Example 3 (Grid-in)

15. If Josiah drove 10 miles at a speed of 20 miles per hour, then drove 30 miles at a speed of 30 miles per hour, what was his average speed, in miles per hour, for the entire trip?

Remember, to find average speed you just need two values: total distance traveled, and total travel time. Total distance traveled is $10 + 30 = 40$ miles. How long did it take him to go 40 miles? Well, to go 10 miles at 20 mph takes 0.5 hours, and to go 30 miles at 30 mph takes 1 hour. So his total time is 1.5 hours.

$$\text{Average Speed} = \frac{40 \text{ miles}}{1.5 \text{ hours}} = \frac{80}{3}, \text{ or} \approx 26.7 \text{ miles per hour}$$

Median

The median is the middle value in an ordered list of numbers. If the list of numbers you're given isn't in numerical order, it still has a median, but to find it you're going to have to put it in numerical order first. If the set contains an even number of values, the median is the average of the two middle values. That's it. That's all you need to know about the median. Find the median of each of the following sets. (Answers below.)

✎ {4, 6, 7, 9, 12, 16, 30}

✎ {9, 30, 16, 4, 7, 6, 12}

✎ {2, 200, 300, 700}

✎ {17, 22, 6, 99, 68, 52, 29, 86}

If you've got all those, I guess it's time we tried an SAT-inspired question.

Answers: ● 9 ● 9 (changing the order does not change the median)
● 250 (the avg of 200 and 300) ● 40.5 (the avg of 29 and 52)

Example 4

16. Which of the following CANNOT change the value of the median of a set of five numbers?

(A) Adding the number 0 to the set
(B) Multiplying each value by −1
(C) Increasing the least value only
(D) Increasing the greatest value only
(E) Squaring each value

This isn't the hardest question in the world, and if you've seen a similar one before you probably know the answer instantly. If you haven't, well, now you have, and you'll nail a similar one if you see it on the SAT. You're welcome.

Let's plug in a set to make this easier to comprehend. Say our set is {2, 3, 4, 5, 6}. The original value of the median is 4.

(A) If we add 0 to the set, the median becomes the average of 3 and 4, or 3.5. That's no good.

(B) If we multiply each value by −1, the median becomes −4. That's not the same as 4.

(C) If we increase the least value by enough, then we change the median. What if we increase the least value by 8? That 2 becomes a 10. The median becomes 5 instead of 4.[*]

(D) **Increase the greatest value as much as you like, you won't change the order of the values at all. If we change 6 to 600 or 6,000,000, the median is still 4.**

(E) Obviously, squaring each value changes each value, and thus changes the median value. (It would change from 4 to 16.)

Not so bad, right?

---

[*] Note that since the question says "CANNOT," it doesn't matter that the median wouldn't change if we only increased the least value by 1. If we can come up with a way to change the median by increasing the least value, we can cross off the choice.

Mode

The mode of a list of numbers is the number that appears most in that list. Be aware that it's possible for a list to have multiple modes, but all modes will appear the same number of times, and no other number will appear more often. For example: 5 and 6 are modes in {4, 4, 5, 5, 5, 6, 6, 6, 7, 8}. 4 is not a mode, even though it appears more often than 7 and 8.

Find the mode(s) for each of the following sets. (Answers below.)

✎ {2, 4, 2, 7, 9, 3, 2}

2 - X3

✎ {2, 4, 2, 7, 9, 7, 3, 2, 7}

2 - X3
7 - X3

✎ {1, 1, 200, 300, 400}

1 - x2

✎ {p, q, r, s, t, t, s, t}

t - X3
s - x2

Again, if you're good on those, let's try some SAT-type stuff (which you will probably *not* encounter on test day—mode questions are rare).

Example 5 (Grid-in)

$$\{2, 3, 9, 4, 11, 4m - 8, 3n - 4\}$$

15. The modes of the set above are 2 and 11. If m and n are constants, what is one possible value of $m + n$?

Answers: ● 2 ● 2 *and* 7 (both appear 3 times) ● 1 ● *t*

OK. In order for 2 and 11 to be the modes of the set above, each need to appear an equal number of times, and more often than any other value in the list. Which means one of two things must be true:

$$4m - 8 = 2 \text{ and } 3n - 4 = 11$$
$$\text{—or—}$$
$$4m - 8 = 11 \text{ and } 3n - 4 = 2$$

Let's deal with the first possibility:

$$4m - 8 = 2$$
$$4m = 10$$
$$m = 2.5$$

$$3n - 4 = 11$$
$$3n = 15$$
$$n = 5$$

So one possibility is that $m = 2.5$ and $n = 5$.

$$m + n = 2.5 + 5 = 7.5.$$

I'll spare you the algebra for the second possibility; I'm sure you can handle it on your own. The other acceptable solution is 6.75.

Practice questions: Average, median, and mode

Prove that you are above average.

Note: #12 in the following problem set is a grid-in. Also, it's possible that the SAT will throw median, mode, and average at you all at once. Whatcha gonna do when that happens (like in #20)?

10. The mode of a set of 4 positive integers is 3. What is the least possible value of the sum of these 4 integers?

    (A) 6
    (B) 8
    (C) 9
    (D) 10
    (E) 12

12. The median of a set of 7 consecutive integers is −1. What is the greatest of these 7 integers?

15. The average (arithmetic mean) test score in a class of 12 students was 74. If 4 students who averaged 96 were removed from the class, what would be the new average score of the class?

    (A) 70
    (B) 63
    (C) 58
    (D) 44
    (E) 39

17. The average (arithmetic mean) of 5 numbers is f. The sum of 3 of those numbers is g. What is the average of the remaining numbers?

    (A) $\dfrac{5f-3g}{3}$

    (B) $\dfrac{5f-g}{3}$

    (C) $\dfrac{5f-3g}{2}$

    (D) $\dfrac{f-3}{g}$

    (E) $\dfrac{5f-g}{2}$

18. For the first m days of the month of July, the average (arithmetic mean) of the daily peak temperatures in Culver City was 87° Fahrenheit. If the peak temperature the next day was 93° and the average daily peak temperature for July rose to 89°, what is m?

   (A) 9
   (B) 7
   (C) 6
   (D) 4
   (E) 2

20. The median of a set of 9 real numbers is 17. The mode of the set is 13. The greatest number in the set is 29, and the least is 8. Which of the following could be the average (arithmetic mean) of the set?

   I. 15
   II. 17
   III. 19

   (A) I only
   (B) II only
   (C) III only
   (D) II and III only
   (E) I, II, and III

Answers:

10. **(C)**
12. **2**
15. **(B)**
17. **(E)**
18. **(E)**
20. **(D)**

Solutions on page 325.

The following selected Blue Book questions are examples of this stuff in the wild.

Test	§	p	#	Diff.
1	3	397	3	1
1	8	421	7	3
1	8	423	13	3
2	2	455	12	3
2	5	464	3	2
2	5	467	13	3
3	2	517	11	3
3	5	525	1	1
4	3	584	13	M
4	6	596	10	E
5	2	642	18	H
5	4	654	12	M
6	2	701	5	E
6	2	703	14	M
6	4	713	3	E
6	8	732	11	M
7	3	770	8	H
7	7	786	6	E
8	3	835	18	H
8	7	852	19	H
9	2	888	6	M
9	2	891	16	M
9	5	905	7	M
10	2	953	18	H
10	5	967	7	M
11	3	13	17	4
11	4	18	15	4
11	4	19	19	5

Probability

Probability problems are some of the SAT's most difficult, but they're also some of the most rare. There's a pretty decent chance you won't see a very hard probability question on your test, so prioritize your prep time; don't worry too much about this stuff until you've really nailed the basics. Ironically, this is one of the most involved chapters in this book, but it corresponds to one of the smallest point potentials.

The basics

The probability of an event is equal to the number of ways that event can occur divided by the total number of possible outcomes.[*]

$$\text{Probability}_{\text{Event}} = \frac{\text{Number of ways event can occur}}{\text{Total number of possible outcomes}}$$

So the probability that you will be chosen at random to represent your 30-person class in the hot dog eating contest is $\frac{1}{30}$. Likewise, the probability that your frenemy Ashley will be chosen for the contest is $\frac{1}{30}$.

What if I asked you about the probability that EITHER you OR Ashley would be chosen? Well, now the event we're concerned with happens in 2 of the 30 possible outcomes. It would be satisfied if you were picked, or if Ashley was. Therefore, the probability is $\frac{2}{30}$, which simplifies to $\frac{1}{15}$. **When there are multiple, mutually exclusive ways an event can occur, *ADD* the probabilities of each way to get your overall probability.** Again, this only works if you're talking about events that are *mutually exclusive*. In other words, it only works if both events can't happen at the same time. For example: if you buy lottery tickets, since each ticket you buy has a different number on it, each ticket adds to your probability of holding the winning number.

---

[*] If you're thinking that counting (page 77) might be involved in tough probability calculations, you win the prize! If you're thinking that I'm probably going to tell you just to list things instead of using formalized counting techniques, you win the better prize! Congratulations!

This is important, so make sure you're solid. Work through the following examples to ensure this won't leak out of your brain. (Answers are at the bottom of the page).

✎ What's the probability of rolling an even number on a standard 6-sided die?

✎ What's the probability of rolling a number less than 6 on a standard 6-sided die?

✎ What's the probability of rolling a prime number on a standard 6-sided die?

✎ What's the probability of flipping a coin and getting either heads or tails?

I should note right now that on the SAT, you won't find questions about dice or playing cards. Those are gamblin' tools and the SAT won't condone such behavior. I think they can be a nice way to think about probability, so I'm using them, but if you want to be faithful to the SAT you should think *cubes with numbers 1 through 6 painted on the sides* whenever I write about dice.

Back to the example about you and Ashley. What if, after the hot dog eating contest, there was also vomit cleaning contest, and someone from your class was going to be chosen at random to participate in that one, too. What is the probability that you'll end up in the hot dog eating contest AND that Ashley will end up in the vomit cleaning contest? **When looking for the probability of multiple events occurring together, you *MULTIPLY* their probabilities.** You have a $\frac{1}{30}$ chance of being chosen for the hot dog eating contest, and Ashley has a $\frac{1}{30}$ chance of being chosen for the vomit cleaning contest. The probability that you will be chosen to eat AND she will be chosen to clean is $\frac{1}{30} \times \frac{1}{30} = \frac{1}{900}$. Wow, that's small!

This rule only holds if the events are *independent*; whether one occurs has no effect on whether the other occurs. When an event's occurrence *does* have an effect on the probability of another event's occurrence—we say the events are *dependent*—the rules change a little bit.

Say there was a rule that the winner of the hot dog eating contest was ineligible to be chosen for the vomit cleaning contest. In that case, the probability of Ashley being chosen for the second contest (given that you were chosen for the first contest and thus ineligible) becomes $\frac{1}{29}$ (we don't count you as a possible outcome anymore). So if the hot dog contest winner couldn't be chosen for the vomit contest, the probability that you'd be chosen for the first and Ashley would be chosen for the second would get *very slightly* higher: $\frac{1}{30} \times \frac{1}{29} = \frac{1}{870}$.

We still good? Make sure by trying the following examples (as usual, answers below):

✎ What is the probability of flipping 4 coins and having them all come up heads?

✎ What's the probability of flipping two coins and having one or the other (but not both) come up heads?

✎ John and Sam are both choosing randomly from 5 types of candy: types *A*, *B*, *C*, *D*, and *E*. What is the probability of them both choosing candy type *A*?

✎ To pick teams for a game, 8 names are put into a hat and then removed one at a time. What is the probability that Sven is picked first and then Gretchen is picked second?

Answers: ● 1/16 ● 1/2 ● 1/25 ● 1/56

> ## To summarize:
>
> **Probability of X _or_ Y = (Probability of X) + (Probability of Y)**
> (as long as X and Y are mutually exclusive)
>
> **Probability of X _and_ Y = (Probability of X) × (Probability of Y)**
> (unless X and Y are mutually exclusive—in that case Probability of X _and_ Y = 0)

The big reveal

It's nice to know all that stuff above, *but you don't always need it!* Most of the time, it's sufficient just to list all the possible outcomes, and count the ones that match your conditions, especially on the hardest questions! Seriously, the SAT almost always plays with small numbers (remember: *calculator optional*), so it's never too onerous just to put pencil to paper and *start listing*.

Example 1

17. What is the probability of flipping 3 coins and having 2 of them come up heads and 1 come up tails?

(A) $\frac{1}{8}$

(B) $\frac{1}{3}$

(C) $\frac{3}{8}$

(D) $\frac{5}{8}$

(E) $\frac{7}{9}$

Your math teacher would first use counting to figure out the number of possibilities. Then he'd think really hard about how many ways the desired outcome could occur. In other words, he'd say: "There are $2 \times 2 \times 2 = 8$ total possible outcomes, and there are three ways we could get the results we want: HHT, HTH, or THH. So the answer is (C), $\frac{3}{8}$."

But whenever possible, I don't do questions like these the way a math teacher would. It's too easy to make a mistake that way. Note that some thought is required to come up with the possible outcomes that satisfy the condition. In the time it takes to think about possible HHT combinations (are there *really* only three?), you have time to just list the 8 possible outcomes, and *count* the successful outcomes with your eyeballs and fingers.

<u>Possible results of flipping 3 coins (satisfactory outcomes in **bold**)</u>

HHH	**THH**
HHT	THT
HTH	TTH
HTT	TTT

The simpler you keep a probability question, the less likely you are to make a mistake.

Example 2

18. Phil is holding 4 cards in his hand: 8 of clubs, 5 of hearts, king of hearts, and ace of diamonds. If he places them on a table in random order, what is the probability that the first and last cards will both be hearts?

(A) $\frac{1}{2}$

(B) $\frac{1}{3}$

(C) $\frac{1}{4}$

(D) $\frac{1}{6}$

(E) $\frac{1}{8}$

I'll give you the "mathy" solution in a little bit, but you don't get any bragging rights if you solve it that way. When I take tests myself, and I get my perfect scores, I solve questions like this by listing possibilities. It's just easier for me! So here's the listing solution:

Step 1: Assign numbers to the cards (give 1 and 4 to the hearts for simplicity's sake).

> 1 – 5 of hearts
> 2 – 8 of clubs
> 3 – Ace of diamonds
> 4 – King of hearts

Step 2: List all the possibilities that start with "1" (ones with hearts on the ends bolded).

> **1234**
> 1243
> **1324**
> 1342
> 1423
> 1432

Step 3: Either list all the possibilities that start with "2," or recognize that all the possibilities that begin with "2" or "3" cannot possibly satisfy our condition of having hearts on both ends because "2" and "3" are not hearts, and skip right to listing all the possibilities that begin with 4 (again, bolding the ones with hearts on the ends).

> 4123
> 4132
> 4213
> **4231**
> 4312
> **4321**

Step 4: Count the successful outcomes (there are 4 of them), and count the total possible outcomes (we didn't list the ones that began with 2 or 3, but there are 6 each of them, just like there are 6 that begin with 1 and 6 that begin with 4. Total: 24 possible outcomes.

Answer: The probability of getting hearts at the beginning and end is $\frac{4}{24}$, or $\frac{1}{6}$. That's choice (D). Full possibilities list:

1234	2134	3124	4123
1243	2143	3142	4132
1324	2314	3214	4213
1342	2341	3241	**4231**
1423	2413	3412	4312
1432	2431	3421	**4321**

Take a minute to note the order in which I made my lists. If you practice listing things in order from smallest to greatest, you can get *very* fast at it, which makes a question like this a piece of cake. Start by "anchoring" the first 2 digits, and listing all the possible combinations of the last 2. Then anchor another set of 2 digits at the beginning, and repeat. In other words, list all the outcomes that start with "12" then all the ones that start with "13," then all the ones that begin with "14." Only move on to outcomes that begin with "2" once you've exhausted all the ones that begin with "1."

Yes, this is *really* the way I do these questions when I take the test. I get 2400s. I respect it if you want to solve them the math way every time, but I caution you that such a dogmatic adherence to math on a test that is *not a math test* increases your likelihood of making a mistake under pressure. I see that happen to really smart kids all the time.

So what is the "mathy" solution? I'll actually give you two. First, one that involves counting like we discussed in the chapter on counting and listing way back on page 77. First, lay out four hangman blanks for the four positions:

$$- \quad - \quad - \quad -$$

On the top of those blanks, we're going to count the number of ways we could have hearts on both ends of the row. Underneath those blanks, we're going to calculate the total number of possible arrangements of the four cards. Bottom first, since that's the easy one. If we don't care about any special placements, we'll have 4 choices for the first position, 3 choices for the second position, 2 choices for the third position, and 1 choice for the fourth position:

$$\overline{4} \quad \overline{3} \quad \overline{2} \quad \overline{1}$$

Now let's count the ways we could have a heart on either end. We have two hearts, so for the first position we only have 2 choices. Once we've placed a heart there, we only have one other heart, so we have 1 choice for the fourth position:

$$\overline{\dfrac{2}{4}} \quad \overline{3} \quad \overline{2} \quad \overline{\dfrac{1}{1}}$$

Now that we've taken care of our restricted positions, we have two cards left to place, and it doesn't matter where they go. So we have 2 choices for the second position, and 1 choice for the third:

$$\overline{\dfrac{2}{4}} \quad \overline{\dfrac{2}{3}} \quad \overline{\dfrac{1}{2}} \quad \overline{\dfrac{1}{1}}$$

To calculate the probability, just make the product of the top row your numerator, and make the product of the bottom row your denominator.

$$\frac{2\times2\times1\times1}{4\times3\times2\times1}=\frac{4}{24}=\frac{1}{6}$$

So there's the counting solution. Here's one more you might like. If we have two hearts, and we're looking for the probability they they'll occupy two specific spots, we can treat this as a pure probability question. If we were placing the cards randomly, there would be a $\frac{2}{4}$ (or $\frac{1}{2}$, obviously) probability that a heart would go in the first spot. If that were to happen, then there would only be one heart left out of three cards that might possibly take the fourth spot—a $\frac{1}{3}$ probability of that happening. Since we want both things to happen, we multiply those probabilities:

$$\frac{1}{2}\times\frac{1}{3}=\frac{1}{6}$$

The math solutions are fun and interesting, but I just want to stress once more than I really, honestly do solve problems like this by listing, and I get 800s. You don't have to do everything my way, which is why I provide these alternative solutions, but if you run across a question like this on test day and a math "shortcut" isn't obvious to you, *start listing*. Actually, let me take this exhortation one step further: *if you solve a question like this on test day with a method other than listing, and you have any time at all to check your work, check it by listing.*

Geometric probability

Once in a while (like in a few seconds when you do the following example) you might see a question about the probability of a point falling inside a particular section of a geometric shape. The probability of a point randomly falling into a certain area is simply that area divided by the whole area of the shape.

Example 3 (Grid-in)

13. James is throwing darts, blindfolded, at a circular dartboard that is divided evenly into 20 sections that are numbered 1 through 20. Assuming he cannot aim at a particular section, but does not miss the board completely, what is the probability that James hits section number 12 on his next throw?

You might, for a split second, think you don't have enough information here since you can't calculate the area of the dartboard. But look at the number, and remember that this question isn't supposed to be very hard. If the board is divided evenly into 20 sections, then he has a $\frac{1}{20}$ chance of hitting any particular section of the board. So you would grid in "1/20" (or ".05") to collect your free points.

12. Beatrice bought a bag of janky discount candy that contains Snackers and Milky Daze bars in a ratio of 3:2. If she picks a candy bar at random from the bag, what is the probability that she picks a Milky Daze bar?

(A) $\frac{2}{3}$

(B) $\frac{3}{5}$

(C) $\frac{2}{5}$

(D) $\frac{1}{3}$

(E) $\frac{1}{5}$

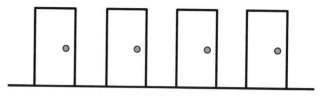

18. The four adjacent offices in the figure above are to be assigned to four employees at random. What is the probability that Scooter and The Big Man (two of the employees) will be placed next to each other?

(A) $\frac{3}{16}$

(B) $\frac{1}{3}$

(C) $\frac{1}{2}$

(D) $\frac{3}{4}$

(E) $\frac{5}{6}$

15. A snake pit contains green and red snakes in equal number and of equal likelihood to attack. Even after a snake bites, it is just as likely to bite again. If Corey falls into the pit, what is the probability that the first 4 snake bites he receives are all from green snakes?

(A) $\frac{1}{2}$

(B) $\frac{1}{4}$

(C) $\frac{1}{8}$

(D) $\frac{1}{16}$

(E) $\frac{1}{32}$

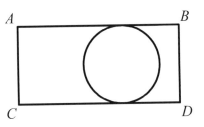

Note: Figure not drawn to scale.

19. In the figure above, a circle is tangent to two sides of a rectangle as shown. If $AB = 5$ and the area of the rectangle is 10, what is the probability (rounded to the nearest hundredth) that a point chosen at random inside the rectangle also falls inside the circle?

(A) 0.63
(B) 0.59
(C) 0.44
(D) 0.31
(E) 0.28

20. Regina rolls two standard 6-sided dice and is astonished to discover that both individual dice show prime numbers, and that their sum is also a prime number. What is the probability of this outcome?

(A) $\dfrac{1}{18}$

(B) $\dfrac{1}{9}$

(C) $\dfrac{1}{8}$

(D) $\dfrac{1}{6}$

(E) $\dfrac{1}{4}$

Answers:
12. **(C)**
15. **(D)**
18. **(C)**
19. **(D)**
20. **(B)**

Solutions on page 327.

The following selected Blue Book questions are examples of this stuff in the wild.

Test	§	p	#	Diff.
1	7	417	11	2
2	8	483	8	3
3	2	514	2	1
4	3	583	7	M
6	8	731	10	M
7	9	795	1	E
8	9	858	5	E
10	8	978	3	E

Notice anything weird? There aren't that many probability questions, in the Blue Book, and there are *no* really hard ones. I know, right? Crazy. That doesn't mean you should let your guard down—probability is fair game and you might get a really hard one on test day even though there are no really hard ones in the Blue Book—but it does mean that you shouldn't obsess *too* much over the hardest probability questions in this book, or elsewhere.

Diagnostic Drill #1

Hopefully, you've taken the time to read and internalize the tips and tricks in this book before jumping straight into these drills. If you haven't, then this is my final suggestion that you do so.

The diagnostic drills in this book are specifically designed to help you identify any weaknesses you're still having with technique-susceptible questions after you've made a first pass through the book—they'll be of more use to you if you've read it than they will if you haven't.

Once you've done this drill, you should use the technique guide that follows to refer back to chapters in this book relevant to the questions you missed before you try Diagnostic Drill #2.

Good luck!

Answer sheet for Diagnostic Drill #1

1. Ⓐ Ⓑ Ⓒ Ⓓ Ⓔ
2. Ⓐ Ⓑ Ⓒ Ⓓ Ⓔ
3. Ⓐ Ⓑ Ⓒ Ⓓ Ⓔ
4. Ⓐ Ⓑ Ⓒ Ⓓ Ⓔ
5. Ⓐ Ⓑ Ⓒ Ⓓ Ⓔ
6. Ⓐ Ⓑ Ⓒ Ⓓ Ⓔ
7. Ⓐ Ⓑ Ⓒ Ⓓ Ⓔ
8. Ⓐ Ⓑ Ⓒ Ⓓ Ⓔ
9. Ⓐ Ⓑ Ⓒ Ⓓ Ⓔ
10. Ⓐ Ⓑ Ⓒ Ⓓ Ⓔ
11. Ⓐ Ⓑ Ⓒ Ⓓ Ⓔ
12. Ⓐ Ⓑ Ⓒ Ⓓ Ⓔ
13. Ⓐ Ⓑ Ⓒ Ⓓ Ⓔ
14. Ⓐ Ⓑ Ⓒ Ⓓ Ⓔ
15. Ⓐ Ⓑ Ⓒ Ⓓ Ⓔ
16. Ⓐ Ⓑ Ⓒ Ⓓ Ⓔ
17. Ⓐ Ⓑ Ⓒ Ⓓ Ⓔ
18. Ⓐ Ⓑ Ⓒ Ⓓ Ⓔ
19. Ⓐ Ⓑ Ⓒ Ⓓ Ⓔ
20. Ⓐ Ⓑ Ⓒ Ⓓ Ⓔ

1. If $f(x) = 8x + 2$, what is $3f(2) + 1$?

   (A) 8
   (B) 17
   (C) 36
   (D) 49
   (E) 55

Month	Account balance
January	$2,500.00
February	$3,200.00
March	$4,000.00
April	$4,700.00
May	$5,700.00
June	$6,600.00

2. The table above shows the balance in Judy's savings account at the end of every month for 6 months. During which period did Judy see the greatest percent change in her account balance?

   (A) From January to February
   (B) From February to March
   (C) From March to April
   (D) From April to May
   (E) From May to June

3. If $x^2 + y^2 = 14$ and $xy = 3$, which of the following is equal to $(x + y)^2$?

   (A) 11
   (B) 17
   (C) 20
   (D) 24
   (E) 28

$$1, 7, 49, 343, \ldots$$

4. Each term in the sequence above after the first is determined by multiplying the previous term by 7. What will be the units (ones) digit of the 96th term?

   (A) 9
   (B) 7
   (C) 5
   (D) 3
   (E) 1

5. A certain sequence is defined such that the nth term in the sequence is equal to $n^2 + 1$. How much greater is the 10th term than the 7th term in the sequence?

(A) 3
(B) 49
(C) 51
(D) 72
(E) 90

x	2	3	4
$f(x)$	11	16	23

7. Based on the table above, which of the following could be an expression of $f(x)$?

(A) $f(x) = 8x - 7$
(B) $f(x) = 5x + 1$
(C) $f(x) = -3x - 9$
(D) $f(x) = x^2 + 7$
(E) $f(x) = 6x - 1$

6. In a class of 6 students, the average (arithmetic mean) height is 5 feet and 8 inches. If a student joins the class and causes the average height of the class to increase by 1 inch, what is the height of the new student? (1 foot = 12 inches)

(A) 6 feet 6 inches
(B) 6 feet 3 inches
(C) 6 feet 0 inches
(D) 5 feet 11 inches
(E) 5 feet 9 inches

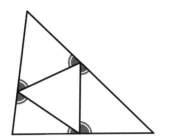

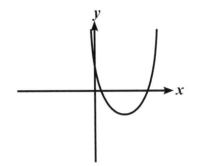

8. What is the sum of the measures of the marked angles in the figure above?

    (A) 180°
    (B) 270°
    (C) 360°
    (D) 450°
    (E) It cannot be determined from the information given.

10. Which of the following could be the equation of the parabola in the figure above?

    (A) $f(x) = x^2 - 7x + 9$
    (B) $f(x) = x^2 - 7x - 9$
    (C) $f(x) = -x^2 + 7x + 9$
    (D) $f(x) = x^2 + 7x - 9$
    (E) $f(x) = -x^2 - 7x - 9$

9. The length of a certain rectangle is increased by 10%, and its width is decreased by 10%. Its new area is what percent of its original area?

    (A) 99%
    (B) 100%
    (C) 101%
    (D) 110%
    (E) It cannot be determined from the information given.

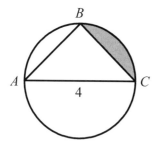

11. In the figure above, $\overline{AC}$ is a diameter of the circle, and $AB = BC$. What is the area of the shaded region?

(A) $4\pi - 2$
(B) $2\pi - 1$
(C) π
(D) $\pi - 1$
(E) $\pi - 2$

12. A certain salad contains croutons, nuts, and raisins. The ratio of croutons to nuts is 3 to 4, and the ratio of raisins to nuts is 3 to 5. What is the ratio of croutons to raisins?

(A) 5 to 4
(B) 4 to 5
(C) 2 to 3
(D) 9 to 20
(E) 3 to 10

13. A circle has an area of $49\pi^3$. What is the length of its diameter?

(A) 7
(B) 14
(C) 7π
(D) 14π
(E) 49π

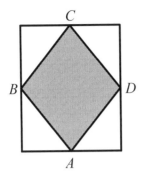

C

B · · D

A

14. The rectangle above has a length of 8 and a width of 10. Points *A*, *B*, *C*, and *D* are the midpoints of the sides upon which they fall. What is the area of the shaded region?

(A) 20
(B) 30
(C) 35
(D) 40
(E) 50

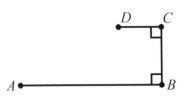

Note: Figure not drawn to scale.

15. In the figure above, *AB* = 14, *BC* = 10, and *CD* = 4. What is the length of $\overline{AD}$ (not shown)?

(A) 10
(B) $10\sqrt{2}$
(C) $10\sqrt{3}$
(D) 12
(E) $12\sqrt{2}$

16. If $x + y = r$ and $x - y = s$, then in terms of x and y, what is $r^2 - s^2$?

  (A) $x^2 + y^2$
  (B) $x^2 - y^2$
  (C) $4xy$
  (D) 2
  (E) 0

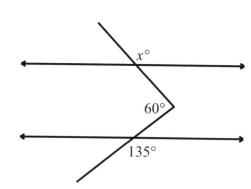

Note: Figure not drawn to scale.

18. The two horizontal lines in the figure above are parallel. What is x?

  (A) 135
  (B) 150
  (C) 165
  (D) 170
  (E) 175

17. Line n has a slope of $-\dfrac{1}{2}$ and a positive y-intercept. Line l passes through the origin, is perpendicular to line n, and intersects line n at the point $(a, a + 2)$. What is the value of a?

  (A) 0.5
  (B) 1
  (C) 1.75
  (D) 2
  (E) 2.5

19. One third of the attendees at a concert left the show before the encore. Twenty more people left during the encore. After the encore, half as many people as had left before the encore left. If 76 people remained in the theater after the concert was over to try to get autographs from the band, how many people, in total, attended the concert?

    (A) 150
    (B) 165
    (C) 192
    (D) 240
    (E) 270

20. For all integers x, let $☼x = 15(x - 5)^2 - 8$. Which of the following is equal to $☼3$?

    (A) $☼(-3)$
    (B) $☼2$
    (C) $☼5$
    (D) $☼7$
    (E) $☼52$

Answers to Diagnostic Drill #1

1   Ⓐ Ⓑ Ⓒ Ⓓ ● → Functions (p114)
2   ● Ⓑ Ⓒ Ⓓ Ⓔ → Percent change (p59)
3   Ⓐ Ⓑ ● Ⓓ Ⓔ → Solving for expressions (p100)
4   Ⓐ Ⓑ Ⓒ ● Ⓔ → Patterns (p87)
5   Ⓐ Ⓑ ● Ⓓ Ⓔ → Patterns (p87), Functions (p114)
6   Ⓐ ● Ⓒ Ⓓ Ⓔ → Average (p211)
7   Ⓐ Ⓑ Ⓒ ● Ⓔ → Functions (p114)
8   Ⓐ Ⓑ ● Ⓓ Ⓔ → Triangles (p165), Plug in (p31)
9   ● Ⓑ Ⓒ Ⓓ Ⓔ → Plug In (p31), Percent change (p59)
10 ● Ⓑ Ⓒ Ⓓ Ⓔ → Parabolas (p140)
11 Ⓐ Ⓑ Ⓒ Ⓓ ● → Circles (p182), Triangles (p165), Shaded regions (p193)
12 ● Ⓑ Ⓒ Ⓓ Ⓔ → Ratios (p64), Plug in (p31)
13 Ⓐ Ⓑ Ⓒ ● Ⓔ → Circles (p182)
14 Ⓐ Ⓑ Ⓒ ● Ⓔ → Right triangles (p175), Shaded regions (p193)
15 Ⓐ ● Ⓒ Ⓓ Ⓔ → Right triangles (p175)
16 Ⓐ Ⓑ ● Ⓓ Ⓔ → Plug in (p31)
17 Ⓐ Ⓑ Ⓒ ● Ⓔ → Lines (p132)
18 Ⓐ Ⓑ ● Ⓓ Ⓔ → Angles (p164)
19 Ⓐ Ⓑ ● Ⓓ Ⓔ → Backsolve (p39)
20 Ⓐ Ⓑ Ⓒ ● Ⓔ → Symbol functions (p126)

Solutions on page 329.

Diagnostic Drill #2

Now that you've completed the first drill, and reinforced any weak areas you discovered in correcting it, let's have a go at another drill.

Again, the value of a drill like this is not only in the doing, it's in the correcting as well. Make sure that you spend time wrestling with the questions you missed (or struggled with), and the relevant chapters from the technique guide at the end of the drill. The key to continued improvement is continued refinement of your skills and techniques.

OK, I've said my piece. Without further blah-blah-ing, here are 20 more moderate-to-tough SAT-type questions. Good luck!

Answer sheet for Diagnostic Drill #2

1 Ⓐ Ⓑ Ⓒ Ⓓ Ⓔ
2 Ⓐ Ⓑ Ⓒ Ⓓ Ⓔ
3 Ⓐ Ⓑ Ⓒ Ⓓ Ⓔ
4 Ⓐ Ⓑ Ⓒ Ⓓ Ⓔ
5 Ⓐ Ⓑ Ⓒ Ⓓ Ⓔ
6 Ⓐ Ⓑ Ⓒ Ⓓ Ⓔ
7 Ⓐ Ⓑ Ⓒ Ⓓ Ⓔ
8 Ⓐ Ⓑ Ⓒ Ⓓ Ⓔ
9 Ⓐ Ⓑ Ⓒ Ⓓ Ⓔ
10 Ⓐ Ⓑ Ⓒ Ⓓ Ⓔ
11 Ⓐ Ⓑ Ⓒ Ⓓ Ⓔ
12 Ⓐ Ⓑ Ⓒ Ⓓ Ⓔ
13 Ⓐ Ⓑ Ⓒ Ⓓ Ⓔ
14 Ⓐ Ⓑ Ⓒ Ⓓ Ⓔ
15 Ⓐ Ⓑ Ⓒ Ⓓ Ⓔ
16 Ⓐ Ⓑ Ⓒ Ⓓ Ⓔ
17 Ⓐ Ⓑ Ⓒ Ⓓ Ⓔ
18 Ⓐ Ⓑ Ⓒ Ⓓ Ⓔ
19 Ⓐ Ⓑ Ⓒ Ⓓ Ⓔ
20 Ⓐ Ⓑ Ⓒ Ⓓ Ⓔ

$$A = \{\, j, k, l, m, n, p \,\}$$

1. If $j < k < l < m < n < p$, and the median of set A is 0, which of the following must be true?

    I. The product of all of the members of the set is 0

    II. The sum of l and m is 0

    III. The sum of all the members of the set is greater than j and less than p

  (A) I only
  (B) II only
  (C) III only
  (D) I and III only
  (E) II and III only

2. If $f(x)$ is a parabola with a minimum at $f(2)$, which of the following is equal to $f(6)$?

  (A) $f(4)$
  (B) $f(0)$
  (C) $f(-2)$
  (D) $f(-4)$
  (E) $f(-6)$

$$1, 2, 2, 3, 3, 3, 4, \ldots$$

3. In the sequence above, there is one 1, followed by two 2s, three 3s, four 4s, and so on. How many terms fall between the first occurrence of 80 and the first occurrence of 85?

  (A) 243
  (B) 330
  (C) 409
  (D) 413
  (E) 495

$$\frac{x^5 x^{10}}{x^{13}} = 225$$

4. According to the equation above, which of the following equals x^2?

  (A) 225
  (B) 75
  (C) 25
  (D) 15
  (E) 5

$$\frac{x^r}{x^p} = x^{2r}$$

5. If the equation above is true for all values of x, and p and r are constants, which of the following must be true?

    (A) $r + p = 2$

    (B) $r - p = 0$

    (C) $r + p = 0$

    (D) $p - r = 0$

    (E) $\dfrac{r}{p} = 2r$

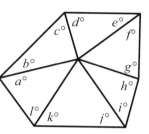

6. In the figure above, an irregular hexagon is divided into six triangles. What is the average (arithmetic mean) of a, b, c, d, e, f, g, h, i, j, k, and l?

    (A) 72
    (B) 60
    (C) 48
    (D) 30
    (E) It cannot be determined from the information given.

7. For all integers m greater than 2, let
   ₪ $m = \dfrac{4m}{m-2}$. Which of the following is true?

   (A) ₪ 3 > ₪ 4
   (B) ₪ 5 + ₪ 6 = ₪ 11
   (C) ₪ 9 ÷ ₪ 3 = ₪ 3
   (D) 4(₪ 3) = 3(₪ 4)
   (E) ₪ (6 + 7) = ₪ 6 + ₪ 7

9. If $f(x) = x^2 - 5$ and $g(x) = 2f(x) + 3$, what is $g(\sqrt{11})$?

   (A) $\sqrt{11} - 2$
   (B) $\sqrt{22} + 3$
   (C) 9
   (D) 15
   (E) 22

Week	1	2	3	4	5	6
Customers	5	9	15	23	33	59

10. The table above shows how many customers came to Sean's new hair salon during his first six weeks in business. When did Sean see his biggest percent increase in customers?

    (A) From week 1 to week 2
    (B) From week 2 to week 3
    (C) From week 3 to week 4
    (D) From week 4 to week 5
    (E) From week 5 to week 6

8. If $3y + 8x = 19$ and $2y - 3x = 11$, what is $y + x$?

   (A) 5.6
   (B) 6
   (C) 8
   (D) 9
   (E) 30

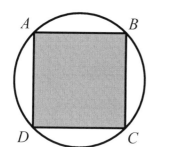

11. In the figure above, $ABCD$ is a square and $\overline{AC}$ and $\overline{BD}$ (not shown) are diameters of the circle. If the area of the shaded region is 16, what is the area of the circle?

(A) $2\pi\sqrt{3}$
(B) 4π
(C) $4\pi\sqrt{2}$
(D) 8π
(E) 16π

$$3x + 2y + 2z = 21$$
$$5 + y + z = 8$$

12. Based on the system of equations above, what is $3x$?

(A) 5
(B) 15
(C) 22
(D) 28
(E) 38

13. At the Biltmore Hotel, 86 rooms have king size beds and 57 rooms have bathtubs. If 83 rooms have only a bathtub OR a king size bed but not both, how many rooms have both features?

(A) 60
(B) 56
(C) 36
(D) 30
(E) 27

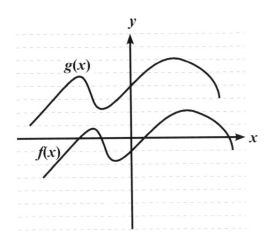

14. The graphs of $y = f(x)$ and $y = g(x)$ are shown above. Which of the following could define the relationship between f and g?

(A) $f(x) = g(x + 1) - 4$
(B) $f(x) = g(x - 1) - 4$
(C) $f(x) = g(x - 4) - 1$
(D) $f(x) = g(x - 4) + 1$
(E) $f(x) = g(x + 1) + 4$

15. A teacher assigns certain students the duty of feeding the class hamster every day. The students decide to take turns, and decide that Alex will feed the hamster on the first day, followed by Bradley, Corinne, Dilip, and Ella, and then the pattern will repeat. Who will be responsible for feeding the hamster on the 99th day of class?

(A) Alex
(B) Bradley
(C) Corinne
(D) Dilip
(E) Ella

16. The equation of a certain parabola is $y = ax^2 + bx + c$. If $a > 0$ and $c < 0$, which of the following could be the graph of the parabola?

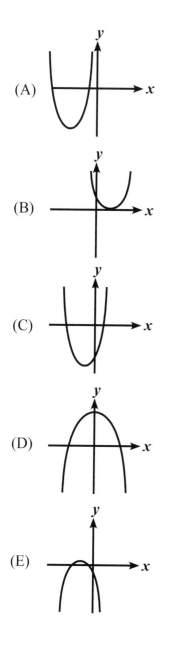

(A)

(B)

(C)

(D)

(E)

17. When p and r are divided by 7, the remainders are 3 and 6, respectively. What is the remainder when pr is divided by 7?

(A) 1
(B) 2
(C) 4
(D) 5
(E) 6

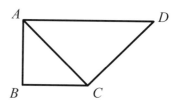

18. In the figure above, $\overline{AD} \parallel \overline{BC}$ and $\overline{AB} \perp \overline{BC}$. If $AB = 2$ and AC and CD both equal $2\sqrt{2}$, what is the perimeter of $ABCD$?

(A) $8 + 2\sqrt{2}$
(B) $8\sqrt{2}$
(C) $6 + 4\sqrt{2}$
(D) $10 + 2\sqrt{2}$
(E) $10\sqrt{2}$

19. In the xy-coordinate plane, the point $(2, r)$ is a distance of 13 from the point $(14, 2)$. Which of the following could equal r?

(A) 15
(B) 6
(C) 5
(D) −1
(E) −3

20. Which of the following sets of points forms a line that is perpendicular to the line $8x + 2y = 12$?

(A) $(6, 2)$ and $(8, 9)$
(B) $(-2, -2)$ and $(3, 1)$
(C) $(1, 4)$ and $(2, 8)$
(D) $(2, 10)$ and $(4, 11)$
(E) $(5, 3)$ and $(1, 2)$

Answers to Diagnostic Drill #2

1 Ⓐ ● Ⓒ Ⓓ Ⓔ → Median (p216), Plug in (p31)
2 Ⓐ Ⓑ ● Ⓓ Ⓔ → Parabolas (p140)
3 Ⓐ Ⓑ ● Ⓓ Ⓔ → Patterns (p87)
4 ● Ⓑ Ⓒ Ⓓ Ⓔ → Exponents (p106)
5 Ⓐ Ⓑ ● Ⓓ Ⓔ → Exponents (p106)
6 Ⓐ ● Ⓒ Ⓓ Ⓔ → Triangles (p165), Plug in (p31)
7 ● Ⓑ Ⓒ Ⓓ Ⓔ → Symbol functions (p126)
8 Ⓐ ● Ⓒ Ⓓ Ⓔ → Solving for expressions (p100)
9 Ⓐ Ⓑ Ⓒ ● Ⓔ → Functions (p114)
10 ● Ⓑ Ⓒ Ⓓ Ⓔ → Percent change (p59)
11 Ⓐ Ⓑ Ⓒ ● Ⓔ → Circles (p182), Guesstimate (p47)
12 Ⓐ ● Ⓒ Ⓓ Ⓔ → Solving for expressions (p100)
13 Ⓐ Ⓑ Ⓒ ● Ⓔ → Backsolve (p39)
14 Ⓐ ● Ⓒ Ⓓ Ⓔ → Functions (p114)
15 Ⓐ Ⓑ Ⓒ ● Ⓔ → Patterns (p87)
16 Ⓐ Ⓑ ● Ⓓ Ⓔ → Parabolas (p140)
17 Ⓐ Ⓑ ● Ⓓ Ⓔ → Plug in (p31)
18 ● Ⓑ Ⓒ Ⓓ Ⓔ → Right triangles (p175)
19 Ⓐ Ⓑ Ⓒ Ⓓ ● → Backsolve (p39), Right triangles (p175)
20 Ⓐ Ⓑ Ⓒ Ⓓ ● → Lines (p132)

Solutions on page 336.

Interlude: So, you want an 800?

Before we really get into this, let's get one thing straight: *It's incredibly unlikely than an 800 will open any doors for you that a 770 or so won't.* In fact, it's usually not a good idea to think of SAT scores opening doors at all. It's better to think of high scores as preventing admissions doors from being closed: your high score encourages an admissions officer to look into your application further. Nobody secures admission to an elite school on SAT scores alone. So if you're looking at an 800 as a means to an end, you might want to reexamine your priorities. If you're pining after an 800 just because you really like the challenge, though, then you and I are kindred spirits, and you should read on.

* **You'll need to be good at math, but you'll also need a healthy helping of SAT technique.** If you're really going to be ready for *everything* the SAT can throw at you, then you're going to need to be conversant with every technique and math concept in this book. As I keep reminding you in this book, *the SAT is not a math test*, but there is a bunch of math on it, and if you're shooting for perfection you're going to need to be able to switch deftly between math wizard and test taking sage as different questions call for different approaches. I call this nimbleness, and if you're shooting for perfection, it's probably the most important trait you can possess.

* **There is no room for error.** While there are some tests that will bestow an 800 on a student who's missed one math question, most are less forgiving. A single mistake might drop you as low as a 770. So let that extirpate any misgivings you have about guessing: *if you want an 800, you have to guess even if you're completely stumped.* Of course, if you're completely stumped, then you probably

haven't prepped sufficiently to be shooting for an 800 in the first place.

- **It's not enough to get all the hard ones.** An obvious corollary of the rule above is that you're going to have to be perfect on the easy ones, too. It always amazes me when I see a student who is consistently perfect on #15-20 miss #4, but I see it *all the time*. If you rush through the easy ones to get to the hard ones and you make a silly mistake along the way, you can kiss your perfect score goodbye.

- **It only counts on the real thing.** If you can get an 800 on a practice test then I'm impressed, but you don't get to join the club until you've done it on game day. That's because it's different when you take the real thing. Have you ever been to the vet's office with your pet? You know that smell in the waiting room? That's the smell of concentrated animal anxiety, and *it will smell like that in your testing room*. I kid, but only sorta. You have to be able to overcome the pressure, the exhaustion, and the entropy that come along with testing first thing in the morning on a Saturday. Kid next to you has the sniffles? They're mowing the lawn outside the school? The heat is blasting even though it's unseasonably warm outside and you're sweating bullets by section 2? A bird gets into your testing room? All of these have happened.

- **You must practice as you play.** To mitigate some of the difficulties of testing day, you should simulate it as best you can when you practice. Wake up early on a Saturday to take practice tests. Take FULL practice tests—all three subjects. No long internet breaks between sections. No cell phone on your desk. No giving yourself an extra 30 seconds to finish a problem. No starting the next section early if you finish before 25 minutes is up. No smiling.

- **You are not entitled to an 800.** Even if you take every test you can get your hands on, even if you can do probability questions in your sleep, even if circle questions see you coming and just solve themselves to save you the trouble since you're such a monster, the SAT might find a way to throw a question at you that's unlike any you've seen before. That's not unfair; that's just how it works. *You're going to have to wrestle with a few very difficult questions when the pressure is on*, and only if you come out on top will you earn your 800.

- **If it were easy, everyone would be doing it.** I know my tone here has been a bit less rosy than in other places in this book, but that's because I really want to set your expectations: *an 800 is quite an accomplishment; it will* *require toil proportional to its resulting renown.* If you expect to muscle through just because you're really good at math, you might be disappointed. If you expect it all to come together on test day even though your practice tests have been in the low-mid 700s, you might be disappointed. Even if you hit 800 on your last three practice tests, you might be disappointed. But doing so, and *enjoying the process*, is the surest path to success.

Wanna try some hard problems right now? The following two drills are more difficult, but you should be able to rip through them without making any mistakes if you're shooting for 800. Be careful, and good luck!

Diagnostic Drill #3

I'm not going to sugar-coat it—this drill is hard. Don't do anything silly like skip ahead and try this one first. You'll only frustrate yourself and then have less really hard stuff to try once you've gone through all the strategies in this book. You don't want that.

You trusted me enough to buy this guide, right? So trust me enough to take my advice and not try this drill or the next one before you've read the whole book.

Answer sheet for Diagnostic Drill #3

1 Ⓐ Ⓑ Ⓒ Ⓓ Ⓔ
2 Ⓐ Ⓑ Ⓒ Ⓓ Ⓔ
3 Ⓐ Ⓑ Ⓒ Ⓓ Ⓔ
4 Ⓐ Ⓑ Ⓒ Ⓓ Ⓔ
5 Ⓐ Ⓑ Ⓒ Ⓓ Ⓔ
6 Ⓐ Ⓑ Ⓒ Ⓓ Ⓔ
7 Ⓐ Ⓑ Ⓒ Ⓓ Ⓔ
8 Ⓐ Ⓑ Ⓒ Ⓓ Ⓔ
9 Ⓐ Ⓑ Ⓒ Ⓓ Ⓔ
10 Ⓐ Ⓑ Ⓒ Ⓓ Ⓔ
11 Ⓐ Ⓑ Ⓒ Ⓓ Ⓔ
12 Ⓐ Ⓑ Ⓒ Ⓓ Ⓔ
13 Ⓐ Ⓑ Ⓒ Ⓓ Ⓔ
14 Ⓐ Ⓑ Ⓒ Ⓓ Ⓔ
15 Ⓐ Ⓑ Ⓒ Ⓓ Ⓔ
16 Ⓐ Ⓑ Ⓒ Ⓓ Ⓔ
17 Ⓐ Ⓑ Ⓒ Ⓓ Ⓔ
18 Ⓐ Ⓑ Ⓒ Ⓓ Ⓔ
19 Ⓐ Ⓑ Ⓒ Ⓓ Ⓔ
20 Ⓐ Ⓑ Ⓒ Ⓓ Ⓔ

1. If $f(x) = 8x - 9$ and $g(x) = f(2x) + 5$, what is $g(3)$?

   (A) 13
   (B) 34
   (C) 39
   (D) 44
   (E) 52

2. One at a time, Lindsey and Jordan each randomly pull one marble from a bag that contains 3 black marbles, 2 green marbles, and 1 red marble. Assuming they do not return the marbles to the bag after they pick, what is the probability that Lindsey picks a green marble and Jordan picks a red one?

   (A) $\dfrac{1}{5}$

   (B) $\dfrac{1}{6}$

   (C) $\dfrac{1}{10}$

   (D) $\dfrac{1}{15}$

   (E) $\dfrac{1}{30}$

3. After b games, Maurice's basketball team had scored an average (arithmetic mean) of 60 points per game. Then they played 4 games in which they averaged 84 points per game, which changed their overall average to 72 points per game. What is b?

   (A) 2
   (B) 3
   (C) 4
   (D) 5
   (E) 6

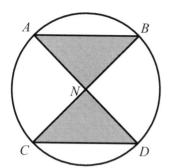

4. In the figure above, points A, B, C, and D lie on the circle, N is the center of the circle, and $\overline{AD} \perp \overline{BC}$. What fraction of the circle is shaded?

(A) $\dfrac{1}{\pi}$

(B) $1 - \dfrac{1}{\pi}$

(C) $\dfrac{1}{2\pi}$

(D) $\dfrac{1}{\pi^2}$

(E) It cannot be determined from the information given.

5. If 6 numbers have an average (arithmetic mean) of –6, and 4 of the numbers have a sum of 10, then what is the average of the other 2 numbers?

(A) 16
(B) 2
(C) –23
(D) –26
(E) –46

6. Line m passes through the points $(3, 2)$ and $(5, p)$, where $p > 2$. If line l is perpendicular to line m, which of the following equations could represent line l?

(A) $y = -\dfrac{2}{p-2}x + 3$

(B) $y = \dfrac{p}{2}x - 1$

(C) $y = -\dfrac{2}{p+2}x - 8$

(D) $y = \dfrac{1}{2p-4}x - 5$

(E) $y = -\dfrac{2}{5+p}x - 3$

7. What is the volume of the smallest cube that could completely contain a sphere with a radius of r?

(A) r^3
(B) $3r^3$
(C) $4r^3$
(D) $5r^3$
(E) $8r^3$

8. In $\triangle ABC$, $AB = 11$ and $BC = 15$. Which of the following could NOT be the perimeter of $\triangle ABC$?

(A) 29
(B) 33
(C) 40
(D) 49.5
(E) 51

9. If $6x - 15y = 18$ and $2x + 7y = 30$, what is $x - y$?

    (A) 1.5
    (B) 6
    (C) 12
    (D) 18
    (E) 48

10. Let $c \approx d$ be defined as $c \approx d = c^2 - 10d$ for all values of c and d. If $11 \approx m = 81$, what is the value of m?

    (A) 9
    (B) 6
    (C) 4
    (D) 2
    (E) 1

11. If $4^{m+n} = q$, then which of the following is equivalent to 4^{2m+2n}?

    (A) $2q$
    (B) $4q$
    (C) q^2
    (D) $2q^2$
    (E) $8q^2$

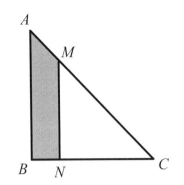

A

M

B   N   C

Note: Figure not drawn to scale.

12. In the figure above, $AB = x$, $BC = y$, and $\overline{AB}$ and $\overline{MN}$ are perpendicular to $\overline{BC}$. If $BN = 0.2y$, what is the area of the shaded region, in terms of x and y?

(A) $0.40xy$
(B) $0.32xy$
(C) $0.25xy$
(D) $0.18xy$
(E) $0.14xy$

13. If $p^2 + q^2 = 18$, and $pq = 9$, what is $(p - q)^2$?

(A) 0
(B) 2
(C) 9
(D) 27
(E) 36

1, 4, 16, 64, ...

14. In the sequence above, each term after the first is determined by multiplying the previous term by 4. Which of the following must be true?

    I.   The nth term in the pattern is equal to 4^n

    II. The nth term in the pattern is equal to $2^{2(n-1)}$

    III. The units digit of the 53rd term is 6

(A) I only
(B) II only
(C) III only
(D) II and III only
(E) I, II, and III

15. In the xy-plane, a circle with center (m, n) touches the y-axis at exactly one point and touches the x-axis at exactly one point. Which of the following must be true?

(A) $m + n = 0$
(B) $m = n$
(C) $m - n = 0$
(D) $mn = m^2$
(E) $|m| = |n|$

16. Sharon has 20 water balloons in her bucket and Michelle has 3 in hers. Sharon is tossing water balloons to Michelle, who is trying her best to catch them and put them in her bucket. If every 3rd toss results in a dropped and broken balloon, how many tosses have to occur for the two girls to have the same number of balloons?

(A) 12
(B) 11
(C) 10
(D) 9
(E) 8

x	$f(x)$	$g(x)$
–2	–7	–9
–1	3	1
0	3	–2
1	2	6
2	–1	–3
3	5	8

17. According to the table above, if $f(1) = n$, what is $g(n - 2)$?

(A) –9
(B) –2
(C) 0
(D) 1
(E) 6

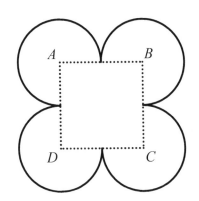

18. In the figure above, $ABCD$ is a square, and A, B, C, and D are the centers of four congruent circles which touch each other but do not overlap. If the area of $ABCD$ is 1, what is the perimeter of the solid-outlined region?

(A) 3π
(B) 4π
(C) 6π
(D) 7π
(E) 9π

19. The length of one leg of a right triangle is increased by 15%, and the length of the other leg is decreased by 20%. The new triangle's area is what percent of the original triangle's area?

(A) 46%
(B) 92%
(C) 95%
(D) 96%
(E) 105%

20. The lowest score on the most recent chemistry exam in Professor Wren's class was a 39, and the highest score was a 75. Which inequality could be used to determine whether a particular score, s, could have come from Professor Wren's class?

(A) $|s - 39| \leq 75$
(B) $|s - 20| \leq 57$
(C) $|s - 18| \leq 55$
(D) $|s - 60| \leq 17$
(E) $|s - 57| \leq 18$

Answers to Diagnostic Drill #3

1. Ⓐ Ⓑ Ⓒ ● Ⓔ → Functions (p114)
2. Ⓐ Ⓑ Ⓒ ● Ⓔ → Probability (p223)
3. Ⓐ Ⓑ ● Ⓓ Ⓔ → Backsolve (p39), Average (p211)
4. ● Ⓑ Ⓒ Ⓓ Ⓔ → Plug in (p31), Circles (p182), Right triangles (p175), Guesstimate (p47)
5. Ⓐ Ⓑ ● Ⓓ Ⓔ → Average (p211)
6. ● Ⓑ Ⓒ Ⓓ Ⓔ → Plug in (p31), Lines (p132)
7. Ⓐ Ⓑ Ⓒ Ⓓ ● → Working in 3D (p199)
8. ● Ⓑ Ⓒ Ⓓ Ⓔ → Triangles (p165)
9. Ⓐ ● Ⓒ Ⓓ Ⓔ → Solving for expressions (p100)
10. Ⓐ Ⓑ ● Ⓓ Ⓔ → Symbol functions (p126)
11. Ⓐ Ⓑ ● Ⓓ Ⓔ → Exponents (p106), Plug in (p31)
12. Ⓐ Ⓑ Ⓒ ● Ⓔ → Plug in (p31), Right triangles (p175), Shaded regions (p193)
13. ● Ⓑ Ⓒ Ⓓ Ⓔ → Solving for expressions (p100)
14. Ⓐ Ⓑ Ⓒ ● Ⓔ → Exponents (p106), Patterns (p87), Logic
15. Ⓐ Ⓑ Ⓒ Ⓓ ● → Plug in (p31), Circles (p182), Absolute value (p148), Logic
16. Ⓐ Ⓑ ● Ⓓ Ⓔ → Backsolve (p39)
17. Ⓐ ● Ⓒ Ⓓ Ⓔ → Functions (p114)
18. ● Ⓑ Ⓒ Ⓓ Ⓔ → Circles (p182)
19. Ⓐ ● Ⓒ Ⓓ Ⓔ → Plug in (p31), Percent change (p59), Triangles (p165)
20. Ⓐ Ⓑ Ⓒ Ⓓ ● → Plug in (p31), Absolute value (p148)

Solutions on page 343.

Diagnostic Drill #4

Buckle your seatbelts, little ones. Strap your helmets on tight. I'm pulling out all the stops for this last drill. If you can traverse this goblin hollow unscathed, then you are truly prepared to PWN the SAT.

Each one of these questions is as hard, or harder, than any #20 you'd find on the SAT. And, since there haven't been any in the diagnostic drills until now, the last 10 problems are grid-ins. Good luck!

Answer sheet for Diagnostic Drill #4

1 Ⓐ Ⓑ Ⓒ Ⓓ Ⓔ
2 Ⓐ Ⓑ Ⓒ Ⓓ Ⓔ
3 Ⓐ Ⓑ Ⓒ Ⓓ Ⓔ
4 Ⓐ Ⓑ Ⓒ Ⓓ Ⓔ

5 Ⓐ Ⓑ Ⓒ Ⓓ Ⓔ
6 Ⓐ Ⓑ Ⓒ Ⓓ Ⓔ
7 Ⓐ Ⓑ Ⓒ Ⓓ Ⓔ
8 Ⓐ Ⓑ Ⓒ Ⓓ Ⓔ

1. Seven years ago, Thom was half as old as Phil and three times as old as Melanie. If Thom is 19 years old now, in how many years will Melanie be half as old as Phil?

   (A) 8 years
   (B) 9 years
   (C) 12 years
   (D) 16 years
   (E) 18 years

2. In a certain right triangle, the difference between the square of the length of the hypotenuse and the square of the length of the longer leg is equal to $x^2 - 2xy + y^2$. What is the length of the shorter leg?

   (A) $x^2 - y^2$

   (B) $x^2 + y^2$

   (C) $x - y$

   (D) $4xy$

   (E) $-2xy$

3. If $2x + y = 8$ and $x < 7$, which of the following must be true?

   (A) $y > -6$
   (B) $y < -6$
   (C) $-6 < y < 7$
   (D) $y < 6$
   (E) $y > 7$

4. The ratio of the lengths of the sides of a certain rectangle is x:y. If x and y are integers, and the sides have integer lengths, which of the following could be the area of the rectangle?

(A) $2xy$
(B) $3(xy)^2$
(C) $5x + 5y$
(D) $9xy$
(E) $xy\sqrt{11}$

5. The sum of six consecutive integers is x. If $x > 0$, what is the smallest possible value of x?

(A) 3
(B) 6
(C) 9
(D) 15
(E) 21

6. Adina keeps track of the number of rats she sees while she waits for the subway every morning. She noticed that there was a *roughly* 46.2% increase in the amount of rats she spotted between Tuesday and Wednesday. If she saw 19 rats on Wednesday, what will be the percent decrease (to the nearest tenth of a percent) in rat sightings if she sees the same number on Thursday that she did on Tuesday?

(A) 46.0%
(B) 35.2%
(C) 32.4%
(D) 31.6%
(E) 19.1%

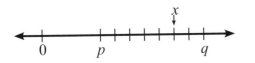

7. On the number line above, the space between p and q is divided evenly into sections. What is x, in terms of p and q?

(A) $\dfrac{5(q-p)}{8}$

(B) $q-\dfrac{2(q-p)}{8}$

(C) $p+\dfrac{q-p}{7}$

(D) $p+\dfrac{5(q-p)}{7}$

(E) $\dfrac{q-p}{7}$

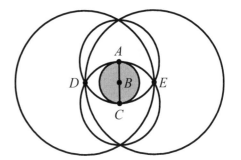

8. In the figure above, B is the midpoint of $\overline{AC}$ and the center of the shaded circle. A, C, D, and E are also the centers of shown circles. If the area of the shaded region is 9π, what is the area of the circle with center E?

(A) 81π
(B) 99π
(C) 108π
(D) 120π
(E) 144π

9. What is the area of the triangle formed by connecting the points (−2, −3), (2, 6), and (2, −2)?

$$x^2 + 14x + c = (x + d)^2$$

10. In the equation above, c and d are constants. If the equation is true for all values of x, what is the value of cd?

11. According to the physical education teacher at Riverdale High school, students are only allowed to use the trampoline if they weigh between 95 and 185 pounds, inclusive. Students in a math class decide to express this same restriction using an inequality of the form $|w - j| \le k$, where w is a student's weight, and j and k are constants. What is jk?

12. In a certain youth soccer league, each team plays each other team exactly once during a season. If there were 28 league games last season, how many teams were in the league?

$$S = \{2, 3, 4, 5, 9, 20\}$$
$$R = \{1, 5, 7, 8, 9, 10\}$$

13. If s is a member of set S, and r is a member of set R, what is the difference between the largest and smallest possible values of $\dfrac{r}{s}$?

14. If $4x + 3y = 20$ and $3y - 2z = 7$, what is $2x + z$?

15. How many positive integers less than 1,000 are NOT divisible by 7?

16. A number is called a "bodacious square" if its square root is the square of an integer. How many bodacious squares are greater than 1 and less than 600?

17. If p^2 is a multiple of both 8 and 35, and p is a positive integer, what is the least possible value of p?

18. Monica spent \$14.13 on bananas and granola at the grocery store. Granola costs four times more than bananas by weight. If she bought five times as many pounds of bananas as pounds of granola, how much, in dollars, did Monica spend on bananas? (Disregard the \$ sign when gridding your answer.)

Answers to Diagnostic Drill #4

1 (A) ● (C) (D) (E) → Setup, then backsolve (p39)
2 (A) (B) ● (D) (E) → Right triangles (p175)
3 ● (B) (C) (D) (E) → Plug in (p31)
4 (A) (B) (C) ● (E) → Ratios (p64), Plug in (p31)

5 ● (B) (C) (D) (E) → Integers (p12)
6 (A) (B) (C) ● (E) → Percent change (p59)
7 (A) (B) (C) ● (E) → Plug in (p31)
8 (A) (B) ● (D) (E) → Circles (p182)

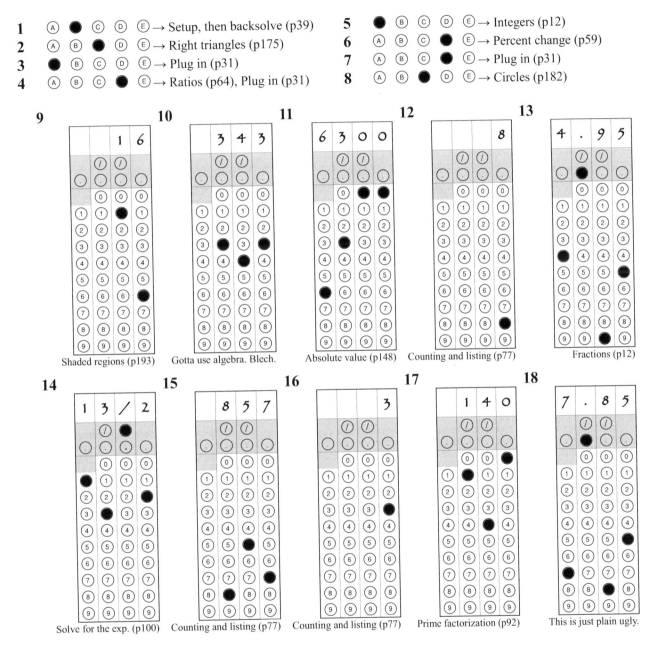

9
Shaded regions (p193)

10
Gotta use algebra. Blech.

11
Absolute value (p148)

12
Counting and listing (p77)

13
Fractions (p12)

14
Solve for the exp. (p100)

15
Counting and listing (p77)

16
Counting and listing (p77)

17
Prime factorization (p92)

18
This is just plain ugly.

Solutions on page 351.

Solutions

On the following pages, you'll find handwritten solutions to all the drill questions in this book. I did this because I've always found it easier to follow math when it's written out by hand, and because I wanted to show that even the scariest questions in this book don't require pages and pages of work.

Some people have told me that they cut this part of the book out to make it easier to compare my work to theirs. If you decide to do that, I suggest you use a pair of scissors or an X-Acto knife[*] or something else similarly designed for the task. If you try to just tear them out like an animal, you run the risk of ripping the pages in half, and it'll be nobody's fault but your own. Gosh, I'm getting depressed just thinking about it.

---

[*] *Carefully.* I almost cut my left thumb off with one of those when I was a kid. I still have a really gnarly scar. I'll show you sometime if you ask.

10. If $r + 9$ is 4 more than s, then $r - 11$ is how much less than s?

make $r > 11$

(A) 9
(B) 11
(C) 16
(D) 20
(E) 24

$r = 12$

$r + 9 = 21$

21 is 4 more than s, so

$s = 17$

$r - 11 = 1$

1 is how much less than 17?

$\boxed{16.}$

12. If Brunhilda went to the casino and lost 40% of her money playing Pai Gow poker before doubling her remaining money playing roulette, the amount of money she had after playing roulette is what percent of the amount of money she started with?

(A) 20%
(B) 40%
(C) 80%
(D) 100%
(E) 120%

Say she started with $100.
After Pai Gow: $60
After roulette: $120

$120 is what percent of $100?

$\boxed{120\%}$

How smart are we to start with 100?

14. If $x^3 = y$, then x^6 is how much greater than x^3, in terms of y?

(A) y^3
(B) y^2
(C) $y(y - 1)$
(D) $2y - y$
(E) $y - 1$

$x = 2$

$2^3 = 8$, so $y = 8$

$x^6 - x^3 = 2^6 - 2^3 = 64 - 8$

$= \boxed{56}$

(A) $8^3 = 512$
(B) $8^2 = 64$
(C) $8(8-1) = 56$ ✓
(D) $2(8) - 8 = 8$
(E) $8 - 1 = 7$

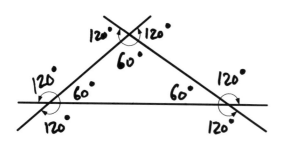

16. What is the sum of the measures of the marked angles in the figure above?

(A) 1080°
(B) 900°
(C) 720°
(D) 540°
(E) 360°

Plug in 60° for the blank angles in the △. Doesn't matter that it's clearly not equilateral!

each marked ∠ is 300°

3 of them = 900°

20. In a certain office, there are c chairs, d desks, and e employees. Five desks are not occupied, and all other desks are occupied by exactly one employee. All but two of the employees have two chairs at their desks, and all the other desks, whether they are occupied or not, have one chair. If $e > 2$, then which of the following expressions is equal to c?

(A) $2(d-5) + e$
(B) $d + e$
(C) $2(d-e)$
(D) $2(d-2)$
(E) $2e + 3$

Start with desks, since desks hold both chairs and employees.

Say d = 10
∴ e = 5
∴ c = 10 + 3 = ⑬
     ↗   ↑
each desk   all but 2 employees
has one   have an extra chair

(A) 2(10-5)+5 = 15
(B) 10+5 = 15
(C) 2(10-5) = 10
(D) 2(d-2) = 16
(E) 2(5)+3 = 13 ✓

13. Rajesh sells only hats and scarves at his store, for which he charges $13 and $7, respectively. On Monday, he sold 15 items and made $123. How many hats did Rajesh sell on Monday?

(A) 3
(B) 4
(C) 5
(D) 6
(E) 7

| | hats | | scarves | | total |
	#	$	#	$	$
(C)	5	65	10	70	135
(B)	4	52	11	77	129
(A)	3	39	12	84	123 ✓

5 hats made Rajesh too much money, so we moved towards (A).

16. From where he lives, it costs Jared $4 more for a round-trip train ticket to Chaska than it does for one to Waconia. Last month, Jared took round-trips to Chaska 7 times and to Waconia 8 times. If he spent a total of $103 on train tickets, how much does Jared spend on one round-trip ticket to Waconia?

(A) $12
(B) $10
(C) $9
(D) $7
(E) $5

| | Waconia | | Chaska | | Total |
	$	×8	$	×7	$
(C)	9	72	13	91	163
(D)	7	56	11	77	133
(E)	5	40	9	63	103 ✓

Choice (C) made it way too expensive. Head towards cheaper fares.

$$V(n) = 8100\left(\frac{7}{6}\right)^n$$

17. A number of years ago, Andy purchased $8,100 worth of stock in PGHH Corporation. The value, in dollars, of his stock n years after purchase is given by the function V, above. If the stock is worth $11,000 now, roughly how many years ago did Andy purchase the stock?

(A) Five
(B) Four
(C) Three
(D) Two
(E) One

(C) $8100\left(\frac{7}{6}\right)^3 = 12862$

too much!

(D) $8100\left(\frac{7}{6}\right)^2 = 11025$ ✓

18. The audience of a reality TV show cast a total of 3.4 million votes, and each vote went to either Brian or Susan. If Susan received 34,000 more votes than Brian, what percent of the votes were cast for Brian?

    (A) 45%
    (B) 49%
    (C) 49.5%
    (D) 49.9%
    (E) 49.95%

B	S	difference
1,683,000	1,717,000	34,000
(49.5%)	(50.5%)	

(C)

Boy, that sure was easy.

19. All the survivors who live in a certain post-apocalyptic settlement spend their miserable days hunting mutant buffalo or growing broccoli, and some do both. If, in total, 45 survivors grow broccoli, 30 hunt, and 37 of them perform only one of those tasks, how many perform both tasks?

    (A) 56
    (B) 38
    (C) 19
    (D) 11
    (E) 9

hunt=30   farm=45

30 - 19 = 11   19   45 - 19 = 26

11 + 26 = 37   yes!

(Drop the answer choice in the middle, use it to fill in the numbers of people doing only one task. If those numbers add up to 37, you're golden.

Note: (B) is 45+30-37.

Way too easy for a #19, and therefore a silly choice. If you picked (B), hang your head in shame.

13. The figure above shows an isosceles right triangle with legs of length m. Which of the following has the greatest area?

(A) Four isosceles right triangles with legs of length m
(B) A square with sides of length $m\sqrt{2}$
(C) A square with a diagonal of length $m\sqrt{2}$
(D) A circle with radius of length m
(E) It cannot be determined from the information given.

Draw

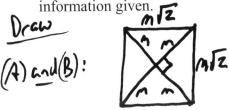

(A) and (B):

(C):

(D):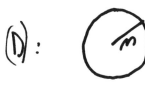

(C) fits inside (A)/(B), which fits inside (D).

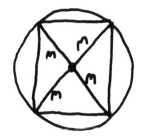

15. In the figure above, $AB + 1 = BC$, $BE - 6 = BD$, and $DE - 3 = BD - 5$. If $AB = 4$, what is the length of $\overline{CD}$?

(A) 3
(B) 4
(C) 5
(D) 7
(E) 8

Hopefully, you used your pencil here.

$\overline{CD}$ is clearly shorter than $\overline{AB}$, so it must be <4 units long.

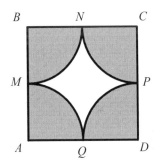

17. In the figure above, $ABCD$ is a square and M, N, P, and Q are midpoints of $\overline{AB}$, $\overline{BC}$, $\overline{CD}$, and $\overline{AD}$, respectively. The arcs shown have centers at A, B, C, and D. If $AB = 6$, what is the area of the shaded regions?

(A) 36π
(B) 18π
(C) 12π
(D) 9π
(E) 6π

Rearrange the pieces. The shaded region makes one full circle with radius 3.

$A = 9\pi$

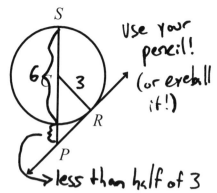

19. In the figure above, the line containing points *P* and *R* is tangent to the circle at *R*, and $\overline{CR}$ is a radius of length 3. If the measure of ∠*RCS* is 135°, what is *SP*?

(A) 5
(B) $4\sqrt{2}$ (approximately 5.66)
(C) 6
(D) $3 + 3\sqrt{2}$ (approximately 7.24)
(E) $6\sqrt{2}$ (approximately 8.49)

$SP = 6 + [\text{less than half of 3}]$
$\quad = [\text{greater than 6 and less than 7.5}]$
$\quad \therefore 6 < SP < 7.5$

The math:

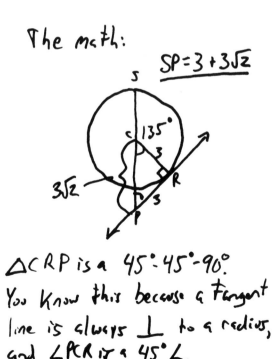

$SP = 3 + 3\sqrt{2}$

$\triangle CRP$ is a 45°-45°-90°. You know this because a tangent line is always ⊥ to a radius, and ∠PCR is a 45° ∠.

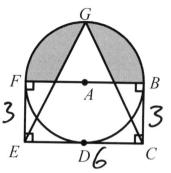

20. In the figure above *A* is the center of the circle, *A* and *D* lie on $\overline{BF}$ and $\overline{CE}$, respectively, and *B, D, F,* and *G* lie on the circle. If *BC* = 3 and $\overline{DG}$ (not shown) bisects $\overline{BF}$, what is the total area of the shaded regions?

(A) $9\pi - 24 \approx 4.3$
(B) $9\pi - 9 \approx 19.3$
(C) $\dfrac{9\pi - 9}{2} \approx 9.6$
(D) $5\pi - 6 \approx 9.7$
(E) $\dfrac{3\pi - 3}{2} \approx 3.2$

this means
$AD = 3$, so
radius = 3.

$A_{whole} = 9\pi \approx 28.3$

We're looking for much less than half of that.

Eliminate (D), because where the heck does 5π come from?

(A) and (E) are too small. (B) is too big. (C) is perfect!

Math hint:

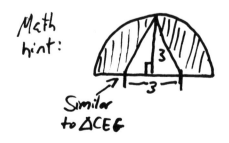

Similar to $\triangle CEG$

9. When Lucy complained to her boss that she was only making $75 per hour while her coworker Steve was making $100 per hour for the same work, her boss gave her a 25% raise. Lucy's hourly wages are now what percent of Steve's?

    (A) 110%
    (B) 100%
    (C) 93.75%
    (D) 75%
    (E) 18.75%

$$75 + \frac{25}{100} \cdot 75 = 93.75$$

That's 93.75% of Steve's wages.

		change
March	$2,000	400
April	$2,400	600
May	$3,000	500
June	$3,500	800
July	$4,300	700
August	$5,000	

14. The table above represents the money Debbie earned, by month, for the last 6 months. When was the percent change in her income the greatest?

    (A) From March to April
    (B) From April to May
    (C) From May to June
    (D) From June to July
    (E) From July to August

(A) $\frac{400}{2000} = 0.20$

(B) $\frac{600}{2400} = 0.25$ ✓

(C) $\frac{500}{3000} = 0.17$

(D) $\frac{800}{3500} = 0.23$

(E) $\frac{700}{4300} = 0.16$

15. What is 500% of 45% of 22% of n?

    (A) $0.0495n$
    (B) $0.099n$
    (C) $0.495n$
    (D) $0.99n$
    (E) $49.5n$

$$\frac{500}{100} \cdot \frac{45}{100} \cdot \frac{22}{100} \cdot n$$

$$= 5 \cdot 0.45 \cdot 0.22 \cdot n$$

$$= 0.495n$$

17. There are 30 more boys than girls in Monroe Township's intramural soccer league. If there are g girls in the league, then, in terms of g, what percent of participants in the league are girls?

Let's Plug in, and be clever about it!

(A) $\dfrac{g}{g+30}$ %

(B) $\dfrac{g}{2(g+30)}$ %

(C) $\dfrac{g}{100(2g-30)}$ %

(D) $\dfrac{100g}{2g+30}$ %

(E) $\dfrac{100g}{g+30}$ %

$g = 35$
$b = 65$
$total = 100$

35% of the league is female

(A) $\dfrac{35}{35+30}$ % $= 0.53$%

(B) $\dfrac{35}{2(35+30)}$ % $= 0.27$%

(C) $\dfrac{35}{100(2(35)-3)}$ % $= 0.00875$%

(D) $\dfrac{100(35)}{2(35)+30}$ % $= 35$% ✓

(E) $\dfrac{100(35)}{35+30}$ % $= 53.85$%

20. Arnold had m marbles before he gave some to Sophia, who had n marbles, in a strange and misguided attempt at flirtation. After the exchange, Arnold and Sophia each had 60 marbles and to their amazement, they realized that Sophia's percent gain in marbles was *exactly twice* Arnold's percent loss! What is the value of m?

Backsolve!

(A) 77
(B) 80
(C) 90
(D) 103
(E) 119

(C) If Arnold started with 90, he gave away 30 and Sophia gained 30.

Arnold's % loss: $\dfrac{30}{90} \times 100$% $= 33.3$%
Sophia's % gain: $\dfrac{30}{30} \times 100$% $= 100$%

Double? Nope. He gave away too many marbles.

(B) If he started with 80, he gave away 20, and Sophia gained 20.

Arnold's % loss: $\dfrac{20}{80} \times 100$% $= 25$%
Sophia's % gain: $\dfrac{20}{40} \times 100$% $= 50$%

Double? Yes! ✓

10. In Ms. Picker's 3rd grade class, the ratio of boys to girls is 7 to 5. If there are 14 boys in the class, then how many students are in the class?

   (A) 10
   (B) 20
   (C) 24
   (D) 25
   (E) 36

$$\frac{7 \ boys}{5 \ girls} \rightarrow \frac{7 \ boys}{12 \ students}$$

$$\frac{7 \ boys}{12 \ students} = \frac{14 \ boys}{x \ students}$$

$$x = 24$$

12. The ratio of pens to pencils in Dore's drawer is 3 to 1. The ratio of sharpened pencils to unsharpened pencils in the drawer is 2 to 1. If there are 18 pens in the drawer, how many pencils in the drawer are sharpened?

   (A) 2
   (B) 4
   (C) 6
   (D) 10
   (E) 15

$$\frac{3 \ pens}{1 \ pencil} = \frac{18 \ pens}{x \ pencils}$$

$$x = 6 \ pencils \ total$$

$$\frac{2 \ sharpened}{1 \ unsharpened} \rightarrow \frac{2 \ sharpened}{3 \ pencils}$$

$$\frac{2 \ sharpened}{3 \ pencils} = \frac{y \ sharpened}{6 \ pencils}$$

$$y = 4$$

13. A certain Witch's Brew recipe calls for $1\frac{1}{2}$ cups werewolf hair and 1 eye of newt, and makes enough brew to curse 2 princesses. If Cheryl, who is a witch, wants to make enough Witch's Brew to curse 7 princesses, how many cups of werewolf hair will she need?

   (A) $5\frac{3}{4}$
   (B) $5\frac{1}{4}$
   (C) 5
   (D) $4\frac{3}{4}$
   (E) $3\frac{3}{4}$

$$\frac{1.5 \ cups}{2 \ princesses} = \frac{x \ cups}{7 \ princesses}$$

$$10.5 = 2x$$

$$5.25 = x$$

16. The ratio of pennies to quarters in Garrett's pocket is 4 to 1. If there are only pennies and quarters in Garrett's pocket, which of the following could be the amount of money in his pocket?

   (A) $0.19
   (B) $0.54
   (C) $1.12
   (D) $1.45
   (E) $1.66

pennies	quarters	total $
4	1	0.29
8	2	0.58
12	3	0.87
16	4	1.16
20	5	1.45 ✓

Shortcut: the correct answer must be a multiple of $0.29.

19. Andy and Sean are in a fantasy baseball league. Last month, the players on Andy's team struck out 7 times for every 2 home runs they hit. In the same month, Sean's players hit 9 home runs for every 5 home runs Andy's players hit. If Andy's players struck out 105 times last month, how many home runs did Sean's players hit over the same span of time?

   (A) 39
   (B) 45
   (C) 49
   (D) 54
   (E) 63

AK = Andy strikeouts
AH = Andy HRs
SH = Sean HRs

$$\frac{7 \, AK}{2 \, AH} \cdot \frac{5 \, AH}{9 \, SH} = \frac{35 \, AK}{18 \, SH}$$

$$\frac{35 \, AK}{18 \, SH} = \frac{105 \, AK}{x \, SH}$$

$$35x = 1890$$
$$x = 54$$

7. If r and s are directly proportional and $r = 18$ when $s = 15$, what is r when $s = 20$?

   (A) 10
   (B) 13.5
   (C) 18
   (D) 20
   (E) 24

$$\frac{r_1}{s_1} = \frac{r_2}{s_2}$$

$$\frac{18}{15} = \frac{r}{20}$$

$$\frac{18}{15} \times 20 = r$$

$$24 = r$$

13. If k is a nonzero constant, which of the following does NOT represent a proportional relationship between x and y?

   (A) $y = x + k$

   (B) $ky = kx$ Simplifies to $y = x$ *

   (C) $\frac{y}{x} = k$ Simplifies to $y = kx$

   (D) $y = k^2 x$ k^2 is still a constant

   (E) $y = \frac{x}{k}$ $\frac{1}{k}$ is still a constant

In (A), the ratio $\frac{x}{y}$ will not always equal the same thing.

* In $y = x$, 1 is the proportionality constant.

17. Which of the following could represent a directly proportional relationship between x and $f(x)$?

   (A) $f(3) = 5, f(5) = 7, f(15) = 17$
   (B) $f(3) = 6, f(5) = 10, f(15) = 30$
   (C) $f(3) = 9, f(5) = 25, f(15) = 225$
   (D) $f(3) = 5, f(5) = 3, f(15) = 1$
   (E) $f(3) = 10, f(5) = 15, f(15) = 40$

Directly proportional means that $\frac{f(x)}{x}$ will always equal the same thing!

(A) $\frac{5}{3} \neq \frac{7}{5}$

(B) $\frac{6}{3} = \frac{10}{5} = \frac{30}{15}$ ✓

(C) $\frac{9}{3} \neq \frac{25}{5}$

(D) $\frac{5}{3} \neq \frac{3}{5}$

(E) $\frac{10}{3} \neq \frac{15}{5}$

18. If y is <u>inversely</u> proportional to z, and $y = 4$ when $z = 6$, which of the following could NOT equal $y + z$?

(A) 8
(B) 11
(C) 14
(D) 25
(E) 48.5

yz will always be the same product.

$4 \times 6 = 24$, so look at other factors of 24!

y	z	yz	$y+z$
4	6	24	10
3	8	24	11
2	12	24	14
1	24	24	25
$\frac{1}{2}$	48	24	48.5

That's (B)–(E), so (A) must be the answer!

For proof, you can graph.

$yz = 24$ $y + z = \boxed{\dfrac{24}{z} + z}$

$y = \dfrac{24}{z}$ This will never equal 8.

19. If m^{-1} is <u>inversely</u> proportional to n^2, and $m = 2$ when $n = 2$, what is m when $n = \sqrt{2}$?

(A) 8
(B) 4
(C) 2
(D) $\sqrt{2}$
(E) 1

$m_1^{-1} n_1^{2} = m_2^{-1} n_2^{2}$

$(2^{-1})(2^2) = m^{-1}(\sqrt{2}^{2})$

$(\tfrac{1}{2})(4) = m^{-1}(2)$

$2 = 2m^{-1}$

$1 = m^{-1}$

$1 = m$

13. How many positive integers less than 1000 are NOT divisible by 9?

    (A) 111
    (B) 782
    (C) 841
    (D) 888
    (E) 900

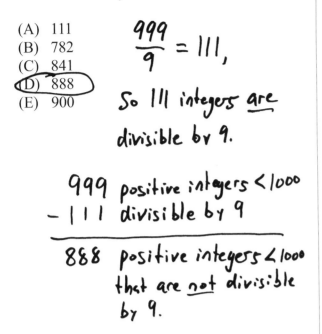

$$\frac{999}{9} = 111,$$

So 111 integers are <u>are</u> divisible by 9.

999 positive integers < 1000
− 111 divisible by 9
——————————
888 positive integers < 1000 that are <u>not</u> divisible by 9.

15. After lunch, 6 friends all shake hands with each other before leaving the restaurant. If nobody shakes hands with anybody else more than once, how many handshakes occurred?

    (A) 10
    (B) 11
    (C) 12
    (D) 14
    (E) 15

Draw + count!

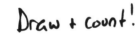

$$5 + 4 + 3 + 2 + 1 = 15$$

17. Alicia is arranging photographs of five family members in a row on her refrigerator. If she wants the photograph of her mother and the photograph of her father to be on opposite ends of the row, how many arrangements for the photographs are possible?

    (A) 120
    (B) 60
    (C) 24
    (D) 21
    (E) 12

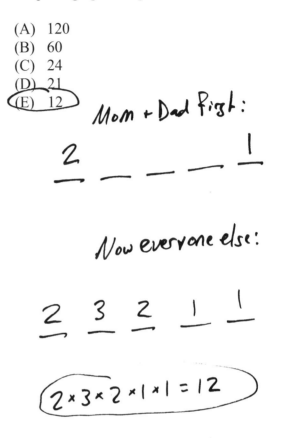

Mom + Dad first:

2 _ _ _ _ 1

Now everyone else:

2 3 2 1 1

$$2 \times 3 \times 2 \times 1 \times 1 = 12$$

18. Alex's favorite restaurant is a buffet-style Chinese restaurant downtown. Each time he goes, he chooses two appetizers and one entree. If the restaurant has four appetizers and five entrees to choose from, how many times could Alex go to the restaurant without choosing the same combination of dishes?

(A) 60
(B) 48
(C) 40
(D) 30
(E) 18

Just start listing and you'll see the pattern

Appetizers   Entrees
A, B, C, D   1, 2, 3, 4, 5

1 A B
1 A C
1 A D   These are all the
1 B C   possible combos for
1 B D   entree #1. There are
1 C D   6 of them. There will
             be 6 for each other
             entree, too.

5 entrees × 6 appetizer combos

= 30 meal possibilities.

19. Brady has ten unique cards in his hand. If he is going to line up four of them in a row on his table, how many arrangements are possible?

(A) 24
(B) 240
(C) 1456
(D) 5040
(E) 6220

How many choices for the 1st card?
    10.
How many choices for the 2nd card?
    9.
For the 3rd?
    8.
For the 4th?
    7. $10 \times 9 \times 8 \times 7 = 5040$

20. How many positive 3-digit integers have a units (ones) digit of 9?

(A) 50
(B) 90
(C) 100
(D) 111
(E) 150

units digit: only 1 choice.
                        1

___ ___ ___

tens digit: 10 choices
            (could be anything)

            10   1

hundreds digit: 9 choices
            (could be anything but 0.
             If it was 0, it
             wouldn't be a 3-digit
             number.)

9   10   1 $9 \times 10 \times 1 = 90$

8, 11, 14, 17, …

10. In the sequence above, each term after the first term is 3 more than the term before it. The 35th term is how much greater than the 29th term?

(A) 12
(B) 15
(C) 16
(D) 18
(E) 21

The actual terms don't matter!

29th term	Start
30th	+3
31st	+3
32nd	+3
33rd	+3
34th	+3
35th	+3
	+18

14. A father decides to set a rule for his 5 children because they're always arguing over the television. Adele gets to decide what to watch on the first night, then Betsy decides what to watch on the second night, Charice decides on the third night, David on the fourth, and Elsie on the fifth. The pattern then begins again. Who gets to decide what to watch on the 38th night after this rule has been set in place?

(A) Adele
(B) Betsy
(C) Charice
(D) David
(E) Elsie

A B C D E ← 5th term
A B C D E ← 10th term
⋮
A B C D E ← 40th term
        ↑
      38th term.

3, –9, 27, …

17. The first term in the sequence above is 3, and every term after the first is –3 times the preceding term. How many terms in the sequence are less than 1000?

(A) 6
(B) 7
(C) 8
(D) 9
(E) More than 9

Uh… a lot more than 9.

Remember that every negative term is less than 1000.

3, 9, 27, 81, …

18. Each term in the sequence above is determined by multiplying the previous term by 3. What will be the units (ones) digit of the 1,000,000,000th term?

(A) 1
(B) 3
(C) 6
(D) 7
(E) 9

Find the pattern in the units digits:

term	value	units digit
1	3	3
2	9	9
3	27	7
4	81	1
5	243	3
6	729	9
7	2187	7
8	6561	1
9	19683	3
⋮	⋮	⋮

The pattern:

3, 9, 7, 1, ← 4th term

3, 9, 7, 1, ← 8th term

⋮

3, 9, 7, 1 ← billionth term

1,000,000,000
is a multiple of 4.

20. Josh goes on a date with Lisette on the first day, Angelique on the second day, Fantasia on the third day, Raquel on the fourth day, Patrice on the fifth day, and Shayla on the sixth day. He begins the patterns again on the seventh day, and repeats it over and over again until he gets hit by a bus. If he was on his way home from a date with Fantasia when he got hit, which of the following could be the number of dates he went on before his accident?

(A) 19
(B) 23
(C) 84
(D) 173
(E) 279

Day	1	2	3	4	5	6	7	8	9
Date	L	A	F	R	P	S	L	A	F

Be careful. The pattern repeats every 6 days, so although F days will always be multiples of 3, not every multiple of 3 will be an F day.

F days will always be 3 days after a multiple of 6. Backsolve:

Ans	-3 days	mult. of 6?
(A) 19	16	no.
(B) 23	20	no.
(C) 84	81	seriously?
(D) 173	170	I hate this.
(E) 279	276	FINALLY! ✓

13. If $45b$ is the square of an integer, which of the following could equal $\dfrac{45}{b}$?

(A) 3
(B) 5
(C) 9
(D) 15
(E) 45

Backsolve!

(C) if $\dfrac{45}{b} = 9$, then $b = 5$.

Is $45(5) = 225$ a perfect square?

$\sqrt{225} = 15$

Yes!

15. If n is a prime number, which of the following COULD NOT be a perfect square?

(A) $13n$
(B) $32n$
(C) $3n^2$
(D) n^4
(E) $49n^6$

(A) could be a perfect square if $n = 13$.

(B) could be a perfect square if $n = 2$.

(D) and (E) will always be perfect squares:

(D) $\sqrt{n^4} = n^2$

(E) $\sqrt{49n^6} = 7n^3$

Remember that n is prime. That means the prime factorization of $3n^2$ will be $3 \times n \times n$. There will never be a partner for that 3.

16. What is the smallest perfect square that is a multiple of both 6 and 10?

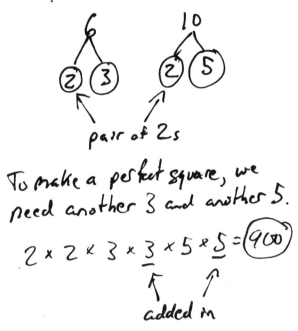

pair of 2s

To make a perfect square, we need another 3 and another 5.

$2 \times 2 \times 3 \times 3 \times 5 \times 5 = 900$

added in

17. What is the smallest multiple of 18 that is the cube of a positive integer?

18

2   9

3   3

$2 \times 3 \times 3 = 18$

We need two additional 2s and one additional 3 for a perfect cube.

$2 \times \underline{2} \times \underline{2} \times 3 \times 3 \times \underline{3} = \boxed{216}$

added in

Remember: prime factors of perfect cubes come in groups of three!

18. If n is a factor of 5445 and $\sqrt{n}$ is an integer, what is the greatest possible value of n?

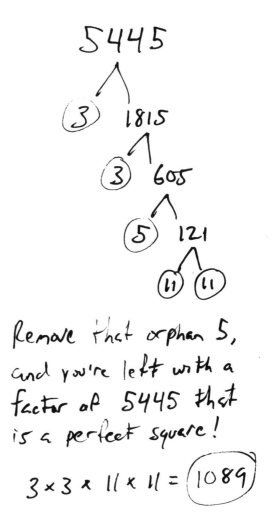

5445

3   1815

3   605

5   121

11   11

Remove that orphan 5, and you're left with a factor of 5445 that is a perfect square!

$3 \times 3 \times 11 \times 11 = \boxed{1089}$

13. If $3x + 7y = 22$ and $2x + 6y = 12$, what is $13x + 13y$?

(A) 34
(B) 58
(C) 72
(D) 130
(E) 156

$$3x + 7y = 22$$
$$-(2x + 6y = 12)$$
$$\overline{\qquad x + y = 10 \qquad}$$

$$13(x + y) = 13(10)$$

$$13x + 13y = 130$$

15. If $p^2 - r^2 = 18$ and $p - r = 2$, what is $p + r$?

(A) 5
(B) 9
(C) 13
(D) 16
(E) 18

pieces of the same puzzle.

$$p^2 - r^2 = 18$$
$$(p+r)(p-r) = 18$$
$$(p+r)(2) = 18$$
↖ substitute!

$$p + r = 9$$

16. If $a + b = -8$ and $a^2 + b^2 = 50$, what is ab?

(A) 14
(B) 10
(C) 9
(D) 8
(E) 7

puzzle pieces

$$a + b = -8$$
$$(a+b)^2 = (-8)^2$$
$$a^2 + 2ab + b^2 = 64$$
$$a^2 + b^2 + 2ab = 64 \text{ (rearrange)}$$
$$50 + 2ab = 64 \text{ (substitute)}$$
$$2ab = 14$$
$$ab = 7$$

$$x + 2y - 3z = 92$$
$$2x - y + z = 36$$
$$4x - y + 2z = 12$$

19. Based on the system of equations above, what is the value of x?

   (A) 11
   (B) 20
   (C) −40
   (D) −42
   (E) It cannot be determined from the information given.

Add 'em up!

$$x + 2y - 3z = 92$$
$$2x - y + z = 36$$
$$+ \ 4x - y + 2z = 12$$
$$\overline{7x + 0 + 0 = 140}$$

$$7x = 140$$
$$x = 20$$

20. If $x + y = m$ and $x - y = n$, then what is $x^2 + y^2$, in terms of m and n?

   (A) mn

   (B) $\dfrac{m^2 + n^2}{2}$

   (C) $(m - n)^2$

   (D) $(m + n)^2$

   (E) $\dfrac{m^2 - n^2}{2}$

Plug in! $x = 3, y = 2$
$\therefore m = 5, n = 1$
$x^2 + y^2 = 3^2 + 2^2 = 13$

(A) $(5)(1) = 5$
(B) $\dfrac{5^2 + 1^2}{2} = 13 \checkmark$
(C) $(5 - 1)^2 = 16$
(D) $(5 + 1)^2 = 36$
(E) $\dfrac{5^2 - 1^2}{2} = 12$

If you crazily crave algebra:

$$x + y = m$$
$$x - y = n$$
$$(x + y)^2 = m^2$$
$$(x - y)^2 = n^2$$
$$x^2 + 2xy + y^2 = m^2$$
$$+ \ x^2 - 2xy + y^2 = n^2$$
$$\overline{2x^2 + 0 + 2y^2 = m^2 + n^2}$$
$$2(x^2 + y^2) = m^2 + n^2$$
$$x^2 + y^2 = \dfrac{m^2 + n^2}{2}$$

$$\frac{x^4 x^6}{x^8} = 81$$

10. According to the equation above, which of the following could equal x^2?

(A) 81
(B) 72
(C) 18
(D) 9
(E) 3

read carefully!

$$\frac{x^4 x^6}{x^8} = 81$$

$$\frac{x^{10}}{x^8} = 81$$

$$x^2 = 81$$

13. If $x^6 = 60$ and $w^{10} = 20$, what is $x^{12} w^{-10}$?

(A) 36
(B) 60
(C) 120
(D) 180
(E) 360

$$x^{12} w^{-10}$$

$$= (x^6)^2 \cdot \frac{1}{w^{10}}$$

$$= 60^2 \cdot \frac{1}{20} \quad (\text{substitute})$$

$$= \frac{3600}{20}$$

$$= 180$$

14. If $a^2 = b$, what is a^4 in terms of b?

(A) $2b$
(B) $b + 2$
(C) $2b + 2$
(D) b^2
(E) $4b$

$$a^4 = (a^2)^2$$

$$a^4 = b^2 \quad (\text{substitute})$$

Plugging in works, too.

$$a = 3$$
$$\therefore b = 9$$
$$3^4 = 81$$
$$81 = 9^2 = b^2$$

If you plug in 2 for a, b will equal 4 and choice (E) will also work. If that happens, don't panic! Just pick a new number.

17. If z, p, and q are each positive integers, which of the following is equivalent to z^q?

(A) $z^{pq} - z^p$

(B) $\sqrt[q]{z^{2q}}$

(C) $\dfrac{z^{pq}}{z^p}$

(D) $\dfrac{z^p}{z^{p-q}}$

(E) $2z^{\frac{q}{2}}$

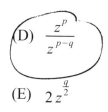

Simplify them all.

(A) doesn't really simplify

(B) $\sqrt[q]{z^{2q}} = \left(z^{2q}\right)^{\frac{1}{q}} = z^{\frac{2q}{q}} = z^2$

(C) $\dfrac{z^{pq}}{z^p} = z^{pq-p} = z^{p(q-1)}$

(D) $\dfrac{z^p}{z^{p-q}} = z^{p-(p-q)} = z^q$ ✓

(E) $2z^{\frac{q}{2}} = 2\sqrt{z^q}$

18. If $(m+n)^2 = m^2 + n^2$, what is $(3^m)^n$?

$(3^m)^n = 3^{mn}$

$(m+n)^2 = m^2 + n^2$

$m^2 + 2mn + n^2 = m^2 + n^2$

$\cancel{m^2} + \cancel{n^2} + 2mn = \cancel{m^2} + \cancel{n^2}$

$2mn = 0$

$mn = 0$

3^{mn}

$= 3^0$

$\boxed{= 1}$

12. If $f(x) = 2x - 1$, what is $f(10) - f(5)$?

    (A) 5
    (B) 9
    (C) 10
    (D) 11
    (E) 19

$f(10) = 2(10) - 1 = 19$
$f(5) = 2(5) - 1 = 9$

$19 - 9 = 10$

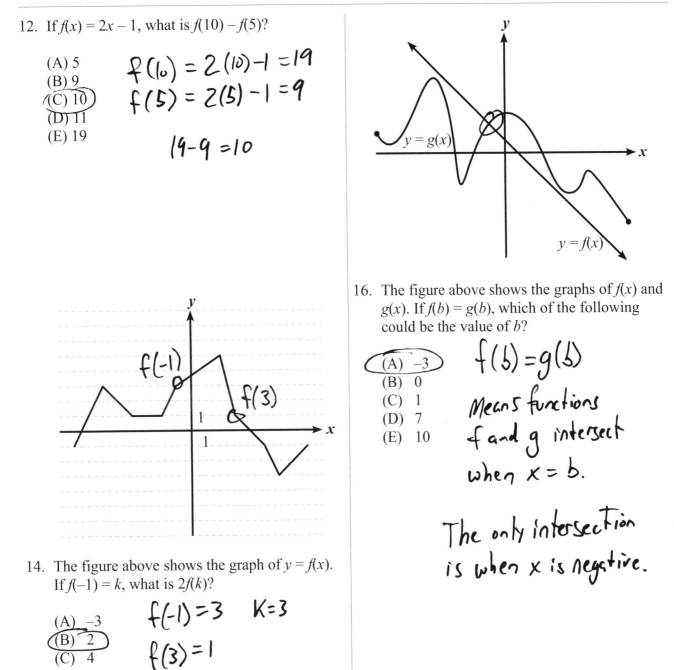

16. The figure above shows the graphs of $f(x)$ and $g(x)$. If $f(b) = g(b)$, which of the following could be the value of b?

    (A) −3
    (B) 0
    (C) 1
    (D) 7
    (E) 10

$f(b) = g(b)$

Means functions f and g intersect when $x = b$.

The only intersection is when x is negative.

14. The figure above shows the graph of $y = f(x)$. If $f(-1) = k$, what is $2f(k)$?

    (A) −3
    (B) 2
    (C) 4
    (D) 6
    (E) 8

$f(-1) = 3$ $K = 3$

$f(3) = 1$

$2f(3) = 2(1) = 2$

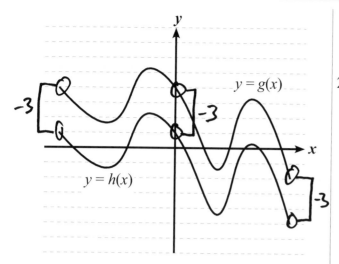

x	1	3	5	7	9
$g(x)$	-2	15	6	-3	-10

20. The table above gives values of the function g for selected values of x. If $f(x) = |g(x)|$, and $f(7) = t$, what is $f(t)$?

(A) -2
(B) 15
(C) 6
(D) -3
(E) -10

$f(7) = |g(7)|$

$g(7) = -3$

$|g(7)| = 3$

$t = 3$

$f(3) = |g(3)|$

$g(3) = 15$

$|g(3)| = 15$

18. The figure above shows the graphs of $y = g(x)$ and $y = h(x)$. Which of the following could be an expression of $h(x)$ in terms of $g(x)$?

(A) $h(x) = g(x + 3)$
(B) $h(x) = g(x - 3)$
(C) $h(x) = g(x) + 3$
(D) $h(x) = g(x - 1) - 2$
(E) $h(x) = g(x) - 3$

$h(x)$ is always 3 less than $g(x)$.

15. For all integers x, let $\diamond x = x^{x+2}$. What is $\diamond 4$?

(A) 16
(B) 64
(C) 256
(D) 4096
(E) 65536

$$\diamond 4 = 4^{4+2}$$
$$= 4^6$$
$$= 4096$$

16. For all integers r and s, let $r \, \text{\textbird} \, s$ be defined as $r \, \text{\textbird} \, s = 4r + 7s$. If $3 \, \text{\textbird} \, p = 33$, which of the following is equal to p?

(A) $3 \, \text{\textbird} \, 21$
(B) $3 \, \text{\textbird} \, 3$
(C) $(-1) \, \text{\textbird} \, 1$
(D) $1 \, \text{\textbird} \, 3$
(E) $7 \, \text{\textbird} \, 4$

$$3 \, \text{\textbird} \, p = 33$$
$$4(3) + 7p = 33$$
$$12 + 7p = 33$$
$$7p = 21$$
$$p = 3$$

$$(c)(-1) \, \text{\textbird} \, 1$$
$$= 4(-1) + 7(1)$$
$$= -4 + 7$$
$$= 3 \quad \text{yes!}$$

18. If $\ominus 3 = 24$ and $\ominus 5 = 38$, which of the following could be the definition of $\ominus x$ for all positive integers x?

(A) $\ominus x = 8x$
(B) $\ominus x = 8x - 2$
(C) $\ominus x = x^2 + 13$
(D) $\ominus x = 7x + 3$
(E) $\ominus x = 10x - 6$

The right answer will work with both:

$\ominus x$	$\ominus 3 = 24$	$\ominus 5 = 38$
(A) $8x$	$8(3) = \underline{24}$	$8(5) = \cancel{40}$
(B) $8x-2$	$8(3)-2 = \cancel{22}$	Don't bother
(C) x^2+13	$3^2+13 = \cancel{22}$	Don't bother
(D) $7x+3$	$7(3)+3 = \underline{24}$	$7(5)+3 = \underline{38}$

yes!

19. Let the ⌐ symbol be defined such that b⌐ equals the sum of the greatest two factors of b. For example, the greatest two factors of 8 are 4 and 8, so 8⌐ $= 4 + 8 = 12$. Which of the following has the greatest value?

(A) 46⌐
(B) 49⌐
(C) 50⌐
(D) 53⌐
(E) 55⌐

(A) 46⌐ $= 23 + 46 = 69$

(B) 49⌐ $= 7 + 49 = 56$

(C) 50⌐ $= 25 + 50 = \boxed{75}$

(D) 53⌐ $= 1 + 53 = 54$

(E) 55⌐ $= 11 + 55 = 66$

Shortcut: Since the answers are so close, the correct one will be the greatest even number.

20. For all integers m, let ♣m be defined to be $m^2 + 10$. Which of the following equals ♣(♣2)?

(A) ♣10
(B) 2(♣10) − 14
(C) (♣4) + 200
(D) ♣196
(E) ♣206 ← Don't you dare.

♣(♣2)

$= ♣(2^2 + 10)$

$= ♣14$

$= 14^2 + 10$

$= 196 + 10$

$= 206$

(A) $10^2 + 10 = 110$

(B) $2(10^2 + 10) - 14$
$= 2(110) - 14$
$= 220 - 14$
$= 206$ ✓

306

6. What is the *x*-intercept of $y = 5x - 20$?

    (A) −20
    (B) −4
    (C) 4
    (D) 5
    (E) 15

    At the x-intercept,

    $y = 0$.

    $0 = 5x - 20$

    $20 = 5x$

    $4 = x$

    Or just graph it on your fancy calculator!

10. Which of the following is the equation of a line that is perpendicular to $y + 3 = 3x - 8$?

    (A) $3y + x = 26$
    (B) $3y - 3x = -8$
    (C) $9y - 6x = 18$
    (D) $y + 3x = 9$
    (E) $y - 3x = 10$

    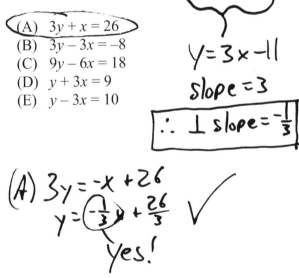

    $y = 3x - 11$

    slope = 3

    $\therefore \perp \text{ slope} = -\frac{1}{3}$

    (A) $3y = -x + 26$

    $y = \left(-\frac{1}{3}\right)x + \frac{26}{3}$ ✓

    Yes!

14. If a line has a slope of −2 and it passes through the point (−3, 2), what is its *y*-intercept?

    (A) 8
    (B) 6
    (C) 0
    (D) −4
    (E) −6

    $\frac{rise}{run} = \frac{-2}{1}$

    Just draw and count!

    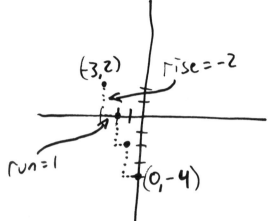

16. Which of the following sets of points forms a line that is parallel to $3y = 2x + 11$?

(A) $(-1, 3)$ and $(3, -1)$
(B) $(12, 4)$ and $(3, -2)$
(C) $(6, 2)$ and $(8, 5)$
(D) $(11, 2)$ and $(11, 3)$
(E) $(7, 4)$ and $(5, 7)$

$y = \dfrac{2}{3}x + \dfrac{11}{3}$

$Slope = \dfrac{2}{3}$

parallel line will have the same slope!

(A) $\dfrac{3 - (-1)}{-1 - 3} = \dfrac{4}{-4} = -1$

(B) $\dfrac{4 - (-2)}{12 - 3} = \dfrac{6}{9} = \dfrac{2}{3}$ ✓

19. Line l has the equation $y = 3x + c$ and line m has the equation $4y - 3x = 11 - d$, for some constants c and d. If lines l and m intersect at $(-3, -2)$, what is the sum of c and d?

(A) -3
(B) -7
(C) 7
(D) 10
(E) 17

Intersection means $(-3, -2)$ is on both lines! So put the point into both equations.

line l: $y = 3x + c$
$-2 = 3(-3) + c$
$-2 = -9 + c$
$7 = c$

line m: $4y - 3x = 11 - d$
$4(-2) - 3(-3) = 11 - d$
$-8 + 9 = 11 - d$
$1 = 11 - d$
$-10 = -d$
$10 = d$

$c + d = 7 + 10 = 17$

Solutions: Parabolas

$$g(x) = -6x^2 + 3x$$

15. Which of the following is true about the graph of the function *g* defined above?

    Graph it! ✓

    I.   It passes through the origin. ✓
    II. It is increasing from $x = 1$ to $x = 6$.
    III. $g(-6)$ is negative. ✓

    (A) I only
    (B) II only
    (C) III only
    (D) I and III only
    (E) I, II, and III

    If you can't graph:

    I. $g(0) = -6(0)^2 + 3(0)$
        $g(0) = 0$ ✓

    II. $g(1) = -6(1)^2 + 3(1)$
        $= -3$ ← *not increasing*
        $g(6) = -6(6)^2 + 3(6)$
        $= -198$ ←

    III. $g(-6) = -6(-6)^2 + 3(-6) = -234$ ✓

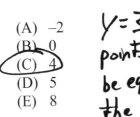

negative x-intercept

16. The parabola in the figure above has its minimum at $x = 2$. Which of the following could be an *x*-intercept of the parabola?

    (A) 2.5
    (B) 3
    (C) 3.5
    (D) 4
    (E) 4.5

    Since the x-intercept on the left is negative, the x-intercepts are more than 2 units away from the line of symmetry.
    Only 4.5 is more than 2 away from 2.

17. If a parabola passes through the points $(0, 3)$ and $(8, 3)$, and has its minimum at $(p, -2)$, what is *p*?

    (A) −2
    (B) 0
    (C) 4
    (D) 5
    (E) 8

    y = 3 at both points, so they must be equidistant from the line of symmetry.

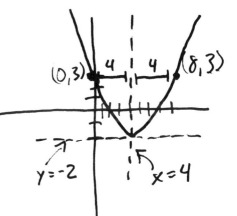

$y = -2$ $x = 4$

18. If a and b are constants, and the graph of $g(x) = (x - a)^2 + b$ has its minimum at $g(6)$, which of the following pairs of points could also be on the graph of $g(x)$?

(A) $(5, -9)$ and $(8, -9)$
(B) $(0, 6)$ and $(10, 10)$
(C) $(5, 6)$ and $(7, 8)$
(D) $(2, -5)$ and $(10, -5)$
(E) $(-2, 0)$ and $(14, 2)$

points must have the same
Y-value, and x-values
equidistant from the line
of symmetry at $x = 6$.

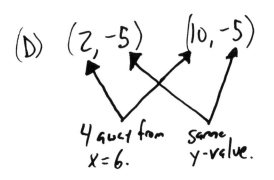

(D) $(2, -5)$ $(10, -5)$

4 away from   same
$x = 6$. y-value.

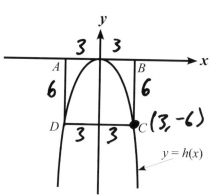

Note: Figure not drawn to scale.

20. In the figure above, $ABCD$ is a square that intersects the graph of $h(x)$ at points C and D. A and B lie on the x-axis. If the area of $ABCD$ is 36 and $h(x) = kx^2$, what is k?

(A) 3
(B) $\frac{1}{3}$
(C) $-\frac{1}{6}$
(D) $-\frac{1}{3}$
(E) $-\frac{2}{3}$

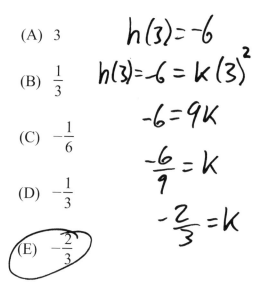

$h(3) = -6$
$h(3) = -6 = k(3)^2$
$-6 = 9k$
$\frac{-6}{9} = k$
$-\frac{2}{3} = k$

13. If $|a| + |b| = 7$ and a and b are integers, which of the following could NOT equal $a + b$?

(A) 7 $3 + 4$
(B) 5 $-1 + 6$
(C) 0
(D) -3 $-5 + 2$
(E) -7 $-7 + 0$

Shortcut: To make an odd number like 7, you need to add an even and an odd number. You can not make an even number like 0 that way.

14. If $h(x) = 2x - 10$, which of the following is NOT true?

(A) $h(3) < |h(3)|$
(B) $h(1) = |h(1)|$
(C) $h(10) = |h(10)|$
(D) $h(10) = |h(0)|$
(E) $-h(10) = h(0)$

(A) $2(3) - 10 < |2(3) - 10|$
    $-4 < 4$ True.

(B) $2(1) - 10 = |2(1) - 10|$
    $-8 = 8$ FALSE.

(C) $2(10) - 10 = |2(10) - 10|$
    $10 = 10$ True.

(D) $2(10) - 10 = |2(0) - 10|$
    $10 = |-10|$
    $10 = 10$ True.

(E) $-(2(10) - 10) = 2(0) - 10$
    $-10 = -10$ True.

17. All the bowlers on Robbie's bowling team, Strike Force, have average scores between 215 and 251. Which of the following inequalities can be used to determine whether a bowler with an average score of s could be on the team?

(A) $|s - 233| < 36$
(B) $|s - 251| < 215$
(C) $|s - 18| < 233$
(D) $|s - 233| < 18$
(E) $|s - 223| < 18$

Middle of range $= \dfrac{215 + 251}{2} = \underline{233}$

Distance to ends $= 251 - 233 = \underline{18}$

Confirm (D):

$|s - 233| < 18$

$-18 < s - 233 < 18$
$+233 \quad +233 \quad +233$

$215 < s < 251$ ✓

(You could also do some careful plugging in.)

x	$g(x)$
3	−3
5	8
9	12
13	−11
17	15

18. The table above shows a few values for the function g. According to the table, which of the following statements is NOT true?

    (A) $|g(3)| = 3$
    (B) $|g(5)| > g(5)$
    (C) $g(17) - g(9) = |g(3)|$
    (D) $|g(13)| < g(9)$
    (E) $|g(17)| = g(17)$

(A) $|g(3)| = 3$
$$|-3| = 3 \quad \text{True.}$$

(B) $|g(5)| > g(5)$
$$|8| > 8 \quad \text{FALSE.}$$

(C) $g(17) - g(9) = |g(3)|$
$$15 - 12 = |-3|$$
$$3 = 3 \quad \text{True.}$$

(D) $|g(13)| < g(9)$
$$|-11| < 12 \quad \text{True.}$$

(E) $|g(17)| = g(17)$
$$|15| = 15 \quad \text{True.}$$

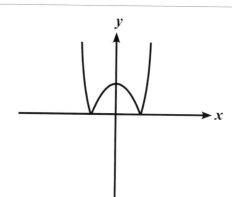

19. Which of the following could be the equation of the graph above?

    (A) $y = |-x^2 + 4|$
    (B) $y = |x^2| - 4$
    (C) $y = |x^2 + 4|$
    (D) $y = -|x^2 - 4|$
    (E) $y = |-x^2 - 4|$

If you can, use your calculator to graph these.

If you can't graph, note that there are two different parabolas that could produce the graph above:

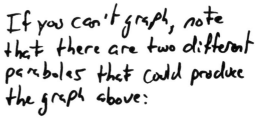

Choice (A) is the absolute value of the second one.

10. If $(a + b)x^3 = cx^3$ for all values of x, which of the following must be true about constants a, b, and c?

(A) $b - a = c$
(B) $a - b = c$
(C) $b - c = a$
(D) $a - c = b$
(E) $c - a = b$

$$a + b = c$$
$$-a \qquad -a$$
$$\overline{\qquad\qquad}$$
$$b = c - a$$

Plugging in works nicely here, too! Say $a = 2$, $b = 3$, $c = 5$. Only (E) is true!

$$(x - 5)(x - 7) = x^2 + mx + n$$

13. The equation above is true for all values of x; m and n are constants. Which of the following equals $n - m$?

(A) 2
(B) 12
(C) 23
(D) 30
(E) 47

$$(x - 5)(x - 7)$$
$$= x^2 - 12x + 35$$

$$x^2 - 12x + 35$$
$$= x^2 + mx + n$$

$$m = -12$$
$$n = 35$$

$$n - m = 35 - (-12) = 47$$

$$ax^2 - bx + c = rx^2 + sx + t$$

16. If the equation above is true for all values of x, and a, b, c, r, s, and t are nonzero constants, which of the following is FALSE?

(A) $b = s$
(B) $c = t$
(C) $b^2 = s^2$
(D) $a + c = r + t$
(E) $a + b = r - s$

you know $\begin{cases} a = r \\ -b = s \\ c = t \end{cases}$

So, plug in!

$$a = 2 \qquad r = 2$$
$$b = 3 \qquad s = -3$$
$$c = 4 \qquad t = 4$$

(A) is false: $3 \neq -3$

(B) is true: $4 = 4$

(C) is true: $3^2 = (-3)^2$

(D) is true: $2 + 4 = 2 + 4$

(E) is true: $2 + 3 = 2 - (-3)$

$(x - 3)(x - d) = x^2 - 2dx + m$

17. In the equation above, d and m are constants. If the equation is true for all values of x, what is the value of dm?

$(x-3)(x-d)$
$= x^2 - 3x - dx + 3d$
$= x^2 - (3+d)x + 3d$

$x^2 - (3+d)x + 3d$
$= x^2 - 2dx + m$

$-(3+d) = -2d$
$3 + d = 2d$
$3 = d$

$3d = m$
$3(3) = m$
$9 = m$

$dm = (3)(9) = 27$

18. If a and b are positive integer constants, and $x^2 + ax + bx + 40$ is equivalent to $(x + 8)(x + 5)$, what is the greatest possible value of a?

$(x + 8)(x + 5)$
$= x^2 + 13x + 40$

$x^2 + 13x + 40$
$= x^2 + (a+b)x + 40$

$13 = a + b$

a and b are positive integers so the greatest possible value of a is 12.

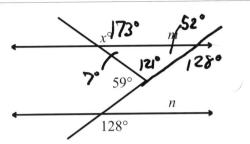

Note: Figure not drawn to scale.

13. In the figure above, m ∥ n. What is x?

(A) 128
(B) 159
(C) 167
(D) 171
(E) 173

Wouldn't a Transversal be convenient?

MAKE ONE.

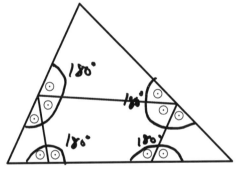

16. What is the sum of the measures of the marked (⊙) angles in the figure above?

(A) 360°
(B) 720°
(C) 900°
(D) 1080°
(E) 1200°

$4 \times 180° = 720°$

You could also plug in.

17. If △RST is isosceles, RS = 9, and RT and ST are integers, then which of the following is NOT a possible perimeter of △RST?

(A) 15
(B) 19
(C) 22
(D) 33
(E) 69

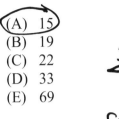

Sadness gap.

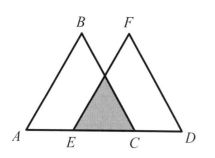

Note: Figure not drawn to scale.

18. In the figure above, $\triangle ABC$ and $\triangle DEF$ are congruent equilateral triangles. If E is the midpoint of $\overline{AC}$, and $AB = 14$, what is the perimeter of the shaded region?

(A) 7

(B) 14

(C) 21

(D) 28

(E) $\dfrac{49\sqrt{3}}{2}$

Because $\triangle ABC$ and $\triangle DEF$ are equilateral, all their angles measure 60°. That makes 2 of the angles in the shaded $\triangle$ 60°. Foo, so it is also equilateral.

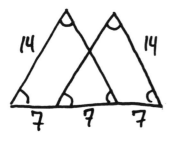

20. In $\triangle PQR$, $PQ > PR$. Which of the following MUST be true?

    I. $PQ - QR < PR$
    II. The measure of $\angle PRQ$ is greater than the measure of $\angle PQR$
    III. $2PR > PQ$

(A) I only
(B) II only
(C) III only
(D) I and II only
(E) II and III only

Who writes a question like this? A jerk, that's who.

I. $\triangle$ inequality theorem says:

$$PQ < PR + QR$$
$$\underline{\;-QR \qquad\quad -QR\;}$$
$$PQ - QR < PR \;\checkmark$$

II. $PQ > PR$

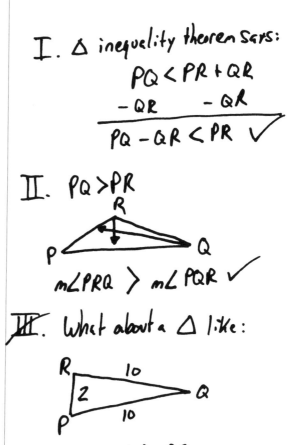

$m\angle PRQ > m\angle PQR \;\checkmark$

III. What about a $\triangle$ like:

$2PR$ is not $> PQ$.

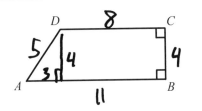

Note: Figure not drawn to scale.

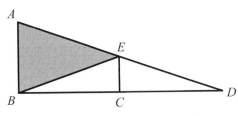

Note: Figure not drawn to scale.

12. In the figure above, $AB = 11$, $AD = 5$, and $DC = 8$. What is the perimeter of quadrilateral $ABCD$?

(A) 24
(B) 28
(C) 29
(D) 30
(E) 33

Can you spot the 3-4-5?

$5 + 8 + 11 + 4 = 28$

15. In the figure above, $\overline{AB} \perp \overline{BD}$, $\overline{EC} \perp \overline{BD}$ and $\overline{EC}$ bisects both $\overline{BD}$ and $\overline{AD}$. If $ED = 13$ and $EC = 5$, what is the area of the shaded region?

(A) 120
(B) 90
(C) 60
(D) 40
(E) 12

Know your triples!

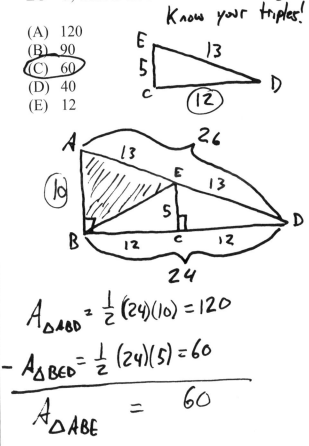

$A_{\triangle ABD} = \frac{1}{2}(24)(10) = 120$

$- A_{\triangle BED} = \frac{1}{2}(24)(5) = 60$

$A_{\triangle ABE} = 60$

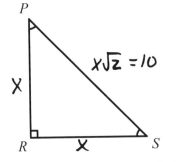

13. In the figure above, $\angle RPS$ and $\angle RSP$ each measure $45°$. If $PS = 10$, what is RS?

(A) $5\sqrt{2}$
(B) $5\sqrt{3}$
(C) 7
(D) 10
(E) $10\sqrt{2}$

Know your 45°-45°-90° side ratios!

$10 = x\sqrt{2}$, what is x?

$\frac{10}{\sqrt{2}} = x$

rationalize $\rightarrow$ denominator $\frac{10\sqrt{2}}{\sqrt{2}\sqrt{2}} = \frac{10\sqrt{2}}{2} = 5\sqrt{2}$

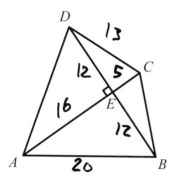

Note: Figure not drawn to scale.

17. In the figure above, point E is the midpoint of $\overline{BD}$. If $CD = 13$, $BD = 24$, and $AC = 21$, what is AB?

(A) $13\sqrt{2}$
(B) $10\sqrt{5}$
(C) 20
(D) 21
(E) 22

Know your triples!

$\triangle CDE$ is a 5-12-13

Since $AC = 21$ and
$CE = 5$, $AE = 16$

$\triangle ABE$ is a 12-16-20

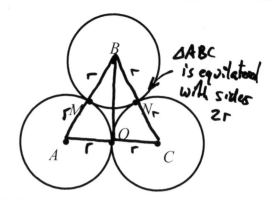

$\triangle ABC$ is equilateral with sides $2r$

20. In the figure above, three congruent circles with centers A, B, and C are tangent to each other at M, N, and O. If $BO = 18$, what is the area of one of the circles?

(A) $18\pi\sqrt{3}$
(B) $36\pi\sqrt{2}$
(C) 72π
(D) 81π
(E) 108π

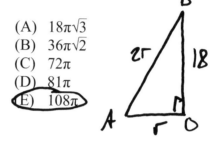

$r^2 + 18^2 = (2r)^2$
$r^2 + 324 = 4r^2$
$324 = 3r^2$
$108 = r^2$

$A_{circle} = \pi r^2$
$\quad = \boxed{108\pi}$

Note: $\triangle ABO$ is also a $30°$-$60°$-$90°$,
So $r = \dfrac{18}{\sqrt{3}}$.

16. If a circle is divided evenly into 12 arcs, each measuring 3 cm long, what is the degree measure of an arc on the same circle that measures 8 cm long?

(A) 64°
(B) 72°
(C) 80°
(D) 96°
(E) 112°

$\underline{Circumference}$

12 arcs × 3cm = 36cm

$$\frac{8cm}{36cm} = \frac{x°}{360°}$$

$$x = 80$$

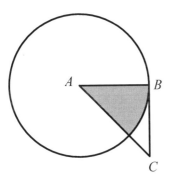

17. In the figure above, A is the center of the circle, $\overline{BC}$ is tangent to the circle at B, and $AB = BC$. If $AC = 8$, what is the area of the shaded region?

(A) 4π
(B) 8π
(C) 10π
(D) 16π
(E) 24π

∴ m∠ABC = 90°

∴ ΔABC is 45°-45°-90°

Hypotenuse = 8, So

legs = $\frac{8}{\sqrt{2}}$

radius = $AB = \frac{8}{\sqrt{2}}$

$\underline{Area\ of\ \bigcirc}$

$$\pi\left(\frac{8}{\sqrt{2}}\right)^2 = 32\pi$$

$$\frac{45°}{360°} = \frac{x}{32\pi}$$

$$4\pi = x$$

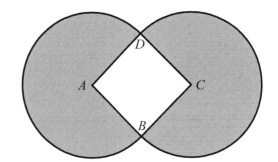

18. In the figure above, $ABCD$ is a square, and A and C are the centers of the circles. If $AB = 2$, what is the total area of the shaded regions?

(A) 3π
(B) 6π
(C) 8π
(D) 8π − 4
(E) 9π − 4

m∠BAD = 90°

m∠BCD = 90°

So you have 270° of each circle shaded.

$\underline{Area\ of\ one\ whole\ circle}$

$$r = 2, \quad A = 4\pi$$

$\underline{Shaded\ region\ of\ one\ circle}$

$$\frac{270°}{360°} = \frac{x}{4\pi}$$

$$3\pi = x$$

You have 2 of them, though. So the answer is $\boxed{6\pi}$.

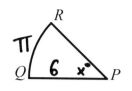

Note: Figure not drawn to scale.

19. In the figure above, P is the center of a circle, and Q and R lie on the circle. If the length of arc QR is π and $PQ = 6$, what is the measure of $\angle RPQ$?

(A) 15°
(B) 20°
(C) 30°
(D) 45°
(E) 80°

find the circumference:

$r = 6, \quad C = 12\pi$

$$\frac{\pi}{12\pi} = \frac{x^\circ}{360^\circ}$$

$$30^\circ = x^\circ$$

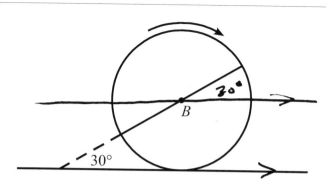

20. In the figure above, a wheel with center B and a radius of 12 cm is resting on a flat surface. A diameter is painted on the wheel as shown. If the wheel begins to rotate in a clockwise direction and rolls along the surface without slipping, how far will B travel before the painted diameter is perpendicular to the surface for the first time?

(A) 2π cm
(B) 4π cm
(C) 8π cm
(D) 12π cm
(E) 16π cm

∴ Circumference = 24π

The wheel must rotate 30° to get to where the diameter is || to the surface. Then, it must rotate 90° more to make the diameter ⊥. That's 120° in total, or $\frac{1}{3}$ of a revolution.

That means B travels $\frac{1}{3}$ of a circumference.

$$\left(\frac{1}{3}\right) 24\pi = 8\pi$$

P W N t h e S A T

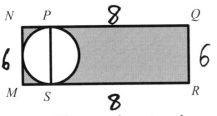

Note: Figure not drawn to scale.

10. In the figure above, a circle with diameter $\overline{PS}$ is tangent to rectangle $MNQR$ on three sides. If $MN = 6$ and $MR = 8$, what is the total area of the shaded regions?

(A) $14 + \pi$
(B) $20 + 3\pi$
(C) $40 - \pi$
(D) $48 - 6\pi$
(E) $48 - 9\pi$

Diameter = 6

∴ r = 3, $A_{circle} = 9\pi$

$A_{whole} = 6 \times 8 = 48$
$- A_{unshaded} = 9\pi$
_____
$A_{shaded} = 48 - 9\pi$

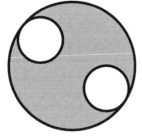

Note: Figure not drawn to scale.
(I'll say...)

11. In the figure above, the smaller circles both have a radius of 3 and are tangent to the larger circle. If the larger circle has a radius of 7, what is the area of the shaded region?

(A) 18π
(B) 31π
(C) 40π
(D) 49π
(E) 64π

$A_{whole} = 49\pi$

$- A_{unshaded} = 2(9\pi)$
_____
$A_{shaded} = 31\pi$

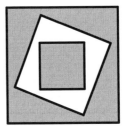

13. In the figure above, three squares have sides of length 6, 10, and 15. What is the total area of the shaded regions?

(A) 289
(B) 225
(C) 189
(D) 161
(E) 89

Slight Modification:

$A_{big} = 15^2 = 225$

$- A_{medium} = 10^2 = 100$
$+ A_{small} = 6^2 = 36$
_____
$A_{shaded} = 161$

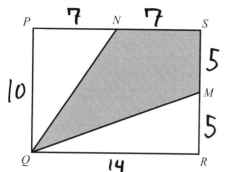

16. In the figure above, *PQRS* is a rectangle, *M* is the midpoint of $\overline{SR}$, and *N* is the midpoint of $\overline{PS}$. If $NS + SM = 12$ and $QR = 14$, what is the area of the shaded region?

(A) 35
(B) 45
(C) 70
(D) 85
(E) 115

Gotta do some figuring:

$$QR = 14$$
$$\therefore PS = 14$$
$$\therefore PN = 7, \; NS = 7$$
$$\therefore SM = 5$$
$$\therefore MR = 5$$
$$\therefore PQ = 10$$

Phew!

$$A_{whole} = 10 \times 14 = 140$$

$$A_{unshaded} = \frac{1}{2}(14)(5) + \frac{1}{2}(10)(7)$$
$$= 35 + 35$$
$$= 70$$

$$A_{whole} - A_{unshaded} = A_{shaded}$$
$$140 - 70 \quad = 70$$

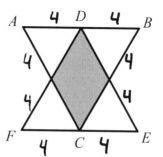

20. In the figure above, $\triangle ABC$ and $\triangle DEF$ are both equilateral triangles with perimeters of 24, and $\overline{AB} \parallel \overline{EF}$. If $\overline{DC}$ (not shown) bisects both $\overline{AB}$ and $\overline{EF}$, what is the area of the shaded region?

(A) $32\sqrt{3} - 4$
(B) $28\sqrt{3}$
(C) $16\sqrt{3}$
(D) $8\sqrt{3}$
(E) $4\sqrt{3}$

$\triangle ABC$ and $\triangle DEF$ are equilateral, so all their angles measure 60°.

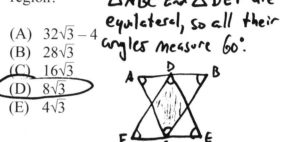

Because $\overline{AB} \parallel \overline{EF}$, there are 4 alternate interior angle pairs that are congruent and also 60°.

From this you know that all the small $\triangle$s are equilateral. Because D and C are midpoints, you know all the small $\triangle$s have sides of 4.

Small $\triangle$:
(30°-60°-90°)

$$A = \frac{1}{2}(4)(2\sqrt{3})$$
$$= 4\sqrt{3}$$

The last trick is to recognize that the shaded region is made up of 2 small $\triangle$s, so $A_{shaded} = 8\sqrt{3}$

13. What is the surface area of a cube with a volume of 27?

(A) 54
(B) 36
(C) 27
(D) 18
(E) 9

$$Volume = s^3$$

$$27 = s^3 \quad (s = \text{edge length})$$

$$3 = s$$

$$Area \text{ of one face} = s^2$$
$$= 3^2$$
$$= 9$$

6 faces: $6 \times 9 = 54$

17. John is a weird kid who likes math and plays with bugs. He is holding a cylindrical cardboard tube in his hand, and two ants are crawling around on it. If the cylinder is 12 inches long and has a radius of 2.5 inches, what is the farthest the two ants could possibly be from each other and still both be on the tube?

(A) 12 inches
(B) 12.25 inches
(C) 13 inches
(D) 14.5 inches
(E) $12\sqrt{2}$ inches

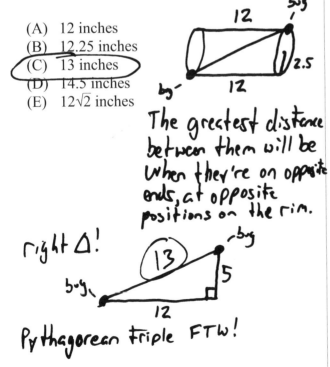

The greatest distance between them will be when they're on opposite ends, at opposite positions on the rim.

right △!

Pythagorean triple FTW!

18. Xorgar H'ghargh is building a pyramid to honor himself on the planet Geometrox. If the pyramid has a square base with edges 50 meters long, and its other four sides are equilateral triangles, how tall will the pyramid be?

(A) $50\sqrt{5}$
(B) $50\sqrt{3}$
(C) $50\sqrt{2}$
(D) $25\sqrt{3}$
(E) $25\sqrt{2}$

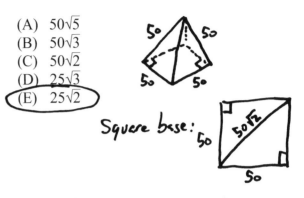

Square base:

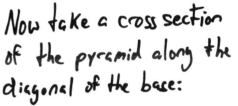

Now take a cross section of the pyramid along the diagonal of the base:

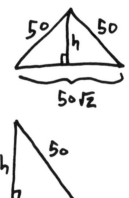

Use the Pythagorean Theorem if you want to prove it to yourself, but this is a 45°-45°-90° △. So the legs are equal: $h = 25\sqrt{2}$.

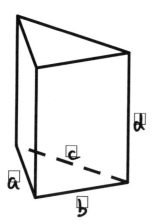

19. In the figure above, each empty box (□) is to be filled by the value of the length of one edge of the right triangular prism. If four unique constants, a, b, c, and d, are needed to fill the squares, and if the surface area of the prism equals $ab + ad + bd + cd$, then which constant represents the length of the longest edge of the prism's base?

(A) a
(B) b
(C) c
(D) d
(E) It cannot be determined from the information given.

This one is pretty tricky.

SA = top + bottom + side 1 + side 2 + side 3.

The 3 sides are rectangles, so each will include the height. The given expression for SA tells us d is the height: $SA = ab + a\underline{d} + b\underline{d} + c\underline{d}$

That means a, b, and c must be the edges of the triangular base, and that means ab = top + bottom. Since the top and bottom are the same, the area of one of them equals $\frac{1}{2}ab$. So the base must be a right △ with legs a and b, and hypotenuse c. Therefore, the longest side is c.

20. What is the volume of the largest cube that can be contained by a sphere of radius 4?

(A) 16
(B) $64\sqrt{3}$
(C) $\frac{64}{3}$
(D) $512\sqrt{2}$
(E) $\frac{512\sqrt{3}}{9}$

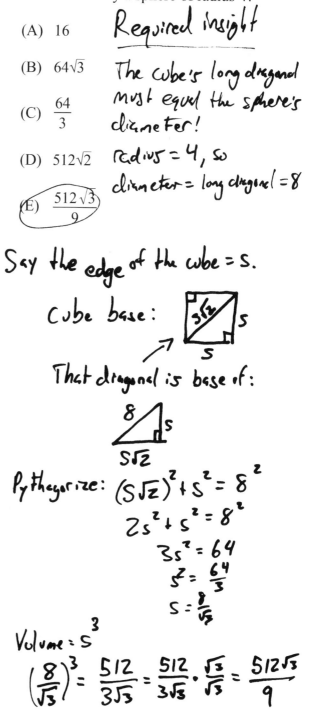

Required insight

The cube's long diagonal must equal the sphere's diameter!

radius = 4, so
diameter = long diagonal = 8

Say the edge of the cube = s.

Cube base:

That diagonal is base of:

Pythagorize: $(s\sqrt{2})^2 + s^2 = 8^2$
$2s^2 + s^2 = 8^2$
$3s^2 = 64$
$s^2 = \frac{64}{3}$
$s = \frac{8}{\sqrt{3}}$

Volume $= s^3$
$\left(\frac{8}{\sqrt{3}}\right)^3 = \frac{512}{3\sqrt{3}} = \frac{512}{3\sqrt{3}} \cdot \frac{\sqrt{3}}{\sqrt{3}} = \frac{512\sqrt{3}}{9}$

10. The mode of a set of 4 positive integers is 3. What is the least possible value of the sum of these 4 integers?

(A) 6
(B) 8
(C) 9
(D) 10
(E) 12

lowest value: 1

one mode means you can't have $\{1,1,3,3\}$.

So the lowest 4 number set: $\{1,2,3,3\}$

$1+2+3+3 = \boxed{9}$

12. The median of a set of 7 consecutive integers is −1. What is the greatest of these 7 integers?

Build from the middle.

-1

$-2, -1, 0$

$-3, -2, -1, 0, 1$

$-4, -3, -2, -1, 0, 1, \boxed{2}$

Set of 7

15. The average (arithmetic mean) test score in a class of 12 students was 74. If 4 students who averaged 96 were removed from the class, what would be the new average score of the class?

(A) 70
(B) 63
(C) 58
(D) 44
(E) 39

#n	× avg	= sum
12	74	888
-4	96	-384
8	63	504

17. The average (arithmetic mean) of 5 numbers is f. The sum of 3 of those numbers is g. What is the average of the remaining numbers?

(A) $\dfrac{5f-3g}{3}$

(B) $\dfrac{5f-g}{3}$

(C) $\dfrac{5f-3g}{2}$

(D) $\dfrac{f-3}{g}$

(E) $\dfrac{5f-g}{2}$

#n	× avg	= sum
5	f	5f
-3		-g
2	$\frac{5f-g}{2}$	5f-g

(It might help to plug in, but doing so isn't necessary.)

Tip: Eliminate (A), (B), and (D) because they have the wrong denominator.

18. For the first m days of the month of July, the average (arithmetic mean) of the daily peak temperatures in Culver City was 87° Fahrenheit. If the peak temperature the next day was 93° and the average daily peak temperature for July rose to 89°, what is m?

(A) 9
(B) 7
(C) 6
(D) 4
(E) 2

#n x avg = sum

#n	avg	sum
m	87	87m
+1	93	93
$m+1$	89	

2 ways to fill in the box, and they must equal each other!

$$\frac{Sum\ of\ column}{87m + 93} = \frac{product\ of\ row}{89(m+1)}$$

$$87m + 93 = 89(m+1)$$
$$87m + 93 = 89m + 89$$
$$4 = 2m$$
$$2 = m$$

Backsolve works, too.

20. The median of a set of 9 real numbers is 17. The mode of the set is 13. The greatest number in the set is 29, and the least is 8. Which of the following could be the average (arithmetic mean) of the set?

	avg	sum	
I.	15	135	
II.	17	153	✓
III.	19	171	✓

(A) I only
(B) II only
(C) III only
(D) II and III only
(E) I, II, and III

you're given:

$$\underline{8} \ \underline{\ } \ \underline{13} \ \underline{\ } \ \underline{17} \ \underline{\ } \ \underline{\ } \ \underline{\ } \ \underline{29}$$

13 will also be in one of these spots.

SUM: 80

Find the range of possible sums.*

• Smallest:
$$\underline{8} \ \underline{8.1} \ \underline{13} \ \underline{13} \ \underline{17} \ \underline{17.1} \ \underline{17.2} \ \underline{17.3} \ \underline{29}$$
Sum = 139.7

• biggest:
$$\underline{8} \ \underline{13} \ \underline{13} \ \underline{16.9} \ \underline{17} \ \underline{28.7} \ \underline{28.8} \ \underline{28.9} \ \underline{29}$$
Sum = 183.3

So basically, it's just a matter of playing with the numbers to get Sums of 153 or 171. It's not possible to get a sum of 135.

* I know there are smaller and bigger possible numbers. Full range: $139 < Sum < 184$.

12. Beatrice bought a bag of janky discount candy that contains Snackers and Milky Daze bars in a ratio of 3:2. If she picks a candy bar at random from the bag, what is the probability that she picks a Milky Daze bar?

(A) $\frac{2}{3}$

(B) $\frac{3}{5}$

(C) $\frac{2}{5}$

(D) $\frac{1}{3}$

(E) $\frac{1}{5}$

This is really a ratios problem!

$$\frac{Milky\ Daze}{Snackers} = \frac{2}{3}$$

$$\frac{Milky\ Daze}{all\ candy} = \frac{2}{5}$$

15. A snake pit contains green and red snakes in equal number and of equal likelihood to attack. Even after a snake bites, it is just as likely to bite again. If Corey falls into the pit, what is the probability that the first 4 snake bites he receives are all from green snakes?

(A) $\frac{1}{2}$

(B) $\frac{1}{4}$

(C) $\frac{1}{8}$

(D) $\frac{1}{16}$

(E) $\frac{1}{32}$

Prob that 1st snake is green: $\frac{1}{2}$

AND prob that 2nd is green: $\frac{1}{2}$

AND prob that 3rd is green: $\frac{1}{2}$

AND prob that 4th is green: $\frac{1}{2}$

$$\frac{1}{2} \times \frac{1}{2} \times \frac{1}{2} \times \frac{1}{2} = \frac{1}{16}$$

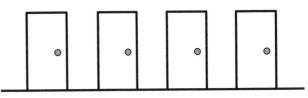

18. The four adjacent offices in the figure above are to be assigned to four employees at random. What is the probability that Scooter and The Big Man (two of the employees) will be placed next to each other?

(A) $\frac{3}{16}$

(B) $\frac{1}{3}$

(C) $\frac{1}{2}$

(D) $\frac{3}{4}$

(E) $\frac{5}{6}$

Say Scooter and Big Man are 1 and 2.

List possible arrangements:

①②③④	②①③④
①②④③	②①④③
①③②④	②③①④
①③④②	②③④①
①④②③	②④①③
①④③②	②④③①

③①②④	④①②③
③①④②	④①③②
③②①④	④②①③
③②④①	④②③①
③④①②	④③①②
③④②①	④③②①

$$\frac{12}{24} = \frac{1}{2}$$

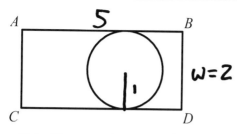

Note: Figure not drawn to scale.

19. In the figure above, a circle is tangent to two sides of a rectangle as shown. If $AB = 5$ and the area of the rectangle is 10, what is the probability (rounded to the nearest hundredth) that a point chosen at random inside the rectangle also falls inside the circle?

(A) 0.63
(B) 0.59
(C) 0.44
(D) 0.31
(E) 0.28

$$A_{rectangle} = lw = 10$$

$$5w = 10$$

$$w = 2$$

So radius = 1

$$A_{circle} = \pi$$

Probability of landing in circle:

$$\frac{A_{circle}}{A_{rectangle}} = \frac{\pi}{10} \approx .31$$

20. Regina rolls two standard 6-sided dice and is astonished to discover that both individual dice show prime numbers, and that their sum is also a prime number. What is the probability of this outcome?

(A) $\frac{1}{18}$

(B) $\frac{1}{9}$

(C) $\frac{1}{8}$

(D) $\frac{1}{6}$

(E) $\frac{1}{4}$

Remember: 1 is not prime!

The most foolproof way to solve this is to list!

Combinations

1,1 2,1 3,1 4,1 5,1 6,1
1,2 2,2 3,2 4,2 5,2 6,2
1,3 2,3 3,3 4,3 5,3 6,3
1,4 2,4 3,4 4,4 5,4 6,4
1,5 2,5 35   4,5 5,5 6,5
1,6 2,6 3,6 4,6 5,6 6,6

36 combos

Combos where both dice
show prime: 2+2=4
            2+3=5 ✓
            2+5=7 ✓
            3+2=5 ✓
            3+3=6
            3+5=8
            5+2=7 ✓
            5+3=8
            5+5=10

} 4 hits

$$\frac{4}{36} = \frac{1}{9}$$

1. If $f(x) = 8x + 2$, what is $3f(2) + 1$?

    (A) 8
    (B) 17
    (C) 36
    (D) 49
    (E) 55

$f(2) = 8(2) + 2 = 18$

$3f(2) + 1 = 3(18) + 1$
$= 55$

Month	Account balance	Change
January	$2,500.00	700
February	$3,200.00	800
March	$4,000.00	700
April	$4,700.00	1000
May	$5,700.00	900
June	$6,600.00	

2. The table above shows the balance in Judy's savings account at the end of every month for 6 months. During which period did Judy see the greatest percent change in her account balance?

    (A) From January to February
    (B) From February to March
    (C) From March to April
    (D) From April to May
    (E) From May to June

% change
is $\frac{change}{original} \times 100\%$.

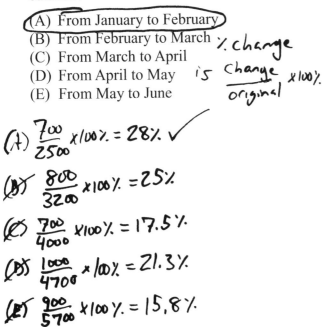

(A) $\frac{700}{2500} \times 100\% = 28\%$ ✓

(B) $\frac{800}{3200} \times 100\% = 25\%$

(C) $\frac{700}{4000} \times 100\% = 17.5\%$

(D) $\frac{1000}{4700} \times 100\% = 21.3\%$

(E) $\frac{900}{5700} \times 100\% = 15.8\%$

3. If $x^2 + y^2 = 14$ and $xy = 3$, which of the following is equal to $(x + y)^2$?

    (A) 11
    (B) 17
    (C) 20
    (D) 24
    (E) 28

puzzle pieces

$(x+y)^2 = x^2 + 2xy + y^2$
$= x^2 + y^2 + 2xy$
$= 14 + 2(3)$
$= 20$

1, 7, 49, 343, …

4. Each term in the sequence above after the first is determined by multiplying the previous term by 7. What will be the units (ones) digit of the 96th term?

    (A) 9
    (B) 7
    (C) 5
    (D) 3
    (E) 1

Find the pattern in the units digits

term #	term	Units digit
1	1	1
2	7	7
3	49	9
4	343	3
5	2401	1
6	16807	7
7	117649	9
8	823543	3
⋮	⋮	⋮

Every 4th term has a units digit of 3. 96 is a multiple of 4, so the 96th term will have a units digit of 3.

5. A certain sequence is defined such that the nth term in the sequence is equal to $n^2 + 1$. How much greater is the 10th term than the 7th term in the sequence?

(A) 3
(B) 49
(C) 51
(D) 72
(E) 90

Treat this like a function question!

10th term = $10^2 + 1 = 101$

7th term = $7^2 + 1 = 50$

$101 - 50 = 51$

x	2	3	4
$f(x)$	11	16	23

7. Based on the table above, which of the following could be an expression of $f(x)$?

(A) $f(x) = 8x - 7$
(B) $f(x) = 5x + 1$
(C) $f(x) = -3x - 9$
(D) $f(x) = x^2 + 7$
(E) $f(x) = 6x - 1$

$f(x)$	$f(2)$	$f(3)$	$f(4)$
(A) $8x-7$	~~9~~	~~17~~	~~25~~
(B) $5x+1$	11	16	~~21~~
(C) $-3x-9$	~~-15~~	~~-18~~	~~-21~~
(D) x^2+7	11	16	23 ✓
(E) $6x-1$	11	~~17~~	23

Note: I filled out the whole table but obviously you should eliminate a choice as soon as you see an inconsistency.

6. In a class of 6 students, the average (arithmetic mean) height is 5 feet and 8 inches. If a student joins the class and causes the average height of the class to increase by 1 inch, what is the height of the new student? (1 foot = 12 inches)

(A) 6 feet 6 inches
(B) 6 feet 3 inches
(C) 6 feet 0 inches
(D) 5 feet 11 inches
(E) 5 feet 9 inches

5ft 8in = 68 in

∴ new avg height = 69 in

#n × avg = sum

6	68	408
+1	x	+x
7	69	483

x = 75 in, or 6ft 3in

PWN the SAT

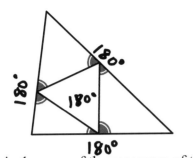

8. What is the sum of the measures of the marked angles in the figure above?

(A) 180°
(B) 270°
(C) 360°
(D) 450°
(E) It cannot be determined from the information given.

$180° \times 3 - 180° = 360°$

3 straight   1△
lines

Plugging in is also a good way to go. Make all the angles 60° and then all your straight lines and triangles easily add up to 180°.

9. The length of a certain rectangle is increased by 10%, and its width is decreased by 10%. Its new area is what percent of its original area?

(A) 99%
(B) 100%
(C) 101%
(D) 110%
(E) It cannot be determined from the information given.

Plug in!

10
A=100   10

(yes, you can use a square.)

↓
11
A=99   9

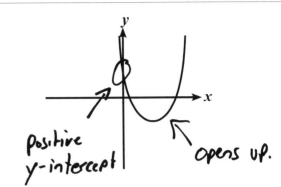

Positive
y-intercept   opens up.

10. Which of the following could be the equation of the parabola in the figure above?

(A) $f(x) = x^2 - 7x + 9$
(B) $f(x) = x^2 - 7x - 9$
(C) $f(x) = x^2 + 7x + 9$
(D) $f(x) = x^2 + 7x - 9$
(E) $f(x) = x^2 - 7x - 9$

$f(x) = ax^2 + bx + c$
     ↑   ↑
Must be   Must be
positive   positive

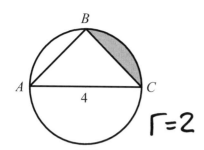

$r = 2$

11. In the figure above, $\overline{AC}$ is a diameter of the circle, and $AB = BC$. What is the area of the shaded region?

(A) $4\pi - 2$
(B) $2\pi - 1$
(C) π
(D) $\pi - 1$
(E) $\pi - 2$

Best to only deal with a quarter of the circle.

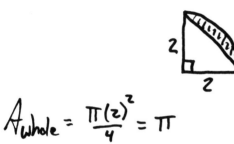

$$A_{whole} = \frac{\pi(2)^2}{4} = \pi$$

$$-A_{unshaded} = \frac{1}{2}(2)(2) = 2$$

$$A_{shaded} = \pi - 2$$

12. A certain salad contains croutons, nuts, and raisins. The ratio of croutons to nuts is 3 to 4, and the ratio of raisins to nuts is 3 to 5. What is the ratio of croutons to raisins?

(A) 5 to 4
(B) 4 to 5
(C) 2 to 3
(D) 9 to 20
(E) 3 to 10

$$\frac{3 \text{ croutons}}{4 \text{ nuts}} \times \frac{5 \text{ nuts}}{3 \text{ raisins}} = \frac{15 \text{ croutons}}{12 \text{ raisins}}$$

Simplify: $\frac{5c}{4r}$

13. A circle has an area of $49\pi^3$. What is the length of its diameter?

(A) 7
(B) 14
(C) 7π
(D) 14π
(E) 49π

read carefully!

$$A = \pi r^2$$

$$49\pi^3 = \pi r^2$$

$$49\pi^2 = r^2$$

$$7\pi = r$$

$$14\pi = d$$

(Backsolving also works.)

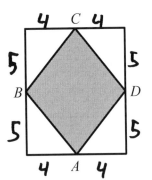

14. The rectangle above has a length of 8 and a width of 10. Points A, B, C, and D are the midpoints of the sides upon which they fall. What is the area of the shaded region?

(A) 20
(B) 30
(C) 35
(D) 40
(E) 50

$$A_{whole} = (10)(8) = 80$$

$$- A_{unshaded} = 4\left[\tfrac{1}{2}(4)(5)\right] = 40$$

$$A_{shaded} = 40$$

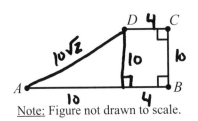

Note: Figure not drawn to scale.

15. In the figure above, $AB = 14$, $BC = 10$, and $CD = 4$. What is the length of $\overline{AD}$ (not shown)?

(A) 10
(B) $10\sqrt{2}$
(C) $10\sqrt{3}$
(D) 12
(E) $12\sqrt{2}$

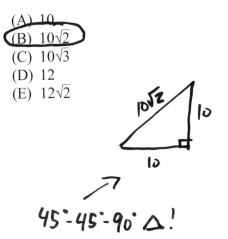

$45°\text{-}45°\text{-}90°\ \triangle$!

16. If $x + y = r$ and $x - y = s$, then in terms of x and y, what is $r^2 - s^2$?

Plug in!

(A) $x^2 + y^2$
(B) $x^2 - y^2$
(C) $4xy$
(D) 2
(E) 0

$X = 3 \quad r = 5$
$y = 2 \quad s = 1$

$r^2 - s^2 = 25 - 1 = \underline{24}$

(A) $9 + 4 = 13$
(B) $9 - 4 = 5$
(C) $4(3)(2) = 24 \checkmark$
(D) 2
(E) 0

17. Line n has a slope of $-\frac{1}{2}$ and a positive y-intercept. Line l passes through the origin, is perpendicular to line n, and intersects line n at the point $(a, a + 2)$. What is the value of a?

(A) 0.5
(B) 1
(C) 1.75
(D) 2
(E) 2.5

Line l's slope = 2

Line l's y-int = 0

∴ equation of line l:

$$y = 2x$$

drop $(a, a+2)$ into the equation: $y = 2x$
$a + 2 = 2a$
$2 = a$

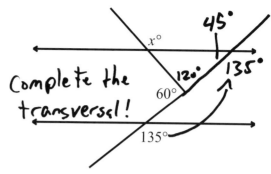

Note: Figure not drawn to scale.

18. The two horizontal lines in the figure above are parallel. What is x?

(A) 135
(B) 150
(C) 165
(D) 170
(E) 175

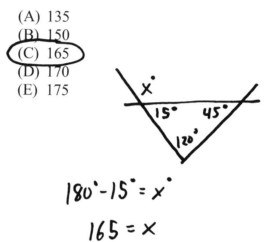

$180° - 15° = x°$
$165 = x$

19. One third of the attendees at a concert left the show before the encore. Twenty more people left during the encore. After the encore, half as many people as had left before the encore left. If 76 people remained in the theater after the concert was over to try to get autographs from the band, how many people, in total, attended the concert?

 (A) 150
 (B) 165
 (C) 192
 (D) 240
 (E) 270

Backsolve.

Try (C) first.

192 were there. $\frac{1}{3}$ leave:
$$\begin{array}{r} 192 \\ -64 \\ \hline 128 \end{array}$$

20 more leave:
$$\begin{array}{r} 128 \\ -20 \\ \hline 108 \end{array}$$

Half as many as left the first time leave. 64 left the first time, so now 32 leave:
$$\begin{array}{r} 108 \\ -32 \\ \hline 76 \checkmark \end{array}$$

So (C) works! Done.

20. For all integers x, let $☼x = 15(x-5)^2 - 8$. Which of the following is equal to $☼3$?

 (A) $☼(-3)$
 (B) $☼2$
 (C) $☼5$
 (D) $☼7$
 (E) $☼52$

Don't even think about it.

$$☼3 = 15(3-5)^2 - 8$$
$$= 15(-2)^2 - 8$$
$$= 15(4) - 8$$
$$= 52$$

You can either try all the choices to see which gives you 52, or you can take a clever shortcut.

In the original $☼3$, the $(3-5)^2$ part became $(-2)^2$, or 4. What other value for x will make that part equal 4?

$$(7-5)^2 = 2^2 = 4.$$

So $☼7 = ☼3$!

$A = \{ j, k, l, m, n, p \}$

1. If $j < k < l < m < n < p$, and the median of set A is 0, which of the following must be true?

   I. The product of all of the members of the set is 0

   II. The sum of l and m is 0 ✓

   III. The sum of all the members of the set is greater than j and less than p

   (A) I only
   (B) II only ⟵ Use your imagination!
   (C) III only
   (D) I and III only
   (E) II and III only

Eliminate I: $\{-3, -2, -1, 1, 2, 3\}$

Eliminate III: $\{-3, -2, -1, 1, 99, 100\}$

(Sum will be greater than 100)

2. If $f(x)$ is a parabola with a minimum at $f(2)$, which of the following is equal to $f(6)$?

   (A) $f(4)$
   (B) $f(0)$
   (C) $f(-2)$
   (D) $f(-4)$
   (E) $f(-6)$

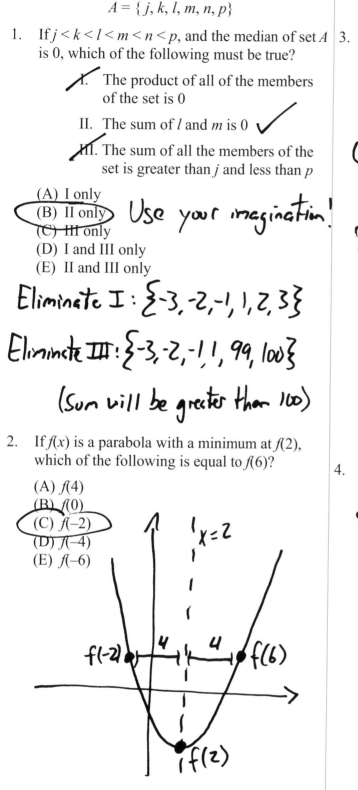

$1, 2, 2, 3, 3, 3, 4, \ldots$

3. In the sequence above, there is one 1, followed by two 2s, three 3s, four 4s, and so on. How many terms fall between the first occurrence of 80 and the first occurrence of 85?

   (A) 243
   (B) 330
   (C) 409
   (D) 413
   (E) 495

The first 80 and the first 85 don't count!

That leaves:

79	80s
81	81s
82	82s
83	83s
+84	84s
409	

$$\frac{x^5 x^{10}}{x^{13}} = 225$$

4. According to the equation above, which of the following equals x^2?

   (A) 225
   (B) 75
   (C) 25
   (D) 15
   (E) 5

Careful!

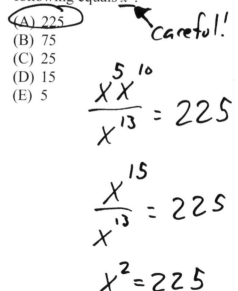

$$\frac{x^5 x^{10}}{x^{13}} = 225$$

$$\frac{x^{15}}{x^{13}} = 225$$

$$x^2 = 225$$

$$\frac{x^r}{x^p} = x^{2r}$$

5. If the equation above is true for all values of x, and p and r are constants, which of the following must be true?

(A) $r + p = 2$

(B) $r - p = 0$

(C) $r + p = 0$

(D) $p - r = 0$

(E) $\dfrac{r}{p} = 2r$

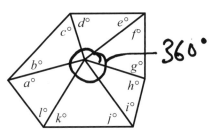
360°

6. In the figure above, an irregular hexagon is divided into six triangles. What is the average (arithmetic mean) of a, b, c, d, e, f, g, h, i, j, k, and l?

(A) 72

(B) 60

(C) 48

(D) 30

(E) It cannot be determined from the information given.

$$\frac{x^r}{x^p} = x^{2r}$$

$$x^{r-p} = x^{2r}$$

$$\therefore \ r - p = 2r$$

$$-p = r$$

$$0 = r + p$$

$$6 \ \triangle s : 180° \times 6 = 1080°$$

$$- \text{unmarked } \angle s \text{ in circle: } 360°$$

$$\overline{}$$

$$12 \text{ marked } \angle s \quad 720°$$

$$Avg = \frac{720°}{12} = 60°$$

7. For all integers m greater than 2, let
₪ $m = \dfrac{4m}{m-2}$. Which of the following is true?

(A) ₪ 3 > ₪ 4
(B) ₪ 5 + ₪ 6 = ₪ 11
(C) ₪ 9 ÷ ₪ 3 = ₪ 3
(D) 4(₪ 3) = 3(₪ 4)
(E) ₪ (6 + 7) = ₪ 6 + ₪ 7

Try 'em until one works!

$(A) \dfrac{4(3)}{3-2} > \dfrac{4(4)}{4-2}$

$\dfrac{12}{1} > \dfrac{16}{2}$

$12 > 8$ ✓

That could have been worse.

8. If $3y + 8x = 19$ and $2y - 3x = 11$, what is $y + x$?

(A) 5.6
(B) 6
(C) 8
(D) 9
(E) 30

$3y + 8x = 19$
$+ 2y - 3x = 11$
_____
$\dfrac{5y + 5x}{5} = \dfrac{30}{5}$

$y + x = 6$

9. If $f(x) = x^2 - 5$ and $g(x) = 2f(x) + 3$, what is $g(\sqrt{11})$?

(A) $\sqrt{11} - 2$
(B) $\sqrt{22} + 3$
(C) 9
(D) 15
(E) 22

$f(\sqrt{11}) = (\sqrt{11})^2 - 5$
$= 11 - 5$
$= 6$

$g(\sqrt{11}) = 2 f(\sqrt{11}) + 3$
$= 2(6) + 3$
$= 15$

Week	1	2	3	4	5	6
Customers	5	9	15	23	33	59

4   6   8   10   26

10. The table above shows how many customers came to Sean's new hair salon during his first six weeks in business. When did Sean see his biggest percent increase in customers?

(A) From week 1 to week 2
(B) From week 2 to week 3
(C) From week 3 to week 4
(D) From week 4 to week 5
(E) From week 5 to week 6

$(A) \dfrac{4}{5} \times 100\% = 80\%$

$(B) \dfrac{6}{9} \times 100\% = 66.7\%$

$(C) \dfrac{8}{15} \times 100\% = 53.3\%$

$(D) \dfrac{10}{23} \times 100\% = 43.5\%$

$(E) \dfrac{26}{33} \times 100\% = 78.8\%$

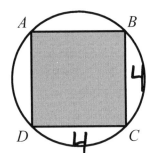

A   B

4

D   4   C

11. In the figure above, *ABCD* is a square and *AC* and *BD* (not shown) are diameters of the circle. If the area of the shaded region is 16, what is the area of the circle?

(A) $2\pi\sqrt{3}$
(B) 4π
(C) $4\pi\sqrt{2}$
(D) 8π
(E) 16π

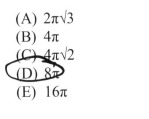

$4\sqrt{2}$ 4

4

$$r = 2\sqrt{2}$$

$$A_0 = \pi(2\sqrt{2})^2$$

$$= 8\pi$$

$3x + 2y + 2z = 21$
$2[5 + y + z = 8]$

12. Based on the system of equations above, what is $3x$?

(A) 5   ← careful!
(B) 15
(C) 22
(D) 28
(E) 38

$$3x + 2y + 2z = 21$$
$$-[10 + 2y + 2z = 16]$$
$$\overline{3x - 10 = 5}$$

$$3x = 15$$

13. At the Biltmore Hotel, 86 rooms have king size beds and 57 rooms have bathtubs. If 83 rooms have only a bathtub OR a king size bed but not both, how many rooms have both features?

(A) 60
(B) 56
(C) 36
(D) 30
(E) 27

Backsolve!

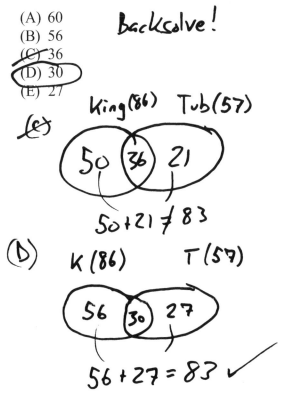

King (86)   Tub (57)

(e)

50   (36)   21

$50 + 21 \neq 83$

(D)   K (86)   T (57)

56   (30)   27

$56 + 27 = 83$ ✓

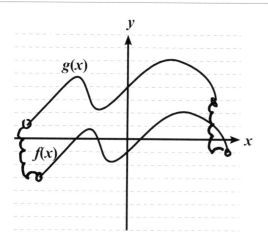

14. The graphs of $y = f(x)$ and $y = g(x)$ are shown above. Which of the following could define the relationship between f and g?

(A) $f(x) = g(x + 1) - 4$
(B) $f(x) = g(x - 1) - 4$
(C) $f(x) = g(x - 4) - 1$
(D) $f(x) = g(x - 4) + 1$
(E) $f(x) = g(x + 1) + 4$

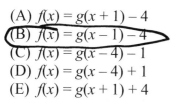

15. A teacher assigns certain students the duty of feeding the class hamster every day. The students decide to take turns, and decide that Alex will feed the hamster on the first day, followed by Bradley, Corinne, Dilip, and Ella, and then the pattern will repeat. Who will be responsible for feeding the hamster on the 99th day of class?

(A) Alex
(B) Bradley
(C) Corinne
(D) Dilip
(E) Ella

A B C D E ← 5th
A B C D E ← 10th
⋮
A B C (D) E ← 100th
↑
99th

16. The equation of a certain parabola is $y = ax^2 + bx + c$. If $a > 0$ and $c < 0$, which of the following could be the graph of the parabola?

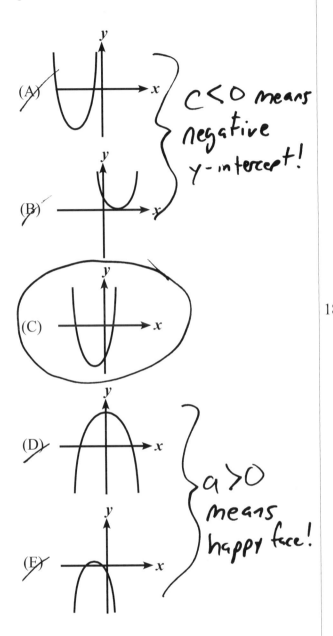

(A)

(B)

(C)

(D)

(E)

$c < 0$ means negative y-intercept!

$a > 0$ means happy face!

17. When p and r are divided by 7, the remainders are 3 and 6, respectively. What is the remainder when pr is divided by 7?

(A) 1
(B) 2
(C) 4
(D) 5
(E) 6

plug in

$p = 10$
$r = 13$
$pr = 130$

$18 R 4$
$7 \overline{)130}$
$\underline{-7}$
60
$\underline{-56}$
4

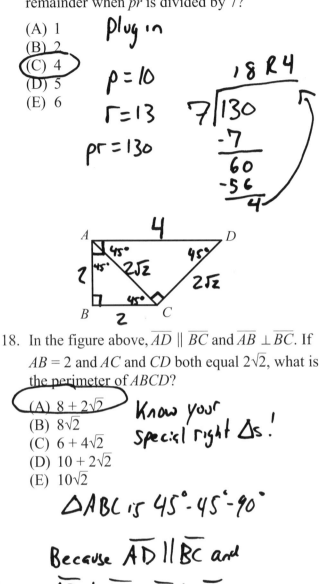

18. In the figure above, $\overline{AD} \parallel \overline{BC}$ and $\overline{AB} \perp \overline{BC}$. If $AB = 2$ and AC and CD both equal $2\sqrt{2}$, what is the perimeter of $ABCD$?

(A) $8 + 2\sqrt{2}$
(B) $8\sqrt{2}$
(C) $6 + 4\sqrt{2}$
(D) $10 + 2\sqrt{2}$
(E) $10\sqrt{2}$

Know your special right $\triangle$s!

$\triangle ABC$ is $45°$-$45°$-$90°$

Because $\overline{AD} \parallel \overline{BC}$ and $\overline{AB} \perp \overline{BC}$, $\overline{AB} \perp \overline{AD}$ too.

$m\angle CAD = 45$; so $m\angle CDA = 45°$ because the $\triangle$ is isosceles.

So $\triangle ACD$ is also $45°$-$45°$-$90°$.

19. In the xy-coordinate plane, the point $(2, r)$ is a distance of 13 from the point $(14, 2)$. Which of the following could equal r?

(A) 15
(B) 6
(C) 5
(D) –1
(E) –3

Know your Pythagorean triples!

5-12-13!

20. Which of the following sets of points forms a line that is perpendicular to the line $8x + 2y = 12$?

(A) $(6, 2)$ and $(8, 9)$
(B) $(-2, -2)$ and $(3, 1)$
(C) $(1, 4)$ and $(2, 8)$
(D) $(2, 10)$ and $(4, 11)$
(E) $(5, 3)$ and $(1, 2)$

$y = -4x + 6$

$\therefore$ need to find slope $= \frac{1}{4}$

(A) $\frac{9-2}{8-6} = \frac{7}{2}$

(B) $\frac{1-(-2)}{3-(-2)} = \frac{3}{5}$

(C) $\frac{8-4}{2-1} = 4$

(D) $\frac{11-10}{4-2} = \frac{1}{2}$

(E) $\frac{2-3}{1-5} = \frac{-1}{-4} = \frac{1}{4}$ ✓

1. If $f(x) = 8x - 9$ and $g(x) = f(2x) + 5$, what is $g(3)$?

    (A) 13
    (B) 34
    (C) 39
    (D) 44
    (E) 52

$$g(3) = f(2 \cdot 3) + 5$$
$$= f(6) + 5$$
$$f(6) = 8(6) - 9$$
$$= 39$$
$$g(3) = 39 + 5$$
$$= 44$$

2. One at a time, Lindsey and Jordan each randomly pull one marble from a bag that contains 3 black marbles, 2 green marbles, and 1 red marble. Assuming they do not return the marbles to the bag after they pick, what is the probability that Lindsey picks a green marble and Jordan picks a red one?

    (A) $\frac{1}{5}$

    (B) $\frac{1}{6}$

    (C) $\frac{1}{10}$

    (D) $\frac{1}{15}$

    (E) $\frac{1}{30}$

Multiply the Probabilities

L picks green: $\frac{2}{6}$

J picks red: $\frac{1}{5}$

(L's marble already removed)

$$\frac{2}{6} \times \frac{1}{5} = \frac{1}{15}$$

Note: if they pick in the reverse order, the answer is the same!

3. After b games, Maurice's basketball team had scored an average (arithmetic mean) of 60 points per game. Then they played 4 games in which they averaged 84 points per game, which changed their overall average to 72 points per game. What is b?

    (A) 2
    (B) 3
    (C) 4
    (D) 5
    (E) 6

#n × avg = sum

b	60	$60b$
$+4$	84	336
$b+4$	72	

2 ways to fill the box!

$$\frac{\text{Sum of column}}{60b + 336} = \frac{\text{product 1st row}}{72(b+4)}$$

$$60b + 336 = 72b + 288$$
$$48 = 12b$$
$$4 = b$$

Backsolve works, too.

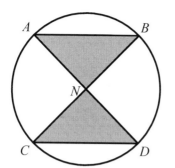

4. In the figure above, points A, B, C, and D lie on the circle, N is the center of the circle, and $\overline{AD} \perp \overline{BC}$. What fraction of the circle is shaded?

(A) $\dfrac{1}{\pi}$

(B) $1 - \dfrac{1}{\pi}$

(C) $\dfrac{1}{2\pi}$

(D) $\dfrac{1}{\pi^2}$

(E) It cannot be determined from the information given.

Plug in + Guesstimate.

Say $r = 3$, $A_o = 9\pi$

The shaded regions can be rearranged to make a square:

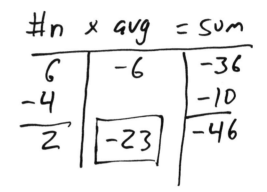

Area = 9

$\dfrac{A_{shaded}}{A_{whole}} = \dfrac{9}{9\pi} = \dfrac{1}{\pi}$

5. If 6 numbers have an average (arithmetic mean) of –6, and 4 of the numbers have a sum of 10, then what is the average of the other 2 numbers?

(A) 16
(B) 2
(C) –23
(D) –26
(E) –46

#n × avg = sum

#n	avg	sum
6	–6	–36
–4		–10
2	–23	–46

6. Line *m* passes through the points (3, 2) and (5, *p*), where *p* > 2. If line *l* is perpendicular to line *m*, which of the following equations could represent line *l*?

(A) $y = -\dfrac{2}{p-2}x + 3$

(B) $y = \dfrac{p}{2}x - 1$

(C) $y = -\dfrac{2}{p+2}x - 8$

(D) $y = \dfrac{1}{2p-4}x - 5$

(E) $y = -\dfrac{2}{5+p}x - 3$

Plug In!

$p = 3$

Slope of line m:

$p \to \dfrac{3-2}{5-3} = \boxed{\dfrac{1}{2}}$

So ⊥ slope is $\boxed{-2}$.

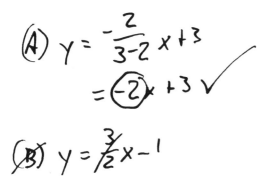

(A) $y = \dfrac{-2}{3-2}x + 3$

$= \boxed{-2}x + 3$ ✓

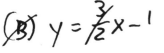

(B) $y = \dfrac{3}{2}x - 1$

(C) $y = \dfrac{-2}{3+2}x - 8$

$= \dfrac{-2}{5}x - 8$

(D) $y = \dfrac{1}{2(3)-4}x - 5$

$= \dfrac{1}{2}x - 5$

(E) $y = -\dfrac{2}{5-3}x - 3$

$= -x - 3$

7. What is the volume of the smallest cube that could completely contain a sphere with a radius of *r*?

(A) r^3

(B) $3r^3$

(C) $4r^3$

(D) $5r^3$

(E) $8r^3$

Picture a box that barely contains a basketball. Its length, width, and height would all have to be the diameter of the sphere.

$d = 2r$

$V = \ell w h$

$= (2r)(2r)(2r)$

$= 8r^3$

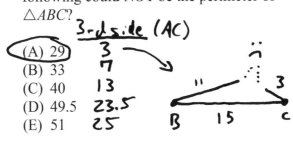

8. In △*ABC*, *AB* = 11 and *BC* = 15. Which of the following could NOT be the perimeter of △*ABC*?

(A) 29

(B) 33

(C) 40

(D) 49.5

(E) 51

3rd side (AC)

3
7
13
23.5
25

Sadness gap

9. If $6x - 15y = 18$ and $2x + 7y = 30$, what is $x - y$?

   (A) 1.5
   (B) 6
   (C) 12
   (D) 18
   (E) 48

$$6x - 15y = 18$$
$$+ \ 2x + 7y = 30$$
$$\overline{\ 8x - 8y = 48\ }$$
$$\frac{8x}{8} \qquad \frac{48}{8}$$
$$x - y = 6$$

10. Let $c \gtrless d$ be defined as $c \gtrless d = c^2 - 10d$ for all values of c and d. If $11 \gtrless m = 81$, what is the value of m?

   (A) 9
   (B) 6
   (C) 4
   (D) 2
   (E) 1

$$11^2 - 10m = 81$$
$$121 - 10m = 81$$
$$-10m = -40$$
$$m = 4$$

Backsolve works, too.

11. If $4^{m+n} = q$, then which of the following is equivalent to 4^{2m+2n}?

   (A) $2q$
   (B) $4q$
   (C) q^2
   (D) $2q^2$
   (E) $8q^2$

$$4^{m+n} = q$$
$$\left(4^{m+n}\right)^2 = q^2$$
$$4^{2m+2n} = q^2$$

Plug in works, too!

$$m = 2 \qquad 4^{2+3} = 4^5 = 1024$$
$$n = 3 \qquad \therefore \ q = 1024$$

$$4^{2(2)+2(3)} = 4^{10}$$

$$= 1,048,576$$

$$(c) \ 1024^2 = 1,048,576 \ \checkmark$$

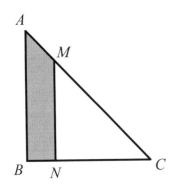

Note: Figure not drawn to scale.

12. In the figure above, $AB = x$, $BC = y$, and $\overline{AB}$ and $\overline{MN}$ are perpendicular to $\overline{BC}$. If $BN = 0.2y$, what is the area of the shaded region, in terms of x and y?

(A) 0.40xy
(B) 0.32xy
(C) 0.25xy
(D) 0.18xy
(E) 0.14xy

If $BN = .2y$,
then $NC = .8y$.

The triangles are
Similar. They Share
$\angle C$ and $m\angle ABC = m\angle MNC = 90°$

So $\dfrac{MN}{AB} = \dfrac{NC}{BC}$

$\dfrac{MN}{x} = \dfrac{.8y}{y}$

$MN = .8x$

$A_{whole} - A_{unshaded} = A_{shaded}$

$\frac{1}{2}xy \quad \frac{1}{2}(.8x)(.8y)$

$.5xy - .32xy = .18xy$

13. If $p^2 + q^2 = 18$, and $pq = 9$, what is $(p - q)^2$?

(A) 0
(B) 2
(C) 9
(D) 27
(E) 36

puzzle pieces

$(p-q)^2$

$= p^2 - 2pq + q^2$

$= \underbrace{p^2 + q^2}_{} - \underbrace{2pq}_{}$

$= 18 - 2(9)$

$= 0$

1, 4, 16, 64, ...

14. In the sequence above, each term after the first is determined by multiplying the previous term by 4. Which of the following must be true?

   I. The nth term in the pattern is equal to 4^n

   II. The nth term in the pattern is equal to $2^{2(n-1)}$

   III. The units digit of the 53rd term is 6

(A) I only
(B) II only
(C) III only
(D) II and III only
(E) I, II, and III

say n = 4. 4th term = 64

I. $4^4 \neq 64$

II. $2^{2(4-1)} = 2^6 = 64$ ✓

III. See the pattern?
even numbered terms have units digits of 4, and odd numbered terms have units digits of 6 (after the first term). So the 53rd term will have a units digit of 6. ✓

15. In the xy-plane, a circle with center (m, n) touches the y-axis at exactly one point and touches the x-axis at exactly one point. Which of the following must be true?

(A) $m + n = 0$
(B) $m = n$
(C) $m - n = 0$
(D) $mn = m^2$
(E) $|m| = |n|$

4 ways this could happen:

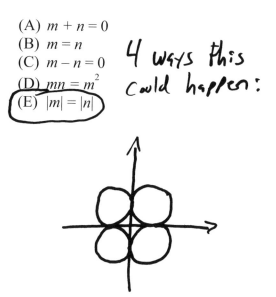

16. Sharon has 20 water balloons in her bucket and Michelle has 3 in hers. Sharon is tossing water balloons to Michelle, who is trying her best to catch them and put them in her bucket. If every 3rd toss results in a dropped and broken balloon, how many tosses have to occur for the two girls to have the same number of balloons?

(A) 12
(B) 11
(C) 10
(D) 9
(E) 8

S	M	toss # (start)
20	3	
19	4	1
18	5	2
17 (break)	5	3
16	6	4
15	7	5
14 (break)	7	6
13	8	7
12	9	8
11 (break)	9	9
10	10	10

x	$f(x)$	$g(x)$
-2	-7	-9
-1	3	1
0	3	-2
1	2	6
2	-1	-3
3	5	8

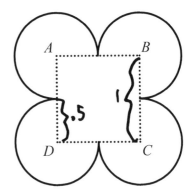

17. According to the table above, if $f(1) = n$, what is $g(n-2)$?

(A) -9
(B) -2
(C) 0
(D) 1
(E) 6

$f(1) = 2$

$n = 2$

$g(n-2)$

$= g(2-2)$

$= g(0) = -2$

18. In the figure above, $ABCD$ is a square, and A, B, C, and D are the centers of four congruent circles which touch each other but do not overlap. If the area of $ABCD$ is 1, what is the perimeter of the solid-outlined region?

(A) 3π
(B) 4π
(C) 6π
(D) 7π
(E) 9π

$r = .5$

$C = 2(.5)\pi$

$= \pi$

$\dfrac{270°}{360°} = \dfrac{\text{arc length}}{\pi}$

$\dfrac{3}{4}\pi = \text{arc length}$

But that's only for one arc. 4 of them make up the perimeter.

$4\left(\dfrac{3}{4}\pi\right) = 3\pi$

19. The length of one leg of a right triangle is increased by 15%, and the length of the other leg is decreased by 20%. The new triangle's area is what percent of the original triangle's area?

(A) 46%
(B) 92%
(C) 95%
(D) 96%
(E) 105%

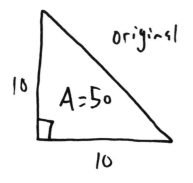

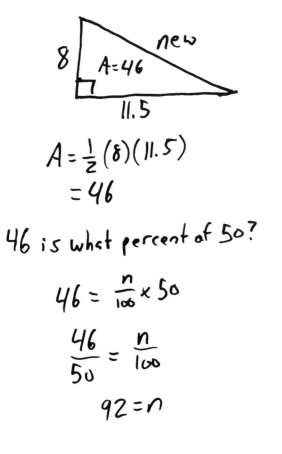

$A = \frac{1}{2}(8)(11.5)$
$= 46$

46 is what percent of 50?

$46 = \frac{n}{100} \times 50$

$\frac{46}{50} = \frac{n}{100}$

$92 = n$

20. The lowest score on the most recent chemistry exam in Professor Wren's class was a 39, and the highest score was a 75. Which inequality could be used to determine whether a particular score, s, could have come from Professor Wren's class?

(A) $|s - 39| \le 75$
(B) $|s - 20| \le 57$
(C) $|s - 18| \le 55$
(D) $|s - 60| \le 17$
(E) $|s - 57| \le 18$

middle of range = $\frac{75 + 39}{2} = \underline{57}$

distance to ends = $75 - 57 = \underline{18}$

Confirm (E):

$|s - 57| \le 18$

$-18 \le s - 57 \le 18$
$+57 \quad +57 \quad +57$

$39 \le s \le 75$ ✓

1. Seven years ago, Thom was half as old as Phil and three times as old as Melanie. If Thom is 19 years old now, in how many years will Melanie be half as old as Phil?

(A) 8 years
(B) 9 years
(C) 12 years
(D) 16 years
(E) 18 years

Follow the arrows.

	M	T	P
7 years ago	4 ←12→ 24		
Today	11	19	31
(C) +12 years	23		43

(No, she's already more than half as old as him.)

(B) +9 years | 20 | 40

(20 is half of 40. Bingo.)

2. In a certain right triangle, the difference between the square of the length of the hypotenuse and the square of the length of the longer leg is equal to $x^2 - 2xy + y^2$. What is the length of the shorter leg?

(A) $x^2 - y^2$
(B) $x^2 + y^2$
(C) $x - y$
(D) $4xy$
(E) $-2xy$

From the question:
$c^2 - b^2 = x^2 - 2xy + y^2$

From Pythagoras:
$c^2 - b^2 = a^2$

So: $a^2 = x^2 - 2xy + y^2$
$a^2 = (x-y)^2$ ← binomial square!
$a = x - y$

3. If $2x + y = 8$ and $x < 7$, which of the following must be true?

(A) $y > -6$
(B) $y < -6$
(C) $-6 < y < 7$
(D) $y < 6$
(E) $y > 7$

Plug in.

If $x = 7$:
$2(7) + y = 8$
$14 + y = 8$
$y = -6$

But x is really less than 7!

If $x = 6$:
$2(6) + y = 8$
$12 + y = 8$
$y = -4$

$-4 > -6$, so $y > -6$ if $x < 7$

4. The ratio of the lengths of the sides of a certain rectangle is $x:y$. If x and y are integers, and the sides have integer lengths, which of the following could be the area of the rectangle?

(A) $2xy$
(B) $3(xy)^2$
(C) $5x + 5y$
(D) $9xy$ ⟵ circled
(E) $xy\sqrt{11}$

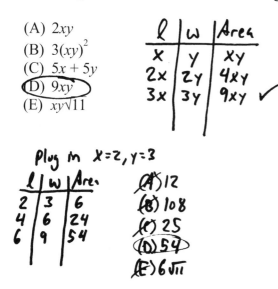

ℓ	w	Area
x	y	xy
$2x$	$2y$	$4xy$
$3x$	$3y$	$9xy$ ✓

Plug in $x=2, y=3$

ℓ	w	Area
2	3	6
4	6	24
6	9	54

(A) 12
(B) 108
(C) 25
(D) 54 ⟵ circled
(E) $6\sqrt{11}$

5. The sum of six consecutive integers is x. If $x > 0$, what is the smallest possible value of x?

(A) 3 ⟵ circled
(B) 6
(C) 9
(D) 15
(E) 21

x can be positive even if you use some negative integers!

$(-2) + (-1) + 0 + 1 + 2 + 3 = 3$

Sum of these 5 = 0

6. Adina keeps track of the number of rats she sees while she waits for the subway every morning. She noticed that there was a *roughly* 46.2% increase in the amount of rats she spotted between Tuesday and Wednesday. If she saw 19 rats on Wednesday, what will be the percent decrease (to the nearest tenth of a percent) in rat sightings if she sees the same number on Thursday that she did on Tuesday?

(A) 46.0%
(B) 35.2%
(C) 32.4%
(D) 31.6% ⟵ circled
(E) 19.1%

$\% \text{ change} = \dfrac{\text{change}}{\text{original}} \times 100\%$

Tues: x rats
Weds: 19 rats
Thurs: x rats

Change from Tues to Weds

$0.462 = \dfrac{19 - x}{x}$

$0.462x = 19 - x$

$1.462x = 19$

$x \approx 13$ ⟵ so 13 rats Tues + Thurs!

Change from Weds to Thurs

$\dfrac{13 - 19}{19} \times 100\% = -31.6\%$, or a 31.6% decrease!

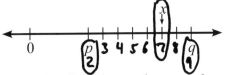

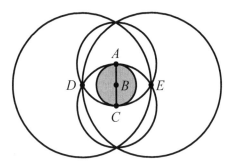

7. On the number line above, the space between p and q is divided evenly into sections. What is x, in terms of p and q?

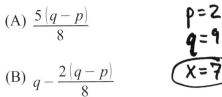

(A) $\dfrac{5(q-p)}{8}$

$p=2$
$q=9$
$\boxed{x=7}$

(B) $q - \dfrac{2(q-p)}{8}$

(C) $p + \dfrac{q-p}{7}$

(D) $p + \dfrac{5(q-p)}{7}$

(E) $\dfrac{q-p}{7}$

(A) $\dfrac{5(9-2)}{8} = \dfrac{35}{8}$ ✗

(B) $9 - \dfrac{2(9-2)}{8} = \dfrac{29}{4}$ ✗

(C) $2 + \dfrac{9-2}{7} = 3$ ✗

(D) $2 + \dfrac{5(9-2)}{7} = \boxed{7}$

(E) $\dfrac{9-2}{7} = 1$ ✗

Holy crap plug in is awesome.

8. In the figure above, B is the midpoint of $\overline{AC}$ and the center of the shaded circle. A, C, D, and E are also the centers of shown circles. If the area of the shaded region is 9π, what is the area of the circle with center E?

(A) 81π
(B) 99π
(C) 108π
(D) 120π
(E) 144π

$AB = BC = 3$
$\therefore AC = 6$

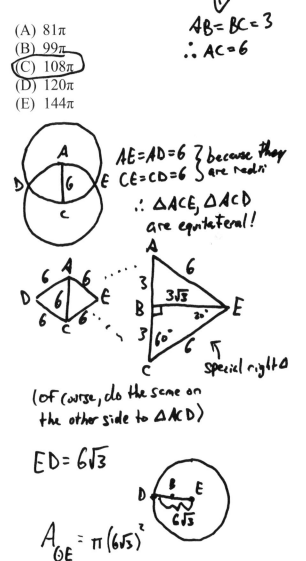

$AE = AD = 6$ } because they are radii
$CE = CD = 6$

$\therefore \triangle ACE, \triangle ACD$ are equilateral!

(of course, do the same on the other side to $\triangle ACD$)

$ED = 6\sqrt{3}$

$A_{\odot E} = \pi(6\sqrt{3})^2$

$= 108\pi$

9. What is the area of the triangle formed by connecting the points $(-2, -3)$, $(2, 6)$, and $(2, -2)$?

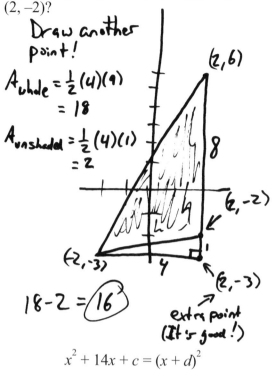

Draw another point!

$A_{whole} = \frac{1}{2}(4)(9)$
$= 18$

$A_{unshaded} = \frac{1}{2}(4)(1)$
$= 2$

$(2,6)$

8

$(2,-2)$

4

$(2,-3)$

4

$(2,-3)$

$18 - 2 = \boxed{16}$

extra point
(It's good!)

$$x^2 + 14x + c = (x + d)^2$$

10. In the equation above, c and d are constants. If the equation is true for all values of x, what is the value of cd?

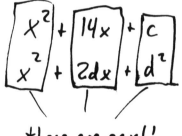

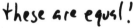

these are equal!

$14x = 2dx$
$14 = 2d$
$7 = d$

$c = d^2$
$c = 49$

$cd = 49 \cdot 7 = \boxed{343}$

11. According to the physical education teacher at Riverdale High school, students are only allowed to use the trampoline if they weigh between 95 and 185 pounds, inclusive. Students in a math class decide to express this same restriction using an inequality of the form $|w - j| \le k$, where w is a student's weight, and j and k are constants. What is jk?

$95 \le w \le 185$ $\frac{95 + 185}{2} = 140$

find middle of range:

$95 - 140 \le w - 140 \le 185 - 140$
$-45 \le w - 140 \le 45$
$|w - 140| \le 45$
$j = 140 \quad K = 45$
$\boxed{jK = 6300}$

12. In a certain youth soccer league, each team plays each other team exactly once during a season. If there were 28 league games last season, how many teams were in the league?

Find the pattern.

2 teams → 1 game   ⟩ +2
3 teams → 3 games   ⟩ +3
4 teams → 6 games   ⟩ +4
5 teams → 10 games
  ⋮
$\boxed{8}$ teams → 28 games

$S = \{2, 3, 4, 5, 9, 20\}$
$R = \{1, 5, 7, 8, 9, 10\}$

13. If s is a member of set S, and r is a member of set R, what is the difference between the largest and smallest possible values of $\frac{r}{s}$?

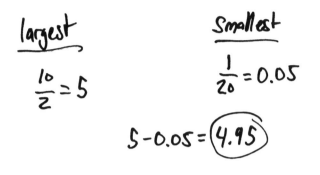

largest

$\frac{10}{2} = 5$

Smallest

$\frac{1}{20} = 0.05$

$5 - 0.05 = \boxed{4.95}$

14. If $4x + 3y = 20$ and $3y - 2z = 7$, what is $2x + z$?

$$4x + 3y \qquad = 20$$
$$-(\quad 3y - 2z = 7)$$
$$\overline{4x + 0 + 2z = 13}$$
$$\frac{4x + 2z}{2} = \frac{13}{2}$$
$$2x + z = \boxed{6.5}$$

15. How many positive integers less than 1,000 are NOT divisible by 7?

Easier to count how many $\underline{are}$.

$999 \div 7 = 142.714\ldots$

That means the biggest multiple of 7 that's less than 1000 is $7 \times 142 = 994$. It also means there are 142 multiples of 7 that are less than 1000.

999 positive integers < 1000
-142 multiples of 7
$\overline{\boxed{857}}$ positive integers < 1000 that are not divisible by 7.

16. A number is called a "bodacious square" if its square root is the square of an integer. How many bodacious squares are greater than 1 and less than 600?

$(2^2)^2 = 16$
$(3^2)^2 = 81$
$(4^2)^2 = 256$
$\cancel{(5^2)^2 = 625} \leftarrow$ oops, too big ¨

$\boxed{3}$

17. If p^2 is a multiple of both 8 and 35, and p is a positive integer, what is the least possible value of p?

Prime factors of perfect squares come in doubles.

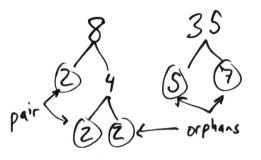

To make a perfect square, we need another 2, another 5, and another 7.

$p^2 = 2 \times 2 \times 2 \times \underline{2} \times 5 \times \underline{5} \times 7 \times \underline{7}$

I added these in.

$p^2 = 19600$

$p = 140$

18. Monica spent $14.13 on bananas and granola at the grocery store. Granola costs four times more than bananas by weight. If she bought five times as many pounds of bananas as pounds of granola, how much, in dollars, did Monica spend on bananas? (Disregard the $ sign when gridding your answer.)

Say 1 unit of bananas costs x. Then 1 unit of granola costs $4x$.

For every 1 unit of granola, Monica bought 5 units of bananas, so we can say:

$5x + 4x = \$14.13$

bananas total cost   granola total cost

$9x = \$14.13$
$x = \$1.57$

$5x = \$7.85$

bananas total cost

$\underbrace{(x)(x)(x)(x)(x)}_{banana} \quad \underset{granola}{(4x)}$

Blue Book Breakdown

What follows is a listing of every question in the Blue Book and which techniques or concepts in this guide apply. This section is meant to be used as an after-test reference, not as a during-test road map. Work through the tests on your own, and then use this section to keep track of the history of your mistakes by highlighting the questions you missed, guessed on, or struggled with before getting right. Later in your prep process, use this section to revisit the questions that used to gave you trouble, to make sure that the lessons you learned from them stuck.

Please note that, whether I say so about a particular question or not, algebra is almost always also an option. For example, I might say #1 is a backsolve question, because it *could* be solved that way, but it might just be a solve-it-in-your-head algebra question for you. *That's fine.* Even if you're not going to use these techniques on the easiest questions, it's good for you to recognize opportunities to apply them. This is how it becomes easier for you to recognize the same opportunities on harder questions. This is part of becoming nimble.

Note also that there are a few questions (like pictograph and spatial reasoning questions) that just don't lend themselves nicely to any of the techniques or concepts in this book. In that case, I won't try to shoe-horn questions into technique applications that don't fit. I'll just give you a few words about how I'd approach the problem instead.

Finally, note that I keep a running database of Blue Book questions that I've solved thoroughly on my Q&A website, which you can find at http://qa.pwnthesat.com/BlueBookSolutionLinks. Chances are very good that if you find a math problem you can't solve in the Blue Book, I've explained it in detail on the Q&A page. If I haven't, all you need to do is ask!

Test 1

Date taken:_____   Score:_____

correct:_____   # incorrect:_____   Raw score:_____

§	p	#	Techniques and concepts	Diff.
3	396	1	Try every answer choice.	1
3	396	2	Read the question carefully.	1
3	397	3	Average (p211), Backsolve (p39)	1
3	397	4	Read the graphs and question carefully.	2
3	397	5	Read the graph and question carefully.	1
3	397	6	Read the graph and question carefully.	2
3	398	7	Solving for expressions (p100)	2
3	398	8	Circles (p182)	2
3	398	9	Backsolve (p39)	3
3	398	10	Angles (p164)	2
3	399	11	Plug in (p31)	3
3	399	12	Read the graphs and question carefully.	3
3	399	13	Just list out the pattern terms (p87).	3
3	399	14	Solving for expressions (p100)	3
3	400	15	Guesstimate (p47)	3
3	400	16	Solving for expressions (p100)	3
3	400	17	Right triangles (p177)	4
3	400	18	Functions (p114), Exponents (p106)	4
3	401	19	Working in three dimensions (p199)	5
3	401	20	Percents (p57), Plug in (p31)	5
7	413	1	Read the graph carefully.	1
7	413	2	Angles and triangles (p164)	1
7	414	3	Backsolve (p39)	2
7	414	4	Plug in (p31) for m if you're stuck.	2
7	414	5	Circles (p182)	3
7	415	6	Lines (p132)	3
7	415	7	Triangles (p165)	3
7	415	8	Backsolve (p39)	5
7	416	9	Do the algebra.	1
7	416	10	Um...rounding?	2
7	417	11	Ratios (p64), Probability (p223)	2
7	417	12	Draw it carefully, then guess and check.	3
7	417	13	There are 30 days in April and you're told what happens every 5 days. Use ratios (p64).	3
7	417	14	Figure out the difference between each term (it's 20). Take no prisoners.	4
7	418	15	Absolute value (p148)	3
7	418	16	Be super careful and use trial and error. Starting point: X is the biggest.	4
7	418	17	Angles and triangles (p164)	4
7	418	18	Don't be fooled, this question is easy as long as you can read function notation (p114).	5
8	419	1	Read the graph carefully. Boy, there sure are a lot of these in this test!	1
8	419	2	Circles (p182), Angles and triangles (p164)	1
8	420	3	Symbol functions (p126)	1
8	420	4	Draw it. The sides of the square are 4.	2
8	420	5	Make four blanks, and fill them in based on what the question says.	1
8	421	6	Angles (p164)	3
8	421	7	Average (p211)	3
8	422	8	Exponents (p106)	3
8	422	9	Functions (p114)	3
8	422	10	Plug in (p31), Solving for expressions (p100)	3
8	423	11	Working in three dimensions (p199)	3
8	423	12	Plug in (p31)	4
8	423	13	Median (p216)	3
8	424	14	Counting and listing (p77)	4
8	424	15	Plug in (p31)	5
8	424	16	Functions (p114), Backsolve (p39)	4

Test 2

Date taken:_____   Score:_____

correct:_____   # incorrect:_____   Raw score:_____

§	p	#	Techniques and concepts	Diff.
2	452	1	Patterns (p87)	1
2	452	2	Ratios (p64)	1
2	453	3	Read the graph and the question carefully.	1
2	453	4	Circles (p182)	3
2	453	5	Actually turn the book on your desk and see what the shape looks like once it's rotated.	2
2	454	6	Do the algebra: $2x + 3 = 10$, what is $4x$?	2
2	454	7	Plug in (p31)	2
2	454	8	Break it into two rectangles.	2
2	454	9	Backsolve (p39)	2
2	455	10	Angles and triangles (p164)	3
2	455	11	First, read the graph carefully: the scales on the axes are different! Lines (p132)	2
2	455	12	Median (p216), Mode (p218)	3
2	455	13	Read the Venn diagram carefully. It might help to darken the boundaries of Y and Z.	3
2	456	14	Plug in (p31), Exponents (p106)	3
2	456	15	Symbol functions (p126)	4
2	456	16	Backsolve (p39)	3
2	456	17	Absolute value (p148)	3
2	457	18	Working in three dimensions (p199)	4
2	457	19	This one is a pain, but backsolving (p39) works if you don't want to do algebra.	4
2	457	20	Lines (p132)	5
5	463	1	Well, x must be 0, right?	1
5	463	2	Ratios (p64), Circles (p182)	1
5	464	3	Plug in (p31), Average (p211), Sets (p12)	2
5	464	4	Plug in (p31)	2
5	464	5	Plug in (p31)	2
5	464	6	Ratios (p64), Lines (p132)	3
5	465	7	Graph amplification (p120), or just plug in (p31) and graph if your calculator can.	3
5	465	8	Counting and listing (p77)	4
5	466	9	Do the algebra: $2x + 5 = 14$, solve for x.	2
5	466	10	Angles (p164)	3
5	467	11	How many times does 0.25 fit into 8?	2
5	467	12	Solving for expressions (p100)	4
5	467	13	Average (p211)	3
5	467	14	Absolute value (p148), Functions (p114), Plug in (p31)	3
5	468	15	Just walk through each choice keeping the goal in mind (and write everything down).	3
5	468	16	Counting and listing (p77)	4
5	468	17	Do the algebra: $1 + 0.07(t - 20) = 0.06t$, solve for t.	4
5	468	18	Tricky (but fun!): $p = 16k$ (count carefully) and $a = 10k^2$. Set them equal and solve for k.	5
8	481	1	Simplifying fractions?	1
8	481	2	Guesstimate (p47), Right triangles(p175)	1
8	482	3	Functions (p114), Lines (p132)	1
8	482	4	Plug in (p31)	2
8	482	5	Angles (p164)	2
8	483	6	Plug in (p31)	2
8	483	7	It might help to plug in (p31), but make sure your numbers make sense on the diagram.	3
8	483	8	Probability (p223)	3
8	484	9	Graph reflection (p120)	2
8	484	10	Backsolve (p39) carefully, or solve for the expression (p100).	3
8	484	11	Inequalities (p12)	3
8	485	12	Picture that circle as a wheel rolling along. Those rectangles could be at any orientation.	4
8	485	13	Plug in (p31), Exponents (p106)	4
8	485	14	Triangles (p165)	5
8	486	15	Figure out what Tom paid for the room using percents (p57), then multiply that by 4.	5
8	486	16	Patterns (p87)	5

Test 3

Date taken:_____   Score:_____

correct:_____   # incorrect:_____   Raw score:_____

§	p	#	Techniques and concepts	Diff.
2	514	1	I suppose you could backsolve (p39) if you wanted to.	1
2	514	2	Probability (p223)	1
2	515	3	Spatial reasoning is fun!	1
2	515	4	25% is a quarter. A quarter of a circle is a right angle. Which angles are acute?	2
2	515	5	Angles and triangles (p164)	2
2	516	6	Solving for expressions (p100)	2
2	516	7	Guesstimate (p47)	2
2	516	8	If you're not immediately sure what $(-0.5)^2$ is, just put it in your calculator.	2
2	516	9	Plug in (p31)	3
2	517	10	Functions (p114)	3
2	517	11	Average (p211)	3
2	517	12	Read the Venn diagram carefully. It might help you to darken the boundaries of A and B.	3
2	517	13	Percents (p57), Backsolve (p39)	3
2	518	14	Backsolve (p39)	3
2	518	15	Percents (p57)	3
2	518	16	Functions (p114)	4
2	518	17	Guesstimate (p47), Circles (p182), Shaded regions (p193)	4
2	519	18	Counting and listing (p77)	4
2	519	19	Functions (p114)	4
2	519	20	Plug in (p31)	5
5	525	1	Average (p211)	1
5	525	2	Circles (p182), Guesstimate (p47)	1
5	526	3	Plug in (p31)	1
5	526	4	Read the question carefully.	1
5	526	5	Special right triangles (p177)	4
5	527	6	Proportionality (p70)	3
5	527	7	Draw it carefully.	4
5	527	8	FOIL it. Corresponding coefficients will be equal (p156), so $(-8 - k) = -5k$ and $m = 8k$.	5
5	528	9	Ratios (p64)	1
5	528	10	Circles (p182)	2
5	529	11	Exponents (p106)	2
5	529	12	Lines (p132)	3
5	529	13	This is a tricky graph. Read it carefully.	2
5	529	14	Write the equation: $5n = n + 5$. Solve for n.	3
5	530	15	Angles (p164)	4
5	530	16	Patterns (p87)	4
5	530	17	For every 4 inches of strip, there are 5 inches of edge. Use ratios (p64).	4
5	530	18	Square's side = 8, so R is (4, 8). Plug into the equation to solve for a. Parabolas (p140).	4
8	543	1	Do the algebra: $(3/4)n = 18$.	1
8	543	2	Symbol functions (p126)	2
8	544	3	Read the graph carefully.	1
8	544	4	Read the question carefully.	2
8	544	5	Solving for expressions (p100)	2
8	545	6	Angles and triangles (p164)	2
8	545	7	Backsolve (p39), Absolute value (p148)	2
8	545	8	Special right triangles (p177)	2
8	545	9	Ratios (p64)	3
8	546	10	Lines (p132)	3
8	546	11	Corresponding coefficients in equivalent polynomials (p156)	3
8	547	12	Reasoning: Can they all be negative? No. All but one? Yes, if the one is big enough.	3
8	547	13	Counting and listing (p77)	4
8	547	14	Graph amplification (p120)	3
8	548	15	Follow the pattern (p87) remembering that all negative values are less than 100.	4
8	548	16	Working in three dimensions (p199)	5

Test 4

Date taken: _____   Score: _____

correct: _____   # incorrect: _____   Raw score: _____

§	p	#	Techniques and concepts	Diff.
3	581	1	Backsolve (p39)	E
3	581	2	Backsolve (p39), Exponents (p106)	E
3	581	3	Plug in (p31)	E
3	582	4	Spatial reasoning, schmatial schmeasoning.	E
3	582	5	Draw them carefully, counting as you go.	E
3	582	6	Do the algebra.	E
3	583	7	Probability (p223)	M
3	583	8	Plug in (p31)	M
3	583	9	Patterns (p87)	M
3	583	10	Functions (p114)	M
3	584	11	Angles (p164)	M
3	584	12	Lines (p132)	M
3	584	13	Median (p216)	M
3	584	14	Angles and triangles (p164)	M
3	585	15	Prime factorization (p92)	M
3	585	16	Lines (p132)	M
3	585	17	Symbol functions (p126)	M
3	585	18	Plug in (p31)	H
3	586	19	Circles (p182)	H
3	586	20	Plug in (p31), Percents (p57)	H
6	593	1	Backsolve (p39)	E
6	593	2	Angles (p164)	E
6	594	3	Read the table carefully.	E
6	594	4	Functions (p114)	E
6	594	5	You *could* plug in (p31), but you should know the transitive property of equality, dawg.	M
6	594	6	Ratios (p64)	M
6	595	7	Simplify the radical and straight on 'til morning.	M
6	595	8	Know your triangles (p165), plug in (p31), or note that those angles make a quadrilateral.	H
6	596	9	Multiply.	E
6	596	10	Average (p211)	E
6	597	11	Triangles (p165)	M
6	597	12	Solving for expressions (p100): solve for $(x - y)$, then find x from there.	M
6	597	13	Circles (p182)	M
6	597	14	Patterns (p87)	M
6	597	15	Triangles (p165), Plug in (p31)	M
6	597	16	Functions (p114)	H
6	598	17	In that period, clocks will chime at 7:30, 8:00, and 8:30. The nth hour will be the 8th hour.	H
6	598	18	Counting and listing (p77)	H
9	609	1	Backsolve (p39)	E
9	609	2	Lines (p132)	E
9	610	3	Divide.	E
9	610	4	I don't know why you wouldn't want 3 extra donuts, but pay attention to the *exactly* 21 bit.	E
9	610	5	Functions (p114)	E
9	610	6	Angles (p164)	M
9	611	7	Exponents (p106)	M
9	611	8	It's a semicircle, but just like parabola questions (p140), it's the symmetry that's important.	M
9	611	9	Backsolve (p39)	M
9	611	10	It's a trap! If you picked 25, you fell for it. Count: 1, 2, ..., 10, 11, <u>12</u>, 11, 10, ..., 2, 1.	M
9	612	11	Parabolas (p140)	M
9	612	12	You can plug in (p31), just pick lengths so the part of *PR* that's inside the rectangle is 4.	M
9	613	13	Percents (p57), Plug in (p31)	M
9	613	14	Solving for expressions (p100): The equation you should write is $4w = w + 4$; you want $3w$.	M
9	613	15	Right triangles (p175)	M
9	613	16	Plug in (p31)	H

Test 5

Date taken:_____   Score:_____

correct:_____   # incorrect:_____   Raw score:_____

§	p	#	Techniques and concepts	Diff.
2	638	1	Backsolve (p39)	E
2	638	2	Backsolve (p39)	E
2	639	3	Counting and listing (p77)	E
2	639	4	Functions (p114)	E
2	639	5	Ratios (p64)	E
2	639	6	Draw it, then plug in (p31)	E
2	640	7	By the transitive property, $2r = 6t$. Divide by 2 for your answer!	E
2	640	8	Plug in (p31)	M
2	640	9	Angles (p164)	M
2	640	10	Backsolve (p39)	M
2	641	11	Circles (p182)	M
2	641	12	Ratios (p64)	M
2	641	13	Functions (p114), Backsolve (p39)	M
2	641	14	Plug in (p31)	M
2	642	15	Triangles (p165)	M
2	642	16	Plug in (p31)	M
2	642	17	Lines (p132)	M
2	642	18	Average (p211)	H
2	643	19	Right triangles (p177), Circles (p182)	H
2	643	20	Remainders (p12)	H
4	650	1	Plug in (p31)	E
4	650	2	Work in 3-D (p199)	E
4	651	3	Read the graph carefully.	E
4	651	4	Backsolve (p39)	E
4	651	5	Triangles (p165)	M
4	652	6	Exponents (p106)	M
4	652	7	Right triangles (p177)	M
4	652	8	Parabolas (p140)	H
4	653	9	Figure out the total number of bottles needed, pick the lowest multiple of 3 that covers it.	E
4	653	10	Absolute value (p148)	E
4	654	11	Angles (p164)	M
4	654	12	Median (p216)	M
4	654	13	Functions (p114)	M
4	654	14	Angles and triangles (p164)	M
4	655	15	Ratios (p64)	M
4	655	16	Percents (p57)	H
4	655	17	Figure out which fraction the arrow points to and square it.	H
4	655	18	Draw point B and a line at $y = 3$, make a right triangle, use Pythagorean Theorem (p175).	H
8	667	1	Sets (p12)	E
8	667	2	Backsolve (p39)	E
8	668	3	Ratios (p64)	E
8	668	4	Angles and triangles (p164)	E
8	668	5	Read the graph and the question carefully—change can mean increase or decrease.	E
8	669	6	Functions (p114)	M
8	669	7	Exponents (p106)	M
8	669	8	Circles (p182)	M
8	669	9	Absolute value (p148)	M
8	669	10	Volume (p199)	M
8	670	11	Symbol functions (p126)	M
8	670	12	Percents (p57)	M
8	670	13	Even and odd properties (p12), Plug in (p31)	M
8	670	14	Plug in (p31)	M
8	671	15	Functions (p114), Lines (p132). Read the graph carefully; pay close attention to axis labels.	H
8	671	16	Plug in (p31) very carefully (suggestion: $L = 3$, $W = 2$).	H

Test 6

Date taken:_____   Score:_____

correct:_____   # incorrect:_____   Raw score:_____

§	p	#	Techniques and concepts	Diff.
2	700	1	That's an awful lot of hot dog rolls, Ms. Yun.	E
2	700	2	Draw it and read the question carefully.	E
2	700	3	Solving for expressions (p100)	E
2	701	4	Read the graph carefully. Write out the coordinates and think about what they mean.	E
2	701	5	Average (p211)	E
2	701	6	Plug in (p31), Absolute value (p148)	M
2	701	7	Use your calculator. Also, I think this question gets way easier if you use decimals.	E
2	702	8	Hi, I'm a Cartesian coordinate plane. Have we met? Examine me gently, but carefully.	M
2	702	9	Functions (p114)	M
2	702	10	Plug in (p31)	M
2	702	11	I hate questions like this. You just have to mess with it.	M
2	702	12	Volume (p199)	M
2	703	13	Plug in (p31)	M
2	703	14	Tip: the middle line (p132) will be the median (p216). Only calculate one slope.	M
2	703	15	Convert all times to EST to figure out how long the flights are.	M
2	703	16	Guesstimate (p47), Circles (p182)	M
2	704	17	Graph translation (p120)	M
2	704	18	Angles and triangles (p164)	H
2	705	19	(C) and (D) are clearly equivalent, so plug in (p31) numbers that work for them.	H
2	705	20	Symbol functions (p126)	H
4	712	1	Do the algebra.	E
4	712	2	Plug in (p31)	E
4	713	3	Average (p211)	E
4	713	4	Backsolve (p39): which choice is 1 more than a perfect square?	E
4	713	5	Circles (p182), Triangles (p165)	M
4	713	6	Prime factorization (p92)	M
4	714	7	Plug in (p31), Triangles (p165)	M
4	714	8	Apply exponent rules (p106), then backsolve (p39). Prime factorization (p92) also works!	H
4	715	9	Factors (p12)	M
4	715	10	Ratios (p64)	E
4	716	11	Percent change (p59)	M
4	716	12	Read the question carefully and draw the plot.	M
4	716	13	The algebra: $1x + 2y = 600$, $x = 2y$, where x is # of cheap bulbs; y is # of expensive bulbs.	M
4	716	14	Solving for expressions (p100)	M
4	717	15	Draw it carefully. What is the distance from the center of the circle (p182) to the x-axis?	M
4	717	16	Of course you need to know percents (p57), but this is really about reading carefully.	M
4	717	17	Draw them carefully. Edge and side are *not the same thing* on a 3D figure (p199).	H
4	717	18	Point C must be (1/2, 2). Plug that point into the equation to solve for p.	H
8	729	1	Backsolve (p39)	E
8	729	2	Counting and listing (p77)	E
8	730	3	Read the question carefully.	E
8	730	4	Draw Kerry's path and a circle representing the phone's range. Where can she go?	E
8	730	5	Solving for expressions (p100)	E
8	730	6	Angles (p164)	E
8	731	7	Lines (p132)	M
8	731	8	Functions (p114), Backsolve (p39)	M
8	731	9	Plug in (p31) by multiplying a bunch of integers and eliminate.	M
8	731	10	The probabilities (p223) tell you the total must be a multiple (p12) of both 4 and 6.	M
8	732	11	Average (p211)	M
8	732	12	Each triangle loses 9 for the side of the square that isn't part of the outer perimeter..	M
8	732	13	Functions (p114)	M
8	732	14	Plug in (p31) carefully. That negative is important!	H
8	733	15	Plug in (p31), Angles and triangles (p164)	H
8	733	16	Plug in (p31), Patterns (p87)	H

Test 7

Date taken:_____   Score:_____

correct:_____   # incorrect:_____   Raw score:_____

§	p	#	Techniques and concepts	Diff.
3	768	1	Ratios (p64)	E
3	768	2	Simplify! I like this problem a lot, actually.	E
3	769	3	Plug in (p31): If x were 8, then y would be 22. But x is greater than 8, so...	E
3	769	4	Draw it and Pythagorize it (p175).	M
3	769	5	Patterns (p87)	M
3	769	6	Angles (p164)	M
3	770	7	If you're smart about it, you can plug in (p31) here.	M
3	770	8	Average (p211), Median (p216)	H
3	771	9	Solve for x, read the question carefully, and give them what they want.	E
3	771	10	Half of 256, Broseidon. High five!	E
3	772	11	Read the table carefully.	E
3	772	12	Based on the perimeter, R is (1, 3). Use that in the equation to find a. Parabolas (p140).	M
3	772	13	Just do the algebra.	M
3	772	14	Angles (p164)	M
3	773	15	Counting and listing (p77)	H
3	773	16	Circles (p182), Shaded regions (p193)	H
3	773	17	Plug in (p31), Factors (p12), Prime factorization (p92)	H
3	773	18	You know $c = 106$ because it's the peak height. From there, use $h(0)$ to find d. This q sux.	H
7	785	1	Backsolve (p39)	E
7	785	2	Fold the letters *in your mind*.	E
7	786	3	Plug in (p31)	E
7	786	4	Count the squares carefully, then use a ratio (p64). You got this.	E
7	786	5	Read the graph carefully.	E
7	786	6	Average (p211), Backsolve (p39)	E
7	787	7	Triangles (p165)	E
7	787	8	Read the question carefully.	M
7	787	9	Plug in (p31)	M
7	787	10	Kinda a plug in (p31) and backsolve (p39) combo: the choices tell you what to plug in.	M
7	788	11	Exponents (p106)	M
7	788	12	Guesstimate (p47), Lines (p132)	M
7	788	13	Read the question carefully and remember that a month has at most 31 days.	M
7	788	14	Square both sides and you're basically there.	M
7	789	15	Counting and listing (p77)	M
7	789	16	That's a big ol' 3-4-5 triangle (p177)!	M
7	789	17	Circles (p182)	M
7	789	18	Hint: the sum of all the consecutive integers from –22 to 22 is 0. Backsolve (p39)	H
7	790	19	Exponents (p106)	H
7	790	20	Graph translation (p120)	H
9	795	1	Probability (p223)	E
9	795	2	Angles and triangles (p164)	E
9	796	3	Percents (p57), Ratios (p64)	E
9	796	4	Plug in (p31)	E
9	796	5	Ratios (p64)	E
9	796	6	Read the pictograph carefully. I bet you could draw a nicer looking house.	M
9	797	7	Backsolve (p39)	M
9	797	8	Plug in (p31), Absolute value (p148)	M
9	797	9	Plug in (p31)	M
9	797	10	Plug in (p31)	M
9	798	11	Graph reflection (p120), Lines (p132)	M
9	798	12	Backsolve (p39)	M
9	799	13	Angles and triangles (p164), Plug in (p31)	M
9	799	14	Parabolas (p140)	M
9	800	15	Working in three dimensions (p199)	H
9	800	16	Symbol functions (p126)	H

Test 8

Date taken:_____   Score:_____

correct:_____   # incorrect:_____   Raw score:_____

§	p	#	Techniques and concepts	Diff.
3	830	1	Convert to decimals.	E
3	830	2	Draw them.	E
3	831	3	Angles (p164), Backsolve (p39)	E
3	831	4	Do the algebra, or backsolve (p39). It's your life.	E
3	831	5	Exponents (p106)	M
3	831	6	Read the graph and question carefully.	M
3	832	7	Angles (p164), Right triangles (p175)	M
3	832	8	Read this one super carefully before you go about plugging in (p31).	H
3	833	9	Cross-multiply.	E
3	833	10	Patterns (p87)	E
3	834	11	Draw it carefully.	M
3	834	12	The algebra: $x + (x - 1) + (x - 2) + (x - 3) + (x - 4) = 185$. Or you could guess and check.	M
3	834	13	Percents (p57)	M
3	834	14	Circles (p182)	M
3	835	15	Solving for expressions (p100)	H
3	835	16	Shaded regions (p193), Right triangles (p175)	M
3	835	17	Symbol functions (p126), Remainders (p12)	H
3	835	18	Average (p211)	H
7	847	1	If you got this one wrong, do you want to play me in Scrabble™ ?	E
7	847	2	Solving for expressions (p100)	E
7	848	3	Plug in (p31)	E
7	848	4	Triangles (p165)	E
7	848	5	Percents (p57)	E
7	848	6	Convert to yards before you multiply to make this easier on yourself.	E
7	849	7	I do a solving for expressions (p100) type calculation, but you can also backsolve (p39).	M
7	849	8	Ratios (p64)	M
7	849	9	If it's an intersection point, it's on both graphs, so just substitute 0 for y and go to town.	M
7	849	10	Shortcut: 2 hours is too long but half an hour is way too short. Backsolve (p39) to be sure.	M
7	849	11	Functions (p114)	M
7	850	12	Read the graph, question, and choices carefully.	M
7	850	13	Counting and listing (p77)	M
7	850	14	Lines (p132)	M
7	851	15	Working in three dimensions (p199)	M
7	851	16	Plug in (p31)	M
7	851	17	Backsolve (p39)	H
7	852	18	Don't be intimidated, this pattern (p87) looks way worse than it really is.	M
7	852	19	Median (p216)	H
7	852	20	Guesstimate (p47), Circles (p182)	H
9	857	1	Backsolve (p39)	E
9	857	2	Uhh...I think this is a fundamental identity of mathematics.	E
9	858	3	Angles and triangles (p164)	E
9	858	4	Backsolve (p39)	E
9	858	5	I prefer "yellow" myself, but objections aside, this is a probability question (p223).	E
9	858	6	Proportionality (p70)	M
9	859	7	Triangles (p165), Plug in (p31)	M
9	859	8	Backsolve (p39), Exponents (p106)	M
9	859	9	Lines (p132)	M
9	860	10	Absolute value (p148)	M
9	860	11	Read the table carefully.	M
9	860	12	Triangles (p165)	M
9	861	13	Functions (p114)	M
9	861	14	Functions (p114)	H
9	861	15	Percents (p57)	H
9	861	16	Draw it. Note that $\triangle CDE$ is 1/4 of the rectangle, so $ABED$ must be 3/4. Solve like a boss.	H

Test 9

Date taken:_____   Score:_____

correct:_____   # incorrect:_____   Raw score:_____

§	p	#	Techniques and concepts	Diff.
2	886	1	Count the numbers that are in both sets.	E
2	886	2	Read the question carefully, and make sure you double and halve the right things.	E
2	887	3	Plug in (p31)	E
2	887	4	Lines (p132)	M
2	888	5	Special right triangles (p177)	M
2	888	6	Median (p216)	M
2	888	7	Plug in (p31)	H
2	888	8	The sides are perpendicular, so plug in (p31) for one slope (p134).	H
2	889	9	Read the question carefully.	E
2	889	10	Do the algebra. Gasp!	M
2	890	11	Symbol functions (p126)	E
2	890	12	Plug in (p31) until you find a number that works. In other words, guess and check.	E
2	890	13	Read the question carefully. Red and green must equal half, so blue is half, too.	M
2	890	14	Read the question carefully, draw a diagram, and count (p77).	M
2	891	15	Exponents (p106)	M
2	891	16	To find the greatest possible, assume all others chose the least possible. Average (p211)	M
2	891	17	You're gonna have to do algebra here. $10a + 10c = 17a$. Solve for a/c.	H
2	891	18	Functions (p114)	H
5	903	1	Patterns (p87)	E
5	903	2	Solving for expressions (p100)	E
5	904	3	Read the speedometer carefully—there are 4 divisions between 30 and 60.	E
5	904	4	Counting and listing (p77)	E
5	904	5	Surface area (p201)	E
5	904	6	Backsolve (p39)	E
5	905	7	Average (p211)	M
5	905	8	Guesstimate (p47)	M
5	905	9	Plug in (p31) for x	M
5	905	10	Evaluate each choice, eliminate ones to which you can imagine a counterexample.	M
5	906	11	Circles (p182)	M
5	906	12	Proportionality (p70)	M
5	906	13	Plug in (p31), but only for one variable. Use that one to calculate the rest.	M
5	906	14	Functions (p114)	M
5	907	15	Plug in (p31)	M
5	907	16	Angles and triangles (p164)	H
5	907	17	Do the algebra. Which choice is the same as $n + (n + 2) + (n + 4) = 111$?	M
5	907	18	Circles (p182)	H
5	908	19	Functions (p114), Percents (p57), Backsolve (p39)	H
5	908	20	When you draw $\overline{AC}$, you make four 30º-60º-90º triangles (p177).	H
8	915	1	Backsolve (p39)	E
8	915	2	Backsolve (p39)	E
8	916	3	Angles (p164)	E
8	916	4	Ratios (p64), or just look at the choices and see which one is not a multiple of 5.	E
8	916	5	Backsolve (p39)	E
8	916	6	Plug in (p31)	M
8	917	7	Read the question and graphs carefully. Faster activities have steeper slopes.	M
8	917	8	Do the algebra. Plug the point into the first equation to find k, then into the second for j.	M
8	917	9	Absolute value (p148)	M
8	918	10	The interior angles' sum is $(n - 2)180$, and $n = 2$. Or divide the pentagon into 5 equal $\triangle$s.	M
8	918	11	Ratios (p64)	M
8	918	12	Properties of even and odd numbers (p12), Plug in (p31)	M
8	918	13	Circles (p182), Lines (p132)	M
8	919	14	Hint: $n + 3$ and $n + 10$ are 7 apart from each other.	H
8	919	15	Working in three dimensions (p199)	M
8	919	16	Solving for expressions (p100)	H

Test 10

Date taken:_____   Score:_____

correct:_____   # incorrect:_____   Raw score:_____

§	p	#	Techniques and concepts	Diff.
2	948	1	Do the algebra.	E
2	948	2	Functions (p114), Lines (p132)	E
2	949	3	Circles (p182), Backsolve (p39)	E
2	949	4	Absolute value (p148)	E
2	949	5	Read the graph carefully. What does "less than 40" mean?	M
2	949	6	Plug in (p31)	M
2	950	7	Proportionality (p70)	M
2	950	8	Solving for expressions (p100)	H
2	951	9	Do the algebra.	E
2	951	10	Lines (p132)	E
2	952	11	Ratios (p64)	M
2	952	12	Angles and triangles (p164)	M
2	952	13	Patterns (p87)	M
2	952	14	If you plug in (p31) 100 for z, this is cake.	M
2	953	15	Special right triangles (p177)	H
2	953	16	Ratios (p64)	H
2	953	17	Need a line (p132) with a positive slope lower than shown? Like 0.1? Guesstimate (p47)!	H
2	953	18	Median (p216)	H
5	965	1	Om nom nom nom.	E
5	965	2	Plug in (p31)	E
5	966	3	Angles and triangles (p164)	E
5	966	4	Backsolve (p39)	E
5	966	5	Ostensibly, this is a question about triangles (p165), but it's more of a reading trap.	E
5	966	6	Backsolve (p39)	M
5	967	7	Average (p211), Backsolve (p39)	M
5	967	8	The right answer is the one for which you cannot come up with a counterexample.	M
5	967	9	Do the algebra.	M
5	967	10	Symbol functions (p126)	M
5	968	11	Angles (p164)	M
5	968	12	Backsolve (p39)	M
5	968	13	Try to draw border lines in the big shapes to break them into the small ones.	M
5	969	14	Counting and listing (p77)	H
5	969	15	Right triangles (p175), Solving for expressions (p100)	M
5	969	16	Parabolas (p140)	M
5	969	17	FOIL it. Corresponding coefficients are equal (p156), so $h = 7$ and $1 + h = k$.	H
5	970	18	There's a similar right triangle (p175) with legs length 4 and 10.	H
5	970	19	Functions (p114)	M
5	970	20	Plug in (p31) an *even* number..	H
8	977	1	Counting and listing (p77)	E
8	977	2	Read the question carefully.	E
8	978	3	Probability (p223)	E
8	978	4	INFINITY.	E
8	978	5	Read the graph carefully.	E
8	978	6	Draw D and read the question carefully. Everything will become illuminated.	E
8	979	7	Plug in (p31)	M
8	979	8	Circles (p182)	M
8	979	9	Functions (p114)	M
8	979	10	Working in three dimensions (p199)	M
8	980	11	Exponents (p106)	M
8	980	12	Angles and triangles (p164)	M
8	980	13	Plug in (p31)	M
8	980	14	Angles and triangles (p164), Plug in (p31)	M
8	981	15	Simplify the left side: $n/(n^2 - 1)$. If the top of the right side is 5, then k must be $5^2 - 1$.	H
8	981	16	Plug in (p31)	H

Test 11 (Blue Book DVD)

Date taken:_____   Score:_____

correct:_____   # incorrect:_____   Raw score:_____

§	p	#	Techniques and concepts	Diff.
3	8	1	Factors (p12)	1
3	8	2	You could plug in (p31) here, ya know.	1
3	9	3	In a parallelogram, opposite sides are congruent. Fill in all given lengths.	2
3	9	4	Read the graphs carefully, Percents (p57)	2
3	10	5	Plug in (p31)	3
3	10	6	Patterns (p87)	3
3	10	7	Lines (p132)	3
3	10	8	Exponents (p106)	4
3	11	9	Uh...subtraction?	1
3	11	10	Lines (p132)	2
3	12	11	Triangles (p165)	2
3	12	12	Inequalities (p12)	3
3	12	13	Draw it. (5, 0) is on the circle, so the distance to (13, 0) is 8.	3
3	12	14	At 5 feet you have 2 posts. At 10 feet you have 3 posts. The number of posts is 500/5 + 1.	4
3	13	15	Parabolas (p140)	3
3	13	16	Angles (p164)	3
3	13	17	Median (p216)	4
3	13	18	The key here is to figure out the total journey's time, which is 30 min + 15 min.	5
4	14	1	Solving for expressions (p100)	1
4	14	2	Plug in (p31) to clarify the relationship if you want.	1
4	15	3	Draw it, and then maybe backsolve (p39) if the answer doesn't jump out at you.	2
4	15	4	Backsolve (p39), Exponents (p106)	1
4	15	5	You'll probably just use your head, but your calculator's fraction function is a safety net.	2
4	15	6	Read the graph carefully. Note that the bars add up to more than 100%.	3
4	15	7	Backsolve (p39), or just do the algebra: $x + 1 = 2x - 1$	2
4	16	8	For Pete's sake, just list them (p77)!	2
4	16	9	Patterns (p87)	2
4	16	10	Symbol functions (p126)	3
4	16	11	Logic. You don't know anything about I or II, but if Greta never goes to mysteries, III is true.	3
4	17	12	Absolute value (p148)	3
4	17	13	The ones on the ends add 4 to the perimeter. The others add 3.	3
4	17	14	You probably should just do the algebra here. Combine like terms and you get $2x < 0$.	3
4	18	15	Triangles (p165), Average (p211)	4
4	18	16	Read carefully! Wednesday doesn't work because Anna didn't hit the 5 total servings goal.	4
4	18	17	Plug in (p31)	3
4	18	18	The surface area (p201) of the big cube is 6. The surface area of a small cube is 6/4.	4
4	19	19	Plug in (p31), Average (p211)	5
4	19	20	Guesstimate (p47), or connect big circle centers to make isosceles right triangles (p175).	5
8	32	1	Backsolve (p39)	2
8	32	2	Angles and triangles (p164)	1
8	33	3	Ratios (p64)	3
8	33	4	Solving for expressions (p100)	2
8	33	5	Draw the square and the other diagonal, then draw the points.	2
8	33	6	Plug in (p31), saying the original quantity was 100. You eat questions like this for breakfast.	2
8	34	7	Backsolve (p39)	2
8	34	8	Sets (p12), Multiples (p12). Shortcut: write out all of set T, then look for multiples of 6 in it.	2
8	34	9	Shaded regions (p193), Circles (p182)	3
8	34	10	This is a rare instance of "It cannot be determined." Could have 14 to 26 oatmeal cookies.	1
8	35	11	Functions (p114)	4
8	35	12	Backsolve (p39)	4
8	35	13	Special right triangles (p177)	4
8	36	14	2 is the additional height you get each time a pail is added.	4
8	36	15	Know the properties of even and odd numbers (p12), or plug in (p31) a few possibilities.	5
8	36	16	Quick and dirty: Graph (or look at the table) on your calculator.	5

Thanks for reading!

I hope you've enjoyed working through this book as much as I enjoyed putting it together. If you have any questions, or would just like to say hello, please reach out to me at http://facebook.com/pwnthesat or http://qa.pwnthesat.com. I'd love to hear from you.

Cheers,

Mike

Made in the USA
San Bernardino, CA
30 August 2014